XICONOMICS

Kurt,

Best with

Adrew

Business with China

Series Editor: Kerry Brown

The titles in this series explore the complex relationship between Chinese society and China's global economic role. Exploring a wide range of issues the series challenges the view of a country enclosed in on itself, and shows how the decisions made by Chinese consumers, the economic and political choices made by its government, and the fiscal policies followed by its bankers are impacting on the rest of the world.

Published

Belt and Road: The First Decade
Igor Rogelja and Konstantinos Tsimonis

China's Hong Kong: The Politics of a Global City
Tim Summers

The Future of UK–China Relations: The Search for a New Model
Kerry Brown

Xiconomics: What China's Dual Circulation Strategy Means for Global Business
Andrew Cainey and Christiane Prange

XICONOMICS

What China's Dual Circulation Strategy Means for Global Business

Andrew Cainey and Christiane Prange

agenda
publishing

First published in 2023 by Agenda Publishing

Agenda Publishing Limited
The Core
Bath Lane
Newcastle Helix
Newcastle upon Tyne
NE4 5TF

www.agendapub.com

ISBN 978-1-78821-627-2 (hardcover)
ISBN 978-1-78821-628-9 (paperback)

British Library Cataloguing-in-Publication Data
A catalogue record for this book is available from the British Library

Typeset by Newgen Publishing UK
Printed and bound in the UK by 4edge

Contents

Contents

Preface

Doing business in and with China – never easy – has become much more complicated, volatile and controversial. In 2017 Xi Jinping declared that China had entered a "new era", in which "Xi Jinping Thought on Socialist Economy with Chinese Characteristics" would be the sole guiding principle for financial and economic decision-making. "Xiconomics", for short. In 2020 Xi Jinping announced Dual Circulation Strategy as China's new development pattern, with the priority on China's domestic economy. Business too had entered a new era.

Until recently multinational companies had enjoyed rapid growth and profits in many sectors of the Chinese economy. They did this by adapting to the local context, providing products that Chinese consumers value and demonstrating to the government how their operations supported China's development. This was all part of China's increasing integration in the world economy. What mattered much less was the ideology of the Communist Party of China (CPC), questions of national security and, indeed, in which country a multinational was headquartered. To the extent that shareholders and governments back at home had a view, they supported expansion in China.

Much has now changed in this world. The China context too has transformed. China remains the world's largest market in sector after sector and is the world leader in renewables, electric vehicles and digitization. But the business environment is more uncertain – and, especially for those who have faced Covid-19 travel bans – more opaque. Business leaders now need to know how Party ideology and national security fit into China's economic ambitions. Xi Jinping's leadership pervades all questions of policy and business climate. Geopolitical tensions increase the complexity. Governments, investors, customers and employees outside China no longer automatically support investment in China. Doing more business in China can cause problems back at home, but many multinationals earn sizeable revenues and profit in China. They see further growth potential, while developing alternatives to China takes time and effort even where it is an option.

Uncertainties abound. At the time of writing it is hard to disentangle the economic impact of Covid-19 lockdowns from more deep-seated problems in the real estate sector and elsewhere. At the 20th Party Congress, held in October 2022, Xi Jinping was officially confirmed in his third term as leader. This demonstration of Xi's political dominance was followed a month later by widespread protests against his zero-Covid-19 policy and a rapid policy about-turn. What happens next is uncertain. There is now a reopening of international travel and apparent renewed focus on the economy. But many still expect a tightening of Party control over society and economy, with security remaining the priority and no clear plan to address economic challenges. For the reader, these uncertainties may have mostly resolved themselves. But we can be sure that new ones will come in their place. Against this backdrop, the purpose of this book is to provide a better understanding of the opportunities and challenges for global business in and with China today and then indicate how best to navigate the inherent uncertainty and contradictions.

We wrote this book for several reasons. First, we wanted to break down the barriers between writings on the CPC, national security, ideology and macroeconomic policy, on the one hand, and business strategy and organization, on the other. Historically, many of the former topics have been judged "too political" and so not a matter for business. Such a split is increasingly unsustainable. In today's world, and especially today's China, business leaders need an integrated view. But most cannot easily take time away from the day-to-day of business to understand what matters and what does not. This book summarizes the key points that business leaders need to know, while providing guidance on useful sources for those who want to read further. It draws on our own experience of 25 years living and working in China in both business and academia, investigating and analysing these issues.

Second, Xi Jinping's announcement of Dual Circulation Strategy struck us as timely and of great relevance for today's world of decoupling and disengagement. After decades of increasingly seamless integration across borders, Dual Circulation lays down a clear dividing line between "internal circulation" (the Chinese economy) and "external circulation" (the rest of the world). And it sees the link between the two as something to be managed – for China's advantage. The resurgence of the CPC in leading all aspects of Chinese society reinforces how different the "internal" is and will be from the "external". In contrast to his predecessors, Xi has taken the lead role in economic policy too. Xiconomics goes with Dual Circulation. This book traces a path from academic writings on Dual Circulation and the speeches of Xi Jinping through to the key choices and challenges facing China before examining what this all means for business, both in China and globally.

Finally, the 20th Party Congress has confirmed that security and ideology will play a critical role in China's future economic development – and, therefore, in its business environment. Xi Jinping spoke of the people's security as the "ultimate goal". He placed greater prominence on national security, Marxist-Leninist ideology and Party-building activities, alongside mentions of economic growth and continued opening up to the world. Moreover, Xi has consolidated the power to implement his vision – or, at least, face less resistance: the members of the new Politburo Standing Committee are all Xi loyalists, a change from the past. In CPC phraseology, China's "new era" continues, guided by the "Xi Jinping Thought" of this time. It is an era that can be understood only by looking back at the past and at the full context in which it is unfolding.

We believe that there is value in describing in summary form the ambitions, motivations and choices of China's leaders today, as best we can understand them, while highlighting uncertainty, contradictions and dilemmas. In a world of heated disagreement and partial information, understanding reality from the perspective of others is an aid. Understanding does not imply agreement; rather, it lays the basis for our own principled choices and actions.

We would like to thank all our interview partners in China, Europe and the United States for sharing their experience and perspectives with us. A big "Thank you" also goes to Margaret Siu for her research support and to Alison Howson from Agenda Publishing, who has been extremely supportive from the moment we approached her with our ideas through to the final publication of this book.

Andrew Cainey and Christiane Prange
London and Berlin

Introduction

Two years after the spread of the Covid-19 pandemic, President Xi Jinping started 2022 in expansive mood, speaking at the Davos World Economic Forum by video link from Beijing:

> In two weeks' time, China will celebrate the advent of ... the Year of the Tiger. In Chinese culture, the tiger symbolizes bravery and strength ... To meet the severe challenges facing humanity, we must "add wings to the tiger" and act with the courage and strength of the tiger to overcome all obstacles on our way forward ... The world today is undergoing major [*sic*] changes, unseen in a century ... The world is always developing through the movement of contradictions; without contradiction, nothing would exist ... Economic globalization is the trend of the times. Countries around the world should uphold true multilateralism. We should remove barriers, not erect walls. We should open up, not close off. We should seek integration, not decoupling.[1]

Xi's vaulting ambition shone through. His choice of words was considered and deliberate. Many listeners would not though have grasped their full meaning. This would have required a grounding in the phraseology used by the Communist Party of China (CPC). And, as always, reality has a way of bringing aspirations down to earth.

Despite Xi's appeal to remove barriers, Covid-19 had indeed brought barriers and walls. As he spoke, international travel in and out of China remained at minimal levels and subject to lengthy quarantine, even as travel was recovering quickly in the rest of the world. And, only three months after Xi's Davos speech, he was to order walls and barriers to be built within China too, as stringent lockdowns took effect in Shanghai and other cities in attempts to stave off the omicron variant. Since the arrival of Covid-19, China and the West had been separated, moving to different rhythms dictated by the spread of the virus. Physical separation fuelled increasingly separate information streams, perceptions and attitudes.

Although Xi spoke of opening up and integration, his true ambition was more nuanced – contradictory, even. Xi seeks a China separate from the world and yet connected with it. His Davos speech mentioned the integration. It did not mention the separation. China seeks self-reliance, so that it does not depend on others, while also gaining the benefits of links to the world and, ideally, having others become dependent on China. These messages are much clearer when Xi speaks to his domestic audience. As Xi stated, Party ideology sees contradiction as fundamental to progress. Contradiction does not mean an irreconcilable choice. It is, rather, a call to action to find a way to "have it all". Hard-charging business executives will not find this too unfamiliar: "We need to cut costs and improve service!" "It's not 'either/ or'; we need both." Yet sometimes ambitions are too great and cannot be achieved, regardless of effort.

The year 2020 was one of divergence and difference between China and Western economies. Covid-19 set the economies of the world on their individual paths of lockdowns and openings up, while international air travel ground to a halt. But it was not just Covid-19. On 10 April President Xi Jinping made a speech to the Central Financial and Economic Affairs Commission[2] that seemed designed to highlight the differences between China and the rest of the world. It also made clear where priorities lay. Xi described China's new Dual Circulation Strategy, an approach that divided the world clearly into two: China and the rest. The Chinese words used for "Dual Circulation" (国内国际双循环; *guónèi guójì shuāng xúnhuán*) illuminate the meaning. The literal meaning is "the domestic and the international, two cycles". Left unspoken is the critical question of how the two cycles (or economic domains) link together and interact. After decades of increasing integration, Covid-19 quarantines suddenly made the prospect of continued and extreme separation more imaginable. Yet, at that very moment, trade and investment flows between China and the rest of the world continued to boom. The Chinese automotive and financial sectors were continuing to open up to foreign companies. Tesla was rapidly ramping up production at its Shanghai Gigafactory.

A July 2021 article by Justin Yifu Lin, China's leading development economist and former chief economist of the World Bank, laid out the economic logic and origins of Dual Circulation. It is a framework for describing economic activity and for identifying key strategic choices for steering economic development. But the academic writings of an economist, even one with the extensive practical experience of Justin Lin, are only a part of the story.

The role of Xi Jinping in China's economy today is critical. In the history of the CPC it is the premier rather than the president (and Party secretary-general) who has held the prime responsibility for economic matters. When Xi Jinping came to power, with Li Keqiang as his premier, commentators debated the likely features of "Likonomics", Li's new approach to China's economy. But, instead of Likonomics, Chinese state media writes now of Xiconomics. In 2017 China's key annual economic meeting, the Central Economic Work Conference, concluded by defining its key economic and social policies as "Xi Jinping Economic Thought on Socialism with Chinese Characteristics for a New Era".[3] Xiconomics is broad-ranging and ambiguous indeed. It includes Xi's Davos remarks on globalization. The *China Daily* states that "the economic philosophy of Chinese President Xi Jinping, widely known as 'Xiconomics', emphasizes the market's decisive role in allocating resources; at the same time, Xiconomics allows the government to perform its functions better".[4] It includes Common Prosperity, with its promise of greater equality of opportunity; China's Belt and Road Initiative (BRI); and it even included the zero-Covid-19 policy, with the argument that this was the best route for preserving economic health in the long run.

Above all, Xiconomics takes a holistic view, including security and ideology alongside economic growth as key considerations in economic policy-making. Although policy-making always has a political dimension, Xiconomics means a much greater "mixing of politics with economics".[5] This brings with it at least some echoes of the times of Mao Zedong. Xi's leadership is characterized by the forceful exercise of power to centralize and intervene. This politicization and securitization of economic activity goes hand in hand with the Dual Circulation approach. It marks apart "internal circulation", in which Xi and the CPC hold sway, from "external circulation", in which they do not hold sway and can at best influence and negotiate. It highlights too that, for business in China, the economic is about much more than economics.

In November 2020, on the eve of Ant Financial's initial public offering (IPO), set to be the world's largest ever, the Chinese government withdrew its regulatory approval, so scuppering the deal. The decisive point probably came when Jack Ma, Ant's founder, made an appearance at a financial conference shortly before the listing. What followed was a speech that offended government officials, accusing them of minimizing risks even though, in Ma's words, "there is no innovation in this world without risk". Then, in July 2021, the Chinese government banned for-profit educational tutoring, destroying the entire sector overnight. In 2021 as a whole, China's anti-trust agency, the State Administration for Market Regulation (SAMR), imposed fines of nearly RMB 24 billion in 176 cases "as part of the country's broader efforts to maintain fair market order".[6] Legislation that affected business also came thick and fast: in 2020 the Foreign Investment Law and the Export Control Law; the following year the Anti-Foreign Sanctions Law, the Data Security Law and the Personal Information Protection Law. These laws brought together market liberalization, tighter regulations adapted to a world of data and technology, and issues of national security, often all at the same time.

What did this all mean for business, especially foreign business, uncertain of how to interpret what was happening in China and dealing with increasingly diverse views on China back at headquarters? Change, uncertainty and ambiguity in Chinese business were nothing new. But suddenly all was intensified. Paradoxically, in an environment in which the CPC "leads on everything",[7] it remained difficult to interpret what were often vaguely formulated and poorly communicated policies and ambitions.

"Dual Circulation" is a phrase whose time has come even if its precise meaning remains ambiguous. The explicit focus on separation and linkage – rather than unending integration and seamlessness – is ready-made for a world of US–China rivalry and geopolitical positioning. Xi Jinping's call to focus on internal circulation ahead of external circulation mirrors trends in many Western countries. In the United States and Europe, many argue for a "decoupling" from China, controls over trade and investment and a focus on national security and resilience.

China's Dual Circulation Strategy frames three key questions about the environment in which companies will operate. What sort of business environment will the domestic economy (internal circulation) offer? What role will China play in the rest of the world economy (external circulation)? And how will China and the rest of the world link together? This book explores these questions and then identifies options and implications for companies.

Multinationals have long built successful businesses on the back of globalizing markets, connecting and linking between countries. Now, as well as generating profits, activities in China are causing problems and risks back at headquarters too. Dual Circulation and Xiconomics represent a clear shift of emphasis from the years of reform and opening up. But they are not a "bolt from the blue" – and, by understanding why they have come about and what they mean, many companies will find a way to adapt and prosper. What works for all involved may change suddenly; in the extreme case of Russia and Ukraine, war led to business links breaking overnight. Business needs to be ready.

AN OVERVIEW OF THE BOOK

This book describes the strategic choices and imperatives facing multi-national companies in their China business. It anchors these choices in Xi Jinping's ambitions and policy priorities for China at home and abroad and in the geopolitical context.

Part I explores the meaning of Dual Circulation Strategy and Xiconomics. It examines the intellectual origins of Dual Circulation and its durability as a framework and strategy. It goes on to place this in the broader context of Xiconomics and what we call the China policy puzzle.

In the first chapter we start by defining Dual Circulation, its theoretical underpinnings and the background for the 2020 policy announcement. Dual Circulation divides the economic world into the "internal" (China), the "external" (the rest of the world) and the links between the two. It can usefully be interpreted on three different levels. First, it is a way to frame the workings of the whole economic system and identify policy choices. Second, it is itself a "strategy", reflecting certain policy choices. For China now, the decision has been made to prioritize the domestic economy over the international economy so as to strengthen China's self-reliance, upgrade industrial capabilities and bring about higher living standards. Dual Circulation also emphasizes the value that foreign know-how and capital can still bring to China. Finally, the term has been used as an umbrella phrase under which can be gathered a list of long-standing proposals for economic reform in China.

Chapter 2 then examines the historical roots of Dual Circulation Strategy. The focus on building China's technology capabilities and rebalancing demand from trade towards consumption is one of continuity rather than change. These were clear priorities in 2006 and subsequently. But this focus also harks back to the nineteenth century self-strengthening movement under the Qing dynasty. The ambitions are indeed consistent with the development paths of many countries, especially in east Asia. This chapter provides a brief overview of events in Chinese economic history over the past few centuries, drawing parallels with the framework of Dual Circulation.

Chapter 3 fits Dual Circulation into the broader context of Xiconomics. It describes Xi Jinping's ambition for a "Great Rejuvenation of the Chinese people"[8] at a time of "great changes, unseen in a century"[9] and examines the rationale and history underlying these and other terms. The buzzwords and slogans *du jour* may change, but the underlying ambitions and imperatives for the CPC do not. The chapter slots together the different pieces of this China policy puzzle to clarify these intentions and direction.

Chapter 4 then examines in detail two of Xi Jinping's speeches, focusing on Dual Circulation and Common Prosperity. These give indications of the direction, rationale and implications of these policies. The chapter also serves to illustrate both the value and the limitations of paying attention to Party speeches, to what is actually said. New speeches will come – and business can benefit from staying patient and reading these too, even though some of the language can be uninspiring and hard to penetrate.

Framing economic activity through the lens of Dual Circulation raises three distinct questions for multinational business. Part II explores each of these questions in turn.

First, Chapter 5 addresses the question of what the future business environment within China, the world of internal circulation, will be like. This is where Xi and Xiconomics play the most direct role in creating a more ideological, interventionist and security-focused economy. It is where uncertainty is greatest about the future roles of state and market, both under the umbrella of CPC leadership. Declared CPC ambitions are by no means sufficient to understand this. Business leaders need to understand China's achievements to date, the economic realities of China today, debates on the policy agenda and emerging priorities. Some proposed policies never gain traction; others appear overnight and transform the business environment.

Chapter 6 addresses the question of the role China will play in the rest of the world, in the world of external circulation. China continues to derive significant benefits from the way that the global economy operates today but would also like to shape the ways things work to its own preferences. In some areas, especially technology and data standards, a future of One World, Two Systems is starting to emerge. But establishing new global structures and standards takes effort and requires coalition-building with other countries. The chapter reviews China's priorities, but also notes the limits and constraints that China faces.

Finally, Chapter 7 addresses the question of how internal and external circulation can and will link together. It starts by outlining the ideal interrelationships from the perspective of China, where foreign know-how helps build China's capabilities. This then allows China to take a larger role in the global economy based on accumulated competitive strength. The chapter goes on to consider how other countries see their own interests, and what then the implications are for the interrelationships with China both for countries and companies. There is now much more debate and concern about questions of security, technology competition, values and human rights as well as the economic benefits of trade and investment. Outcomes will rest on mutually beneficial solutions rather than the aspirations of one side alone. China will not get what it seeks without adjustments from its current path.

In Part III, the focus shifts to the implications of Dual Circulation and Xiconomics for global business and how multinational companies need to and can adapt their business models to succeed in a new business environment.

Chapter 8 reviews the importance of China to global business today and how this varies between sectors and companies. It identifies the four different roles that China plays in the global portfolio of multinational companies. Localizers are those companies that serve the Chinese market by building up increasingly integrated operations in China (the "China-for-China" strategy). Exporters simply export to China, without significant operations in the country. Sourcers treat China as a manufacturing base from which to supply the rest of the world. Finally, for some companies, China plays no meaningful role in their business, either in sales or sourcing. These companies are Separators. In practice, most multinationals operate a blend of these strategies across different business units and business lines.

Chapter 9 analyses the impact of Dual Circulation on each of the four strategies. Examples from different industry sectors show how companies are adapting to compete more successfully and how some companies are changing strategy more radically.

Chapter 10 considers the impact of all these changes on multinationals at the global level. As companies adapt to divergent business environments between China and their home markets, they need to become more ambidextrous, behaving differently in different places. But there are limits to such ambidexterity. Issues of legal compliance, reputation, ethics and values pose difficult questions that global business leaders find it increasingly hard to duck. They face too the challenge of how to strengthen connectivity between divergent and more localized country operations, when connectivity is part of the very *raison d'être* of the multinational.

In Chapter 11 we turn to the resilience and agility that multinationals need to develop, both within their China operations and globally. Understanding what is really happening on the ground in China has become more challenging. Shared perspectives between those in the West and those in China on politics, policy and issues of the day are becoming ever more difficult. There is a premium on first-hand information-gathering and synthesis to make sense of conflicting and imperfect data. Scenarios and war games help highlight a wide range of potential outcomes, identify key warning signs and allow contingency plans to be put in place.

The concluding chapter provides a brief summary and identifies a range of scenarios that businesses need to consider. Xi's ambitions for Dual Circulation are clear, but success is not certain. This rests critically on how China's relations with other major economies develop, developments that are in the hands of those from all countries involved and not China alone. China's own domestic economic success is far from assured and is reliant both on the policy priorities that the Chinese leadership actually chooses in practice and on its skill in policy execution. On economic grounds alone, China remains a major commercial and strategic opportunity for multinationals. But these same multinationals will need to navigate much greater uncertainty and complexity to capture it.

Part I

Dual Circulation Strategy and Xiconomics

What is Dual Circulation Strategy?

On 14 May 2020, following a meeting of the Politburo Standing Committee of the Communist Party of China (CPC), Dual Circulation was announced to the world as a "new development programme of mutual benefit through domestic–international dual circulation". In other words, it highlighted the delineation between the domestic and the international economy. A month earlier, at a meeting of the Central Financial and Economic Affairs Commission, Xi had spoken in private of a "new development dynamic that focuses on domestic economic flow and features positive interplay between domestic flow and international engagement".[1]

In October 2020 Han Wenxiu, assistant head of the CPC Central Financial and Economic Affairs Commission office, said that "the proposal for a new development programme that takes the domestic market as the mainstay while letting internal and external markets boost each other is the CPC's practical application of the objective laws of economic development. This is a proactive step, not a passive response; a long-term strategy, not an interim measure."[2]

Ask different analysts – both in China and overseas – what Dual Circulation Strategy really "is" or really "means", and there will come a range of answers. It marks a closing of China to the world, as China seeks to decouple. Or it is really nothing new. It articulates a new form of globalization. Or it is a passing slogan of no import. Some may also observe that mentions of Dual Circulation in policy speeches peaked in 2020 and 2021, and argue that Party rhetoric has moved on to other phrases, such as Common Prosperity and High-Quality Development. Yet the key priorities of Dual Circulation remained clear in Xi's work report to the 20th Party Congress in October 2022. There is indeed much ambiguity about Dual Circulation – not just about the specifics, but also about the nature of the term. Is it best seen as a slogan (perhaps already past its sell-by date), a set of guiding principles or a series of policies and plans? "Dual Circulation" is by no means the only ambiguous phrase in the China policy lexicon. Such ambiguity is almost a defining feature of Chinese policy terms. It runs through discussions on Common Prosperity and the Belt and Road Initiative (BRI) too.

Dual Circulation Strategy is indeed at times a slogan, a mere phrase. But it is also much more than that. More important than the frequency with which these two words are used is the way they reflect underlying realities about China's interests, ambitions and chosen policy approach. Dual Circulation has lasting relevance as a way to frame the world economy from China's perspective and to identify the policy choices that China is making. Referring to Dual Circulation as a "new development programme" or the "practical application of the objective laws of economic development" [3] is not empty rhetoric, even though to the Western reader it may seem that way. In fact, the intellectual effort underpinning the concept appears more significant and robust than for many other Chinese policy phrases. The conceptualization is also well suited to a world in which the United States and other countries talk of "decoupling" and many raise the spectre of a One World, Two Systems splintering of the global economy. It has important implications for the future of multinationals, whose growth has been founded on increasing global integration.

The writings of Justin Yifu Lin on Dual Circulation reinforce this seriousness of intent. Lin is China's leading development economist and dean of the Institute of New Structural Economics at Peking University. He was previously chief economist of the World Bank and received his PhD in economics from the University of Chicago. In 2010 he coined the term "new structural economics" in a paper for the World Bank.[4] Drawing on China's development experience, he argued that "economic development as a dynamic process requires industrial upgrading and corresponding improvements in 'hard' and 'soft' infrastructure at each stage". Lin went on to argue that, "in addition to an effective market mechanism, the government should play an active role in facilitating industrial upgrading and infrastructure improvements". This new structural economics stands in contrast to the free-market economics of much Western development thinking. In his writings on Dual Circulation, Lin links the concept to the intellectual roots of Karl Marx and Adam Smith.[5] Looking forward, Lin writes that Dual Circulation is a core part of China's "new development" paradigm,[6] the approach being promulgated for China's future economic development in this "new era" that Xi Jinping has declared.

UNDERSTANDING DUAL CIRCULATION ON THREE DIFFERENT LEVELS

Dual Circulation is, then, more than a slogan. Yet this statement leaves open the question of what it really "is". It is helpful to separate out three different levels of meaning. At the most fundamental level, Dual Circulation is not so much a strategy as a way of framing the global economic landscape. It draws a sharp line between the internal and the external. Dual Circulation provides a lens through which to identify strategies and policy choices that help China to achieve its ambitions against that global backdrop. The second level of meaning is that Dual Circulation does indeed represent a set of strategic choices for China. Xi Jinping and others have described Dual Circulation in terms of the strategic priorities for China today. Xi states that "internal circulation" – in other words, the domestic economy – should be the "mainstay". These choices are derived from applying the framework to the conditions of the world as the Party leadership judges them to be today. Choices may change as the world changes: the framework remains a constant. Finally, the chosen strategy needs to be translated into specific policies. This is the third level of meaning for the term. In effect, a series of specific, long-standing policies – which pre-date the "Dual Circulation" vocabulary – became bundled into Dual Circulation. Policies such as property taxation or reform of the household registration system (户口; hùkǒu) are effectively "rebadged" with little or no change to the underlying substance. It is at this third level that the phrasing of Dual Circulation is likely to prove the most transient. Here, it is indeed reasonable to view Dual Circulation as a slogan rather than anything new. What matters is whether these policies are implemented or not; the nomenclature has little impact.

LEVEL 1: DUAL CIRCULATION STRATEGY AS A FRAMEWORK

To return to the first level, Dual Circulation proposes a simple framework that fits China's changed position in the world. China is a now much larger economy. Its share of world economic activity is returning to levels not seen since the middle of the nineteenth century. China has its own distinctive model of economic development and is facing tensions and headwinds in the global economy, especially from the United States. This framework has three elements: (a) the internal or domestic cycle (i.e. China); (b) the external or foreign cycle (i.e. the rest of the world); and (c) the "mutually reinforcing" linkages between the internal and the external.

The use of the term "circulation" to describe economic activity has a long intellectual tradition. In his 2021 paper "Dual Circulation: a New Structural Economics view of development",[7] Justin Yifu Lin explores the roots of "circulation" in economic thinking. Lin notes that Adam Smith describes "the division of labour and the accumulation and circulation of capital" as the sources of the wealth of nations.[8] The concept of "circulation" features heavily too in Karl Marx's writings. The second volume of *Das Kapital* is subtitled *The Process of Circulation of Capital* and subdivided into three parts, the first of which is *The Metamorphoses of Capital and their Circuits.* John Maynard Keynes' book *The General Theory of Employment, Interest and Money* also treats national economic activity as the circular flow of income.

The term "cycle" or "circulation" (循环; xúnhuán) emphasizes the flow of activities. It is a dynamic rather than static view. The same word is used for the circulation of the blood or the cycle of the seasons. This framing has more similarities with an engineering perspective (think, for example, of fluid dynamics) than with much of neoclassical economics, which focuses on questions of static resource allocation. Andrew Sheng, a long-time advisor to the Chinese government, describes Dual Circulation as "a strategic process, not a theory".[9] He goes on to state: "Chinese policy-makers, who are more often engineers than lawyers or economists, think about development in terms of an open giant complex system." Indeed, in a speech that Xi Jinping gave to local officials in January 2021, he describes the economic challenges in the following words:

The key to building a new development dynamic is to ensure unimpeded economic flow, just the same as a healthy person needs to keep the blood vessels circulating freely to maintain a good balance of vital energy and blood. Economic activity requires the integration of various production factors at the stages of production, allocation, distribution, and consumption in order to realize a circular flow. Under normal circumstances, smooth economic flow will lead to increased material products, greater social wealth, improved wellbeing among the people, and enhanced national strength, giving rise to an upward spiral of development. When obstructions and breakages emerge, economic flow is disrupted.[10]

This perspective of systems dynamics is also helpful in thinking through the "mutually reinforcing" links between the internal and external, where they can work and where such links bring problems. Xi's mention of "smooth economic flow" is indeed an argument for continued reform and opening up of China and the benefits of free trade. Although, notably, Xi argued the case for globalization at the Davos World Economic Forum in 2017, economic benefits are now increasingly wrapped up with questions of national security. The key proviso in Xi's speech above is perhaps the phrase "under normal circumstances". Chapter 3 explores the broader context for Dual Circulation Strategy, including Xi's belief that the global landscape is undergoing "great changes, unseen in a century".

To return to the framework, it can apply at this level of abstraction to any economy, just as with Marxian and Keynesian economics. It also does not describe a particular policy, emphasis or strategy. All that is stated is that there is an "internal" ("home" or "us") and an external ("foreign" or "them"), and that there is a need to define how and where the two link together to get the best outcomes for the country as whole.

This framing does reflect a choice, however, and a change in how to understand the global economy at this most abstract level. The Dual Circulation framework is the simplest representation of a changed global economic landscape. As with any such abstraction, it simplifies and concentrates on what is most important, omitting the rest. The recent decades of economic globalization were underpinned by an assumption that borders did not really matter much, and that – if they did – they soon would not. Tariffs and non-tariffs barriers were falling. Multinational corporations dispersed their operating activities across different countries in distributed value chains. International negotiations focused on harmonizing or eliminating differential tax policies, industrial subsidies and support to state-owned enterprises.

Dual Circulation frames the world differently. It asserts that the internal and external are indeed distinct – and that they should be treated as such. Linkages between the internal and external also matter. They are to be designed, configured and managed. There are choices to be made in order to secure the benefits of positive linkages and avoid the costs of the negative. Increasingly, the world is not "seamless" or "frictionless". Borders matter. And economic systems are not converging to one, Western, model. This is especially true for the Chinese economy. Governments have more control and influence over what happens domestically than in the international arena. For China, this is especially the case, with Xi Jinping's leadership of an activist, interventionist party-state and an extensive state-owned sector. A new framework makes sense. This has wide-ranging consequences for the corporate world, which has based much of its growth on a world of ever more seamless globalization.

LEVEL 2: PUTTING THE "STRATEGY" INTO DUAL CIRCULATION STRATEGY

The first level highlights the "Dual Circulation" of Dual Circulation Strategy. The second concentrates on the "Strategy". Strategy is about making choices to achieve certain objectives. In an economic landscape split between internal and external, there are, from a top-down perspective, four strategic questions for China's leaders – indeed, for the leaders of any country.

1. Internal circulation: what sort of economic and business environment best supports China's future development?
2. Between internal and external, which offers the greater potential for China's development and where should the greater focus be?

3. External circulation: what role does China seek to play in the world economy?
4. How and for what purpose should the internal and external link together?

The way in which China answers these questions will affect the business environment for global business both in China and the rest of the world. Xi Jinping and the Chinese leadership have espoused reasonably clear views on how to answer each of the questions. In his August 2020 speech Xi Jinping stated: "I proposed to establish a new development paradigm with a large domestic circulation as the mainstay, and the domestic–international dual circulation to reinforce each other." Lin too addresses this strategic choice, in addition to his description of Dual Circulation as a framework. He highlights domestic circulation as "the major driving force for China's sustainable development".[11]

This marks a distinct shift from the way that China has described its economic development since the late 1970s. In 1978 Deng Xiaoping announced the start of "reform and opening up" (改革开放; *gǎigé kāifàng*). This emphasized reducing the differences between China and the rest of the world (through market-based reform) and in increasing the linkages. In 1988 Wang Jian, an economist in the State Development Planning Commission, described this approach – China's export-led growth model – as "taking part in the great international circulation".[12] Of course, during this period many changes took place in China's domestic economy. Internal circulation was by no means ignored. In fact, domestic reforms were the main source of productivity and income gains. The primary orientation, however, was how China would link to the rest of the world, to the "great international circulation". Xi himself has referenced this change. He has contrasted the present need to focus on internal circulation with the previous strategy of "putting both ends of the production process in the world"[13] – in other words, sourcing raw materials from overseas and then exporting back finished goods: 两头在外，打进打出 (*liǎngtóu zàiwài, dǎ jìn dǎchū*). This, he has argued, is no longer feasible or appropriate.

Lin describes the tilt to internal circulation as "the response to new challenges as well as the economic reality that China is facing".[14] It is a consequence both of China's sheer size as a market and of growing protectionism around the world, which limits the opportunities for continued export growth. In other words, the opportunities appear greater close to home. It is also about non-economic considerations. Xi referenced Covid-19's impact on China in a January 2021 speech:

> During my visit to Zhejiang province, I found that global industrial and supply chains had been partially disrupted due to the pandemic ... Many companies were forced to suspend operations because they could not bring in the raw materials and personnel they needed or send their goods overseas. I realized just how much things had changed; the environments and conditions that had facilitated large-scale imports and exports were no longer in place. Given these new circumstances, we needed to come up with new thinking to steer development.[15]

But it is not really Covid-19 that is the problem here – especially not Covid-19 outside China. Even allowing for supply chain interruptions of the kind that Xi describes, China's trade with the rest of the world boomed during 2020 and 2021. It was the China lockdowns of 2022 that had a much larger disruptive impact, impeding internal circulation even more than the external. More fundamental is Xi's concern at China's dependence on the rest of the world, its dependence on external circulation. It is not a coincidence that Dual Circulation emerged in the wake of the actions of the administration of Donald Trump (2017–21) against China. President Trump's focus on the bilateral trade deficit between the United States and China and the resulting tariffs did indeed pose a traditional threat to China's export activity. US restrictions on technology exports were even more significant, however. This has continued, more structured and formalized, under the administration of Joe Biden.

In 2018 the US government imposed sanctions on ZTE, China's second-largest telecommunications equipment manufacturer, for doing business with Iran and North Korea. These sanctions made it illegal for American suppliers to do business with ZTE, cutting off supplies of key components. After accepting the presence of US monitors to validate compliance and paying fines of around US$1 billion, ZTE emerged in July 2018 from an episode that nearly closed down the business.[16]

The much-larger Huawei continues to be the subject of sanctions. Huawei's smartphone business suffered as it lost access to advanced semiconductors and Google services and products. Many Western countries also decided not to buy Huawei 5G network equipment because of concerns over security risks and persistent US pressure. Whatever the merits of these actions, they demonstrated China's vulnerability to US policies in a very tangible manner.

Subsequent US policies have – from the Chinese perspective – served only to increase this sense of risk and exposure and justify China's concerns. As of May 2022 around 1,000 Chinese companies were being penalized in one way or another by the US government for national security or human rights reasons.[17] US objectives are even clearer in the wake of the US CHIPS and Science Act of August 2022 and the subsequent announcement of stringent export controls on all stages of the advanced semiconductor value chain. Jake Sullivan, the US National Security Advisor, has stated that "we have to revisit the long-standing premise ..." whereby the United States "maintained a 'sliding scale' approach ... to stay only a couple of generations ahead". He went on, "[T]hat is not the strategic environment we are in today. Given the foundational nature of certain technologies ... we must maintain as large of a lead [*sic*] as possible."[18] In sum, Xi sees that China is now facing a tougher, more hostile global environment, against which China needs to insulate itself.

Just as Xi emphasizes the primacy of internal circulation, so too he has emphasized the importance of linkages between the internal and the external. The message is clear that such linkages are important in both directions. Focusing on internal circulation does not mean autarky. It does not mean closing the door. For Lin as well, internal and external "are being used to mutually promote and reinforce a higher-quality economic circulation".[19]

In the realm of internal circulation, Xi has advanced an active policy agenda. It is one that focuses on increasing self-reliance and China's ability to produce key technologies for itself and on stimulating domestic demand. Overseas, too, China seeks a more active role. In his January 2021 speech, Xi argued:

> We should ... foster new advantages for China's participation in international economic cooperation and competition

> ... Through competition in the international market, we should boost the competitiveness of our export products and services and promote industrial transformation and upgrading to increase China's influence in global industry chains, supply chains, and innovation chains. Chinese enterprises now have interests that extend to many countries around the world. This requires that we pay more attention to understanding international affairs and carrying out thorough studies on stakeholders, trading partners, and investment destinations, in order to establish a clear picture of potential benefits and risks.[20]

This does not represent a strategic choice to cut China off from the world. The ambition is instead for a China that is more active internationally, more competitive and more successful, based on a better understanding of global affairs. The aim is to blend internationalization and self-reliance, to be separate and also connected. It is a strategy of "hedged integration", in the words of Jude Blanchette and Andrew Polk at the Center for Strategic and International Studies (CSIS), a Washington, DC, think tank. Blanchette and Polk argue that "this model entails engaging international capital, financial, and technological markets when advantages can be gained while simultaneously bolstering indigenous capabilities to avoid overreliance on the global economy – due to national security concerns or the vagaries of global economic cycles".[21]

LEVEL 3: FROM "GRAND STRATEGY" TO POLICY SPECIFICS AND THE TRANSIENCE OF SLOGANS

"Grand strategy" is a reasonable way to describe the four strategic choices within Dual Circulation. It is a grand strategy indeed that boils down the economic choices facing China to a mere four. The policy changes required for China's successful economic development are many, while Dual Circulation sets only the broadest of directions. Lin writes that Dual Circulation "provides policy makers and firms a clear reference point about China's development trajectory in a new era".[22] Prioritizing the internal over the external is indeed a strategic direction. It says nothing about the economic policies that make sense in the domestic economy, however, or for China's engagement with the rest of the world. This is where the ambiguity of Dual Circulation resurfaces – and where it also has the trappings of a transient policy slogan.

As more details emerged on the key policy elements of Dual Circulation, so the list started to look very familiar to any seasoned observer of China's economic policy debates. One key ambition for Dual Circulation is to rebalance demand away from exports and towards domestic demand, in particular towards consumption. *Hukou* reform is to spur labour market mobility and productivity. Industry is to innovate more and shift from lower value-added to higher-value-added products; the service sector is to grow; urbanization is to continue; the health system must be upgraded – especially, after Covid-19, in the area of epidemic prevention and control. Certainly, there are now greater efforts to develop advanced semiconductor manufacturing in China and to establish technology leadership across many new technologies. These are all long-held ambitions, however. Important though the policy ideas are, none of them is new. This should not be surprising, however. China's fundamental economic challenges and choices remain unchanged. The clearest application of "circulation" thinking to the domestic economic reform came in the spring of 2022 with the announcement of renewed policy efforts to create the "national unified market". Covid-19 restrictions and state-backed investment programmes had led to increasing local protectionism and barriers rather than smooth economic flows within China. Circulation was an appealing narrative to force through standardization and domestic opening.

Linking these policy proposals to the concept of Dual Circulation does nothing in itself to advance reform – other than to ensure that they do not "get lost" and retain some form of legitimacy. Already in 2021, as the term "Common Prosperity" gained more prominence, these same ambitions and policies became key elements of Common Prosperity. And then, early in 2022, Common Prosperity was mentioned less in speeches and CPC announcements, until it returned to prominence in the second half of the year and the 20th Party Congress. Yet throughout this time the policy challenges and options remained the same.

2

Dual Circulation: more continuity than change

In 2011 the CEO of a US multinational met a senior Chinese official in a Shanghai Starbucks store. "What impresses you the most about China?" asked the official. "The speed of change. How fast everything moves. How it changes," replied the CEO. "Really? Do you think so?" teased the official. "But we have been talking about the same policy challenges for many years – the need to have more consumption, the need to upgrade our economy and innovate, the need to reduce reliance on debt finance, the ageing population. Not much is changing. And yet – look outside. People are satisfied; things are working; everyone is getting richer. We have time and space to resolve our issues," the official concluded.

The strategic choices that Xi Jinping announced for his Dual Circulation Strategy in 2020 were in fact not so new. Xi highlighted the need to strengthen China's own technological capabilities and to expand domestic consumer demand as the mainstay of China's future growth. Yet 14 years earlier, in 2006, the messages had been the same. China's future growth was to be based on home-grown "indigenous innovation", and the growth of China as a consumer market. Even then the internal was to be favoured over the external. Xi's policy is more continuity than change.

A report by the Carnegie Endowment for International Peace at that time observed that, "in recent years, China has paid more attention to furthering the development of domestic Chinese standards and technologies. It has done so largely to upgrade the country's industrial base, thus retaining more added value, but it has also done so to secure a seat at the table where global standards are set."[1] The 2006 Medium and Long-Term Programme for Science and Technology (MLP) set criteria for the accreditation of so-called national indigenous innovation products (NIIPs). These NIIPs would receive preference in public procurement. The plan included technologies such as biotech, information technology, advanced materials and manufacturing, energy technology, marine technology, laser technology and aerospace technology.

In the very same year, 2006, McKinsey published a report entitled *From 'Made in China' to 'Sold in China': The Rise of the Chinese Urban Consumer.*[2] The report argued that, "while the production side of China's economy has boomed with two decades of 10 per cent growth, the consumer side has yet to live up to its promise". It went on to argue that "China's economy is on the verge of an important transition in which its consumers will begin to take their place on the world stage".

China's consumer markets have indeed grown rapidly in the interim, reaching a level over three times larger than in 2006, adjusted for inflation.[3] The share of household consumption in the economy is little changed, however, accounting for 38 per cent in 2020, a level well below that of other major economies. Domestic demand certainly has played a greater role in China's economic growth, but it has been in the form of increased, debt-financed investment rather than a growing share of consumption in the economy. In 2015 the State Council also announced the launch of the Made in China 2025 initiative (MIC 2025; 中国制造; *zhōngguó zhìzào* 2025).[4] This marked a renewed effort to establish leadership positions for China in ten key industries.[5]

The focus of Dual Circulation on technology upgrading and domestic consumption represents a continuation of previous policy. It is also a quite natural part of China's economic progression. These two elements are a proven path for development. Technological innovation and diffusion provide the basis for higher productivity, and so higher living standards. Increasing consumption – spread broadly across the population or concentrated in certain elites – is both the reward for such productivity and a stimulus for further development through demand growth. A key question for China, as for any country, is how engagement with the rest of the world ("external circulation") can help strengthen China's own prosperity and security.

MAKE THE FOREIGN SERVE CHINA: DUAL CIRCULATION IN HISTORICAL PERSPECTIVE

In 1964 Mao Zedong wrote to students of the Central Conservatory of Music and urged them to "make the foreign serve China". In this instance, Mao meant that they should adopt the good qualities of foreign cultures to enrich Chinese culture.[6] Anne-Marie Brady's book of the same title explores how the CPC has managed its relations with foreigners since 1921.[7] More broadly, throughout its history China has grappled with the question of how best to advance the country's autonomous development, reaping the benefits of engagement beyond China's borders while managing the risks of dependence and foreign influence.

Applying the framework of Dual Circulation retrospectively to China's economic development through history reveals how Xi's strategic choices today find echoes in similar choices over the past several centuries. The focus on "reform and opening up" in an era of globalization is but one part of this story. The explicit division between the internal and the external, in both narrative and substance, is a more enduring feature than the framing of frictionless borders and free-market globalization. This is not just the case for China. Although countries have long sought gains from engaging with the rest of the world, the common purpose has been to support national development and interests as judged by country leaders at the time.

Throughout history China has shifted the balance between focusing on the internal and engaging with the external, at times closing off and at other times opening up. China has had periods of shutting itself off from external developments and foreign influences. At other times it has opened up, to learn from and integrate foreign thinking. For the most part, China's leaders at the time have done this based on their assessment of costs and benefits. Exceptionally, during the "Century of Humiliation" starting from 1839, China lost the ability to make this assessment for itself. China found itself dependent on the choices of others. Rebuilding the capacity to make such decisions for itself became, understandably, a national priority.

DISTINGUISHING BETWEEN THE INTERNAL
AND THE EXTERNAL

Dual Circulation's explicit distinction between the "internal" and the "external" marks a shift from the years of globalization, when most countries sought to integrate "into" the "global economy". It harks back to a prior state of the world. Throughout human history it has been natural for societies to make explicit the difference between the domestic and the foreign. For the Romans, groups outside the Roman Empire were "barbarians", people who dressed differently, ate different foods, had different religions and did not belong to the civilized world. National identity matters.

To the extent that it has looked beyond its borders through history, China too has placed itself at the centre. According to the traditional Chinese conception of the world, the Middle Kingdom stood at the centre of three concentric circles. The inner circle, with China in the middle (thus "middle country": 中国; *zhōngguó*), represented the fully civilized area. From the seventeenth century to the early twentieth this consisted of the then Qing dynasty and its border zones. The next circle out comprised Korea, Burma (now Myanmar), Vietnam, Laos and others, considered to be less civilized countries and asked to pay tribute to the Middle Kingdom. In the outermost circle were more distant countries that, according to the Chinese view, had no contact with Confucianism as the dominant belief system. They were therefore considered uncivilized barbarians. This Sino-centric worldview has helped shape China's understanding of world order. China – like any country – has always sought to define relations with the world around it to its own advantage. Remember too that China was the world's largest economy for many years up to the late nineteenth century, when the United States surpassed it.[8] As a large country with its own distinctive heritage, culture and power structures, China's leaders have determined the role of trading relationships against that backdrop.

MANAGING THE EXTERNAL TO BENEFIT THE INTERNAL

"Our Celestial Empire possesses all things in prolific abundance and lacks no product within its own borders. There was therefore no need to import the manufactures of outside barbarians in exchange for our own produce."[9] This response from Emperor Qianlong to Lord Macartney, the envoy of Britain's King George III, in 1793 is often cited as a demonstration of China's closed approach to the outside world and as a misguided decision not to accept the benefits of trade.

This selective interpretation misses the point. In fact, China had long appreciated the benefits of trade. The ability to purchase stronger horses in exchange for silk lay at the heart of early Silk Road trades.[10] What is missing is the full context for the economic relations that the British were proposing. Emperor Qianlong's letter came in response to broader demands from the British alongside the offer of trade. These included a reduction in tariffs, ceding two territorial bases to Britain and agreeing to receive a British ambassador in the Chinese capital.[11] Taken all together, agreeing to these British demands, and so receiving more "manufactures", was not an exchange that the Chinese emperor found attractive. Since the seventeenth century China had concentrated its trade with the outside world through the southern port of Canton, today's Guangzhou. From 1757 onwards this was formalized into the Canton System, whereby traders from Britain, Portugal and other countries had to conduct business with China only in Canton, subject to Chinese law. Despite the best efforts of countries, especially Britain, to overturn this approach, it persisted until 1842. China both wanted and was able to set the terms on which it engaged with the rest of the world. In 2022 the Chinese Academy of History published research arguing that China's isolation during the Ming and Qing dynasties was motivated by the need to "safeguard territory and culture" and that, "from the contemporary point of view, whether a country should open itself up is an issue within its own sovereignty".[12]

Indeed, China's leaders had earlier also made a different choice to European countries after a period of maritime exploration. In the fifteenth century Emperor Yongle sent Admiral Zheng He on several expeditions aimed at increasing trade and securing tribute from foreign powers. Similar explorations in Europe led to colonization and trade. In China, however, this did not happen. After Zheng He's death, China again closed the door on the outside world. The emperor banned the construction of ocean-going ships and prohibited existing ones from being used for voyages beyond Chinese coastal waters. Several reasons lay behind this. The expeditions cost more than the revenue that they generated and other states appeared unwilling to play the role of tributary state to a Sino-centric "middle kingdom". China also had other priorities, needing to protect itself from the Mongols in the north.[13] Better to cut off contact than have to accept challenges to the established Chinese worldview for no economic gain and at potential risk to national security, given the Mongol challenge.

THE NEED FOR SELF-RELIANCE

It was Britain's growing economic, political and military strength that brought pressure for change that China was no longer able to resist. This culminated in the Opium Wars of the mid-nineteenth century, when Britain fought to continue illegal opium sales in the face of Chinese resistance. Superior British force marked the start of the "Century of Humiliation", when it was foreign nations and not China that set the terms of engagement between China and the rest of the world. The arrival of foreign traders exposed China to Western technologies in mechanization, transportation, steam power and other innovations. It also brought unequal treaties that disadvantaged China and granted concessions to foreign powers, with foreign and not Chinese law holding sway. This historical experience of dependence remains an important part of Chinese education to this day. It also forms a core element of the CPC's narrative on how the Party is leading China away from humiliation and towards national rejuvenation.

In the nineteenth century it was the ruling Qing dynasty rather than the not yet founded CPC that sought to restore the strength of the Chinese people. From 1861 to 1895 three Qing governors-general launched a series of institutional reforms, the so-called "self-strengthening movement", that would draw on Western technologies in order to strengthen the Qing dynasty. The movement drew too on Chinese traditional wisdom, as expressed in the ancient Book of Changes (易经; I Ching). This included phrases such as "the superior man makes himself strong" and "learn the superior technology of the barbarian, in order to control him". These efforts had some impact, especially in the military sphere, but success overall was limited. Those successes that were achieved came to an abrupt end with China's defeat in the First Sino-Japanese War of 1895. Three years later, in 1898, saw the Hundred Days' Reform, a 103-day national, cultural, political and educational reform movement. Reformers under Emperor Guangxu argued that institutional and ideological change was needed in addition to the efforts of the self-strengthening movement. But this reform also failed, following a coup led by Empress Dowager Cixi.

The determinative role of foreign powers continued into the twentieth century. Western nations continued to seek influence over a China that, quite reasonably, resented foreign dominance. This sparked the Boxer Rebellion, an anti-foreign, anti-colonial and anti-Christian uprising against foreign control. Yet the Qing dynasty remained weak. The 1911 Revolution brought to an end the 2,000-year-old imperial system and led to the establishment of the "Republic of China", under the leadership of Sun Yat-sen and the Kuomintang party (KMT).[14] At the Treaty of Versailles in 1919, however, following the First World War, Western countries continued to ignore China's pleas to end territorial concessions and foreign control. Internally, power struggles continued between the KMT and the newly formed Communist Party of China, founded in 1921. In 1931 Japan invaded Manchuria in north-east China and established its own government, under the name "Manchukuo", in 1932. On 7 July 1937 Japan launched a full-scale invasion of China, and by 1939 it controlled most of China's eastern seaboard. By 1941 the United States had begun to help the KMT, which controlled the cities, while the CPC had a strong hold over the countryside. In September 1945 Japan surrendered in China. The civil war within China continued until, on 1 October 1949, as the KMT withdrew to Taiwan, Mao Zedong established the "People's Republic of China". For China, this brought an end to the Century of Humiliation, a century that had brought home the need for China to have the strength to set its own course, not be dependent on others.

SELF-RELIANCE IN PRACTICE: DIFFERENT MEANINGS

Under Chairman Mao's rule, from 1949 to 1976, China entered one of its most closed periods, yet China still did not close itself off completely to foreign influence. China's first Five-Year Plan in 1953 laid out the initial steps towards socialist industrialization.[15] Mao is well known for his espousal of "self-reliance" (自力更生; *zìlì gēngshēng*) as the path forward for China. During the Chinese Civil War, in 1946, Mao had described self-reliance as "the very opposite"[16] of Chiang Kai-shek's dependence on US military aid. Yet Mao later explained that many of the Five-Year Plan policies relied on "copying from the Soviets".[17] Between 1946 and 1960 the Soviet Union delivered aid, transferred technology and sent over 10,000 technical advisors. Paradoxically, the success of the 1953–57 Five-Year Plan encouraged Mao to assert that China could grow more rapidly by giving "primary importance"[18] to self-reliance. This emphasis intensified in the wake of the Sino-Soviet political split of the early 1960s. Yet self-reliance still did not exclude trade with the West if this served China's interests.

In fact, all subsequent leaders – not just Xi Jinping – have supported the doctrine of "self-reliance". Once again, a simple word, "self-reliance", has taken on a variety of meanings to suit the priorities of the time. As Neil Thomas writes, "Self-reliance fundamentally means that the CPC will retain ultimate control over China's economic development – an enduring consensus that has heavily influenced policy across generations of leaders."[19] "Self-reliance is not autarky, i.e. self-reliance can be associated with openness," he continues. The strategic focus of Xi's Dual Circulation on reducing dependence on external circulation and eliminating points of vulnerability has a long history.

REFORM AND OPENING UP IN A GLOBALIZING WORLD

Deng Xiaoping's era of "reform and opening up" brought a new vocabulary and orientation to China's development. It did not, however, renounce self-reliance as a goal. Following Mao's death in 1976, Deng gradually assumed the leadership of China, obtaining full control in 1978. Best known as the architect of China's "open door" policy, Deng launched this policy with the words "only development makes sense".[20] He recognized that China's economy would develop more rapidly with foreign capital, foreign know-how and the opportunity to compete in foreign markets.

This opening was the means to an end, however, rather than an end in itself. Self-reliance remained integral to Deng's thinking. In the

"Resolution on certain questions in the history of our Party since the founding of the PRC",[21] Deng argued against a "closed door policy". He confirmed, however, that "independence and self-reliance" were fundamental to the Chinese nation. The objective of reform and opening up was to use foreign participation and influence to strengthen China's economy and so, in turn, also maintain the legitimacy and rule of the CPC. Self-reliance also formed the driving force of Xi's Made in China 2025 policy. These policies all aim to utilize the external whenever it is helpful in developing the internal. The approaches of both Deng and Xi are consistent with Mao's 1964 edict to "make the foreign serve China".[22]

China's opening up since 1978; the acceleration of globalization that followed the fall of the Berlin Wall in 1989; and China's 2001 accession to the World Trade Organization (WTO) all pointed to a new era of integration and openness between countries. From outside China, then WTO director-general Pascal Lamy observed in 2006 that "China was strong when it opened to the world. When the Middle Kingdom closed its door, it fell behind."[23] The perspective from inside China was subtly different. The reform years were a time of experimentation, a time to engage with external actors and thereby change the country's path. Reforms included a modern tax system, enterprise reforms, the development of commercial banks and social reforms including housing and urban restructuring and the introduction of private property.[24] Following on from Deng, Jiang Zemin and then Hu Jintao maintained the focus on reform and opening up. Even today the phrase remains an important element of government policy. In parallel, Jiang and Hu pursued Deng's mantra that China should "hide its strength, bide its time, never take the lead" (韬光养晦，决不当头; *tāo guāng yǎng huì, jué bù dāng tóu*) in world affairs. China had priorities to address at home. This too has changed under Xi.

3

Xiconomics and the China policy puzzle

At the opening of the 13th National People's Congress in Beijing, the then premier, Li Keqiang, presented the 2022 Government Work Report, which laid out policy priorities for the coming year. China analysts scurried away to count mentions of "Dual Circulation" and of "Common Prosperity", a term that had achieved even greater prominence in 2021. Those looking came back almost empty-handed. Instead, Xinhua described the term "High-Quality Development" as "grabbing the spotlight as one of the catchphrases".[1] At times in China, policy pronouncements seem no more than an alphabet soup of disconnected phrases, falling in and out of fashion. It can be hard to understand which represent lasting priorities and which are simply slogans of the day.

"Dual Circulation" is but one term among many mentioned in policy speeches. How do these different terms fit together? What is the mix between slogan and substance? The consistent element is the central – or, in the phrasing of CPC discourse, "core"[2] – role of Xi Jinping. Rather than an alphabet soup of terms, think of them as pieces of a jigsaw puzzle of Chinese economic policy that together make up Xiconomics. In addition to Dual Circulation, six more jigsaw pieces help make sense of the context, objectives and overall policy agenda of Xi Jinping and the CPC. Fitted together, they highlight the differences between China's domestic environment and the rest of the world. These very differences demonstrate the distinction between the internal and the external. For foreign businesses, they provide substance to the cliché that "China is different" that goes beyond differences in consumer preferences and competitive environment. They reinforce the importance of Dual Circulation as a framework with which to assess the economic and business landscape.

THE CHINA POLICY PUZZLE

This chapter describes these six additional pieces and attempts to fit them together. The first is a simple fact: the CPC rules China and Xi Jinping rules the CPC. Although no individual's hold on power is guaranteed, Xi is widely acknowledged as the most powerful Chinese leader since Mao Zedong. Second is a phrase, the "Great Rejuvenation of the Chinese people". Xi uses this expression to place his CPC agenda for China in the broad sweep of history. The third piece is the new definition of success for China's development. In the language of Party ideology, Xi Jinping has changed the "principal contradiction" that all policy must address. In 2017 Xi declared that "what we now face is the contradiction between unbalanced and inadequate development and the people's ever-growing needs for a better life".[3] Deng Xiaoping had formulated the contradiction as "between the ever-growing material and cultural needs of the people and backward social production".[4] The fourth piece of the puzzle is the assessment that the Chinese leadership has made of the global environment facing China. In this view, the world today faces "great changes, unseen in a century", which presents both opportunity and risk for China. Indeed, since he came to power, Xi Jinping has placed great priority on all matters of national security, the fifth piece of the puzzle. He has defined security in a broad, holistic way to encompass all aspects of society. Finally come Xi Jinping's global "initiatives". Of these, the most important is the Belt and Road Initiative, announced in 2013 as the main plank of China's foreign policy and engagement with the rest of the world. Despite troubled investment projects and pushback around the world, the BRI remains important. Its focus has evolved into the Digital Silk Road, taking China's technological capabilities overseas, especially to lower- and middle-income economies. More recently have come the Global Initiative on Data Security, the Global Development Initiative and the Global Security Initiative.

JIGSAW PIECE 1: THE COMMUNIST PARTY OF CHINA AND XI JINPING'S LEADERSHIP

Since the founding of the People's Republic of China, the CPC has been the ruling party of China. Until Xi Jinping came to power in November

2012, however, there were increasing attempts to distinguish the role of the CPC from that of the state. State structures took a stronger role in governing, while Party ideology became less prominent. Under Xi Jinping, the Party is back in pole position. In 2017 this was made explicit in the CPC constitution: "Party, government, army, society and education – east and west, south and north – the Party leads on everything" (党政军民学，东西南北中，当是领导一切的; *dǎng zhèng jūn mín xué, dōng xī nán běi zhōng, dǎng shì lǐngdǎo yīqiè de*).[5] As of 2021 the CPC had more than 90 million members, with its own separate structure for discipline and investigation, in the form of the Central Commission for Discipline and Inspection (CCDI). Since 2018 the CCDI has worked together with the National Supervisory Commission, which has a remit for Party and non-Party members.

From the late 1950s onwards so-called "leading small groups" (LSGs: 领导小组; *lǐngdǎo xiǎozǔ*) have played an important role in policy, especially on issues that cut across government departments and responsibilities. They bring together the senior figures relevant for a policy area, often with competing interests and perspectives and so both coordinate and force alignment. Under Xi Jinping, LSGs have grown in number and taken on a stronger role, and in 2018 the most important were upgraded to the status of "commission" (委员会; *wěiyuánhuì*).[6] Both LSGs and commissions serve as decision-making and oversight bodies for policy areas such as "Deepening Overall Reform", "Integrated Military and Civilian Development" and "Financial and Economic Affairs" (all these are commissions). New LSGs highlight new policy priorities: in 2021 an LSG for "Peak Carbon and Carbon Neutrality" was created. Xi himself chairs the most important of these commissions and LSGs.

In his first speech as CPC secretary-general, in 2012, Xi identified corruption as the main challenge facing the Party and a threat to the legitimacy of Party rule. "Tigers" and "flies" (senior and junior officials) alike were to be targeted. This focus on corruption has persisted. Since the campaign's inception, 4 million Party officials have been found guilty. In 2021 alone the number reached 627,000.[7] In 2022 Xi again identified the anti-corruption campaign as a top priority, in which "no mercy" would be shown.[8]

The very interpretation of what is "corrupt" lies at the heart of Xi's exercise of power. The campaign has identified many egregious examples of corruption. It has also proved an effective and useful tool for removing or cowing political opponents and ensuring compliance with policy directives. Research by MacroPolo, the in-house think tank of the Paulson Institute in Chicago, has found that half the recent "anti-corruption" cases addressed issues of poor performance and failure to implement policy appropriately rather than traditional examples of graft.[9] The title of its research report: "From fear to behavior modification".

Within the CPC's centralized structure, Xi is acknowledged as the most dominant leader since Mao. In 2018 Xi Jinping Thought was written into the Chinese constitution alongside Mao Zedong and Deng Xiaoping Thought. Only for Mao had this constitutional amendment been made during his lifetime.[10] "Xi Jinping Thought on socialism with Chinese characteristics in a new era" (to use the full name) sets out how CPC leadership and the administrative state bureaucracy should be fused into one integrated system governing China's polity, economy and society.[11] 2018 also saw a rule change that removed term limits on Xi's role as president of China (although the position of CPC secretary-general has no such limit), a move reported as "making Xi president for life".[12] In 2021 this was followed by a new "resolution on history" (历史决议; *lìshǐ juéyì*) at the Sixth Plenum of the CPC's 19th Central Committee. Such resolutions allow the reinterpretation of history in a way that sets the political agenda for the future. In the words of Mao, they "make the past serve the present".[13] Again, only Mao and Deng had previously presided over such a change. The phrase "socialism with Chinese characteristics" has now been replaced in Party narratives with "a new era of socialism with Chinese characteristics with Xi Jinping as core".[14] Xi is the "helmsman" and, at times, "people's leader" – phrases used previously for Mao Zedong.[15]

The resurgence of the Party and Xi Jinping's dominant, centralizing role as leader are the determining factors in understanding the context for policy and business in China today. The impact of this exercise of power is not always clear. When compliance becomes the focus of anti-corruption campaigns, it is hard to disentangle where this helpfully removes roadblocks to welcome reforms and where it ensures that contrary voices dare not point out policy mistakes. Behind the scenes, there remain those who disagree with Xi's leadership – because they seek power for themselves, disagree on policy direction, resent lost political influence or have suffered financially in the crackdown on corruption.

The 20th Party Congress demonstrated the power that Xi has accumulated, however. He secured his third term as leader, and so will remain in power until 2027, at least. The new Politburo Standing Committee is composed entirely of Xi loyalists. Li Qiang, Cai Qi, Ding Xuexiang and Li Xi joined current members Wang Huning and Zhao Leji. There is no apparent successor to Xi among these individuals, though, all of them being men in their 60s. It is also unclear whether, in practice, Xi now has a greater ability to implement policies that faced resistance beforehand, or whether any such opposition always was limited.

JIGSAW PIECE 2: THE GREAT REJUVENATION OF THE CHINESE PEOPLE AFTER THE CENTURY OF HUMILIATION

Restoring the pride and strength of the Chinese people lies at the heart of the CPC's claim to power. The phrase "Great Rejuvenation of the Chinese people" (伟大复兴; *wěidà fùxīng*) recurs in speech after speech. It stands as a counterpoint and response to China's "Century of Humiliation", described in the previous chapter. Xi Jinping's words on the 100th anniversary of the Party's founding illustrate how the CPC defines its role in the context of China's history:

> The Chinese nation is a great nation. With a history of more than 5,000 years, China has made indelible contributions to the progress of human civilization. After the Opium War of 1840, however, China was gradually reduced to a semi-colonial, semi-feudal society and suffered greater ravages than ever before. The country endured intense humiliation, the people were subjected to great pain, and the Chinese civilization was plunged into darkness. Since that time, national rejuvenation has been the greatest dream of the Chinese people and the Chinese nation.
>
> Since the very day of its founding, the Party has made seeking happiness for the Chinese people and rejuvenation for the Chinese nation its aspiration and mission. All the struggle, sacrifice, and creation through which the Party has

39

united and led the Chinese people over the past hundred years has been tied together by one ultimate theme – bringing about the Great Rejuvenation of the Chinese nation. Through tenacious struggle, the Party and the Chinese people showed the world that the Chinese people had stood up, and that the time in which the Chinese nation could be bullied and abused by others was gone forever.

We must uphold the firm leadership of the Party. China's success hinges on the Party. The more than 180-year-long modern history of the Chinese nation, the 100-year-long history of the Party, and the more than 70-year-long history of the People's Republic of China all provide ample evidence that without the Communist Party of China, there would be no new China and no national rejuvenation.[16]

Just before coming to power in 2012, Xi talked of the importance of the "Chinese dream" (中国梦; *zhōngguó mèng*).[17] He argued that "achieving the great revival of the Chinese nation was the greatest dream of the Chinese people in modern times". And he set a clear end date: national rejuvenation was to be achieved by 2049, the centenary of the founding of the People's Republic of China.

Policy speeches repeatedly draw a clear line from this 2049 target to interim targets and to plans and actions in the near term. By 2035 China should have achieved "socialist modernization", following the achievement of a "moderately prosperous society" in 2021. These phrases are stock repetitions of what should happen by distant dates, but they also do service to frame priorities for each five-year plan. Perhaps more importantly, they serve as a reminder of the ambitious and aspirational nature of China's development goals.

JIGSAW PIECE 3: THE NEW PRINCIPAL CONTRADICTION – "MEETING THE PEOPLE'S EVER-GROWING NEEDS FOR A BETTER LIFE" AND COMMON PROSPERITY

Within Party thought, students of both Marx and Mao have long stressed the concept of "contradictions" as a way to express challenges and achieve progress. The dialectic between two opposing forces or facts sets up the basis for resolution through which progress is achieved. The CPC uses the concept of a "principal contradiction" to set the overall direction and priority for policy-making. Deng Xiaoping formulated this principal contradiction as being between "the ever-growing material and cultural needs of the people and backward social production". In other words, economic growth was required to give people what they wanted or needed.

At the 19th Party Congress, in 2017, Xi Jinping introduced a new principal contradiction: that between "unbalanced and inadequate development and the people's ever-growing needs for a better life". The first point to note is that Xi states that development in China remains "unbalanced". This is 11 years after the then premier, Wen Jiabao, used this word to describe the economy and called for action. Words alone do not lead to implementation and change. Second, Xi maintains that people want a better life in all its aspects, not just materially. The definition of a "better life" that Xi gives is broad indeed. He argues that "not only have (the people's) material and cultural needs [increased]" but also "their demands for democracy, rule of law, fairness and justice, security, and a better environment are increasing". Evan Feigenbaum, at the Carnegie Endowment for International Peace, has described this formulation as Xi Jinping's "New Deal" for the Chinese people.[18] Mentioning "demands for democracy" may surprise some, but the CPC maintains that China is indeed a democracy. China is what the CPC calls a "whole-process democracy", a concept explained in *China: Democracy that Works*,[19] a 2021 paper published by the Chinese government.

In 2021 the phrase "Common Prosperity" (共同富; *gòng tóng fù*) gained prominence in speeches and policy statements. This formulation stressed that the "people's ever-growing needs for a better life" applied to all Chinese people. During the period of opening up and reform, Deng Xiaoping had mandated policies to "let some people get rich first",[20] acknowledging the experimentation and entrepreneurship needed to drive economic progress. China today has one of the most unequal income distributions in the world, on a par with the United States. There are concerns that "excessive wealth" and "excessively high income" may spark unrest and discontent. The question remains, as in other countries: what is "excessive" and what is not? Xi Jinping has described the ideal income distribution as being an "olive-shaped distribution structure with large middle and small ends".[21]

What remains unclear is the extent and nature of the policies that Common Prosperity might justify. Western governments grapple with similar issues of income and wealth inequality. Are either the problems or the policy solutions in China so different? One key difference in China is that the same words can be used with radically different meanings. The term "Common Prosperity" was first used by Mao. A 1953 *People's Daily* article implied that collective ownership held in common was a prerequisite for Common Prosperity.[22] For Deng, Common Prosperity meant opening up and the use of incentives for entrepreneurship, company formation and tax reliefs. Xi revived the phrase in an August 2017 speech to mark a new era of economic policy-making but was explicit to reject a Western-style welfare state model.[23] The combination of the usual policy ambiguity with the historical use of the same phrase in very different ways has proved to be a recipe for uncertainty and concern.

In 2021 Chinese regulators intervened suddenly and strongly in business activities, especially in the internet and real estate sectors. Many observers explained these moves as the policy manifestation of Common Prosperity. Some of China's wealthiest entrepreneurs lost billions of dollars in personal wealth as a result. Their companies also paid billions of dollars in so-called "tertiary contributions". These were, in essence, quasi-philanthropic, quasi-forced contributions paid out of profits. Regulators and Party officials informally, yet directly, encouraged and imposed these payments, which entrepreneurs and companies paid in order to avoid further sanctions on businesses or individuals. The Chinese tax authorities also fined famous online influencers and media personalities for tax evasion. The speed, force and ambiguity of the actions brought yet more uncertainty.

By early 2022, however, Common Prosperity was featuring less prominently in the headlines, even though China's underlying inequalities remained. Although mentioned heavily at the October Party Congress, in tougher economic times, the focus turned more to the "prosperity" than the "common".

JIGSAW PIECE 4: MOVING FROM A "TIME OF STRATEGIC OPPORTUNITY" TO "GREAT CHANGES, UNSEEN IN A CENTURY"

China's leaders have historically formulated an explicit perspective on their view of the global context for China's development. This perspective provides the context for policy at home and abroad. In the early 2000s the Chinese leadership judged the external economic environment to be favourable for China's rapid development. Three factors contributed: China's accession to the WTO; the broad liberalizing trend of globalization; and an American focus on the Middle East in response to the 9/11 terror attacks. These all offered China the opportunity to develop its economy and increase its overall strength.[24] This global environment was judged to present a "strategic opportunity" for China.

In 2017 Xi Jinping changed this formulation.[25] At a gathering of China's ambassadors, Xi declared that these opportunities were now "historic" rather than "strategic". He argued instead that China now faced a world experiencing "great changes, unseen in a century" (百年未有之大变局; *bǎinián wèi yǒu zhī dà biànjú*).[26] This would bring both opportunities and risks. The phrase had clear echoes of the words of Li Hongzhang, a Qing-dynasty general, who wrote in 1872 of "great changes unseen in three thousand years". Li spoke of the geopolitical shifts and technological innovations that were then threatening Qing power.[27] Xi's China is now in a much stronger position than under the Qing. "Great changes" now refer more to China's growing strength and the decline of the West, in particular the United States, as revealed by American economic and political polarization, poor handling of Covid-19 and even the January 2021 storming of the US Capitol. "The East is rising, and the West is declining" has gained currency as a phrase among Chinese leaders.[28] The Fifth Plenum in 2020 restated the emphasis on "great changes".[29] At the 20th Party Congress, Xi spoke even more clearly of the adverse external environment that China now faces and the need to "struggle" and show "fighting spirit". This is now a time of "strategic opportunities, risks and challenges", with the need to deal with "worst-case scenarios".[30]

All these "great changes" directly influence Dual Circulation Strategy. At a time of risk and potentially hostile actions, self-reliance and a focus on internal circulation reflect judicious caution. There is an imperative to minimize external dependence and "choke points" for the Chinese economy. Yet it is also the time to engage in the world – and to seek to shape the domain of external circulation, to be more "assertive".

JIGSAW PIECE 5: NATIONAL SECURITY – THE SECURITIZATION OF EVERYTHING

Under Xi Jinping, national security has come to the forefront of policy. This is security in its broadest sense. It goes far beyond the military alone, although military modernization and spending have also featured heavily. Security concerns, in Xi's view, pervade all aspects of society. Security is deeply intertwined with matters of economic prosperity, ideology and values. In consequence, it also underpins the rationale for self-reliance and the focus on internal circulation within Dual Circulation Strategy.

China's 2014 National Security Outlook identified five dimensions of national security: the security of the people; political security; economic security; military, cultural and societal security; and international security.[31] This breadth was captured in the formulation of a "comprehensive national security concept" (总体国家安全观; *zǒngtǐ guójiā ānquán guān*). In 2014 Xi Jinping also established the CPC's National Security Commission (which he chairs) to oversee all such security matters. In 2015 the Politburo approved China's first national security strategy, which the Chinese media heralded as "an important theoretical innovation".[32] In 2018 a book of Xi's collected speeches and writings on national security was published.[33] Legislation has followed, with the introduction of the National Security Law, the National Intelligence Law and the Cybersecurity Law.[34]

The integration of security and economics has become much more explicit. The CPC's Fifth Plenum in 2020 committed to synchronize economic development with security and achieve a higher level in terms of "safe China". In the 14th Five Year Plan, published in 2021, "security and safety" appear as a distinct, new category within economic and social development. Energy and food security are highlighted with binding targets for grain and energy production capacity. The uncertainties caused by US sanctions on Russia following the invasion of Ukraine have served only to heighten this focus. The security aspects of data and technology are under particular scrutiny. China has taken a conservative approach to protecting information that it deems to be "state secrets".[35] Chinese regulators cited data-related security concerns in pressuring Didi, China's equivalent of Uber, to delist from NASDAQ. Chinese regulators have cited "state secrets" as the reason for not sharing in full Chinese audit findings with American regulators for Chinese firms listed on US stock exchanges.

Xi has also sought to strengthen China's military capabilities by applying the advanced capabilities of the business sector to the defence sector through a policy known as military–civil fusion (MCF: 军民融合; *jūnmín rónghé*). This is an expansive initiative including areas such as big data, infrastructure and logistics. Under the most extreme interpretation, this suggests a party-state directive that can and potentially will coerce any Chinese company to serve national military goals. In practice, however, there are limits to how far this goes. The Center for a New American Security, a US think tank, has concluded that MCF relies for the most part on incentivizing rather than coercing participation, and that only a limited proportion of Chinese companies are engaged.[36] This does not rule out significant benefits from applying commercial dual-use technologies to the defence sector, however, especially in advanced technologies. Xi Jinping is not alone, of course, in drawing on his country's economic strengths for security purposes. After all, it was in 1961 that the then US president, Dwight Eisenhower, spoke of the "military-industrial complex".

Despite these caveats, this all-pervasive approach to security means that almost anything can be termed a national security threat. Xiconomics encompasses both economics and security. When decisions need to be made, it is hard for any policy-maker to argue against national security concerns. As a result, both substantive assessments and shifting perceptions of security risk have a major impact on economic and commercial decisions. Paradoxically, security makes business that bit more uncertain.

JIGSAW PIECE 6: THE BELT AND ROAD INITIATIVE
AND BEYOND

China's Belt and Road Initiative is a prominent example of a phrase and a policy that is both ambiguous yet also very specific in certain areas. It is a term that is partly a slogan, in essence a rebranding of existing policies, and in part something markedly new and substantive.

The BRI lies at the heart of China's external engagement in the world. Launched by Xi Jinping in 2013, under the name of the Silk Road Economic Belt, the BRI has mostly been viewed by analysts as an infrastructure initiative. Some have placed it on par with the US Marshall Plan to reconstruct Europe after the Second World War. In fact, it is both less and more than that. Less, because some of the initial, outlandishly large numbers for the scale of infrastructure "investment" will never come to fruition. More, because the BRI has always been about more than infrastructure. In 2017 the BRI was written into the Chinese constitution, and it remains Xi Jinping's hallmark foreign policy initiative. According to the Chinese government, 138 countries have signed up in some form to participate in the BRI, though what this means in concrete terms varies widely.[37]

From the start, China has emphasized five pillars to the Belt and Road Initiative. Infrastructure is but one. The others are policy coordination, unimpeded trade, financial integration and people-to-people exchanges. Together these make up a much broader form of connectivity. The BRI is as much about industrial parks, customs facilitation agreements and cross-border payments as it is about building bridges and railways. One aim has been to strengthen China's domestic economy and companies by creating closer connectivity to the rest of the world. In so doing, this brings access to energy and other resources that China needs, opens up new markets and generates overseas construction contracts for Chinese enterprises. China's less developed western provinces potentially benefit the most from the connectivity. The Belt and Road is a prime example of the ambition for internal and external circulation to "mutually reinforce" one another.

From 2018 onwards, however, the response to the BRI can be best characterized as "pushback", especially in its large infrastructure projects. In Pakistan, Sri Lanka, Malaysia, Kenya, Ethiopia and elsewhere, governments have concluded that project terms were unattractive; construction has fallen behind plan; and extensive evidence of corruption has been uncovered. There have been project cancellations, renegotiated contract terms, debt renegotiations and asset seizures. From 2021 onwards "pushback" turned into "restructuring" as projects failed to deliver promised returns and countries struggled to service the debt. "Pushback" has been accompanied by "pullback" on the Chinese side as the rationale for large-scale, high-risk lending came increasingly into question. The BRI has not stopped but the focus has changed, and the scale of capital investment has fallen. The Digital Silk Road and Health Silk Road are now a higher priority than rail and port investment. The ambiguous definition of the BRI, as with other Chinese policy terms, accommodates such change easily. The Digital Silk Road brings Chinese technology companies (and their standards) to enable economic and social development, while also exporting China's approach to security, surveillance and online censorship. Huawei exports and operates "smart cities" in 52 countries, primarily in sub-Saharan Africa and Asia, mostly in authoritarian states.[38]

"Initiatives" have become a new form of Chinese engagement overseas. In the wake of the Belt and Road, Xi has announced the Global Initiative on Data Security (2020), the Global Development Initiative (2021) and the Global Security Initiative (2022).

PUTTING THE PUZZLE TOGETHER

Fitting together the different pieces of the puzzle, each with its own definitional ambiguities, and adding in Dual Circulation, can feel like "nailing jelly to the wall", in the words of Theodore Roosevelt. Yet the pieces do seem to fit. The role of the CPC and Xi Jinping's leadership (piece 1) set the whole context – hence, too, the aptness of the term "Xiconomics". Together they also demarcate the realm of internal circulation as distinct from the rest of the world. In the longer term, the ambition and drive to achieve the "Great Rejuvenation" (piece 2) means strengthening China's own capabilities at home, while taking advantage of opportunities on the world stage, the dual focus of Dual Circulation. Piece 3 (meeting the needs of the Chinese people for a better life in the face of unbalanced and inadequate development) defines the purpose of further economic development. It places economic and business activity firmly in a broader social context. It also suggests that Common Prosperity will persist as a focus and a rallying cry. That the external environment offers "great changes, unseen in a century" (piece 4) highlights the twin needs to mitigate risks and to capture opportunities from engagement with the world, both elements in Dual Circulation thinking. Xi's comprehensive focus on national security (piece 5) puts the spotlight on the security aspects of all economic decisions. Finally, the Belt and Road Initiative (piece 6), is one, very important, aspect of how China engages in external circulation as part of Dual Circulation Strategy. In his June 2021 paper on Dual Circulation, Justin Yifu Lin places the BRI alongside Dual Circulation Strategy. He writes, "While the Belt and Road Initiative remains the international development and cooperation strategy for China, the adoption of the Dual Circulation Development Paradigm is the response to new challenges as well as the economic reality that China is facing."[39]

4

Putting the "Xi" into Xiconomics

On 23 July 2021 China's State Council issued new rules banning for-profit companies from tutoring in core curriculum subjects and banned foreign investment in the sector. No new licences were to be issued and all existing operators were instructed to register as non-profits. Overnight the share prices of US-listed Chinese commercial education providers fell 60 per cent. Stocks such as New Oriental Education and TAL Education traded more than 90 per cent below their record highs of March 2021. Bloomberg reported that investment analysts were scurrying to read the collected writings of Xi Jinping,[1] the three volumes of his book *The Governance of China*. After all, in 2018 Xi had already written: "The conscientious [education] industry cannot turn into a profit-seeking industry. The off-campus training institutions must be regulated by the law so that they can return to the normal track of educating people." China's regulatory environment was perhaps not so opaque and uncertain after all.

Were all the clues hiding in plain sight? Could the crackdown in the educational sector have been foreseen? In part, yes – although the world is not that simple. Official speeches, books and other writings, many delivered by Xi Jinping or bearing his name, provide a wealth of information on both the rationale and specifics of Chinese policy direction. These materials are frequently designed expressly to provide guidance to Party officials at all levels across China about the priorities and principles that should guide actions and implementation at the local level. In a sense, *The Governance of China* provides the foundation for the governance of business in China, for the role that business is expected to play and the way that it is expected to operate.

Party publications are important too. One particularly significant journal is *Qiushi* (求是: *Seeking Truth*), the CPC's principal official journal. *Qiushi* states that it "serves as an important ideological and theoretical medium for guiding the work of the entire Party and the country as a whole".[2] Many foreign business leaders and analysts underestimate the seriousness and intent behind such statements. Indeed, the often dry, even turgid, style can be off-putting. But familiarity with the arguments and directions that the Party is communicating to its members is a useful starting point for understanding how policies are likely to develop and, from there, the implications for business.

This by no means resolves all uncertainties nor removes risk or the need for judgement. In business and investing, timing is everything. In the three years following the publication of Xi's views on tutoring for profit, the private tutoring sector boomed. In 2020 private equity investors invested US$8.1 billion into the sector – many of these investors themselves Chinese. However sophisticated their understanding of China's political and business context, they too were caught off guard. Xi's book gave no clues as to whether or when his espoused views would become law. In addition, the principles advanced in these materials can verge on the platitudinous. They may articulate an admirable policy goal with which few would disagree but remain vague on the specifics and the immediate policy implications. This ambiguity has the virtue of allowing for local interpretation of what measures make sense in the different and diverse regions of China. But it also lets the Chinese leadership adjust course or declare success as it sees fit. It sets off guessing games as people devote their energies to trying to understand the "true intent" of vague words. Ambiguity can also result in a series of badly executed policies by overly zealous local officials, each seeking to interpret what Xi or the broader Party leadership "really meant".

Nonetheless, with the advent of Dual Circulation Strategy, Common Prosperity and a raft of regulatory reforms and interventions all under Xi's leadership and direction, business leaders are trying to figure out how the business environment in China will develop. These are in part quantitative questions. How rapidly will the economy grow? Which customers and segments will emerge when? How will profit margins develop? More fundamentally, these are questions about the underlying context and structure of the Chinese business environment and the role of foreign business within this. Written into the Chinese constitution is the primacy of the CPC over all aspects of China's society and economy, a primacy that it asserts more actively than do governments in many other countries. It is CPC policy and actions that will shape the environment for business. And it is Xi Jinping – through his 'Thought' and his actions – who plays a determining role in leading the CPC. Again, economics has become Xiconomics.

One way to better understand what Xi wants to achieve is to read selected speeches that he has made. With the caveats already noted, these provide substance on how Xi frames the challenges facing China, his underlying objectives and priority initiatives. Alongside somewhat technocratic descriptions, Xi's speeches also provide some insight into the values and principles that he propounds. Somewhat surprisingly, these go beyond Party ideology alone. The reader should remember, however, that, as with other speeches by political leaders around the world, these speeches are inherently political in nature. They set ambition and direction and they exhort efforts and progress. They say much less about the problems and about how achievable these ambitions are. The speeches cannot be understood in isolation. Finally, there is often a lag of several months between Xi making these speeches in private and their publication for a wider audience.

Two speeches illustrate these points and shine a spotlight on how Xi sees Dual Circulation and Common Prosperity. The first is a speech that Xi gave in April 2020 on economic development that described the aims and key elements of Dual Circulation Strategy and was later published in *Qiushi*.[3] As is common with CPC speeches, it bore a ponderous title: "Certain major issues for our national medium- to long-term economic and social development strategy". The second speech, "Making solid progress towards Common Prosperity", was delivered in August 2021 and later published in *Qiushi*.[4] It provides insights into what is meant by Common Prosperity and Xi's philosophy on how people become prosperous. It does though also leave much unclear and unanswered.

XI'S PRIORITIES FOR DUAL CIRCULATION STRATEGY

In this first speech, Xi describes his ambition for a China with stronger domestic demand, based on a larger, consuming middle class. It is a

China with secure and resilient supply chains, transformed by digitization and with a major role for state-owned enterprises; a continuing urbanization of society; improved science and technology capabilities; a coexistence of people and nature; and an improved public health system. Many points reflect long-standing policy aspirations in China – aspirations that have proved challenging to realize. The influences of Covid-19 and US trade sanctions are clear in other aspects. They show up in the focus on a greater control of key supply chains, on coexisting with nature and on disaster preparedness and public health.

Xi uses "Dual Circulation" as both a strategy and a slogan. He starts by highlighting the need to focus on domestic demand expansion rather than overseas markets. Within this, Xi prioritizes the expansion of consumption over investment. He stresses the need to increase the size of the middle-income population, today numbering around 400 million people. The size of China's economy means that China can build a "new development pattern" based on "domestic great circulation", with a "dynamic balance between aggregate supply and demand". As Chapter 2 argued, this has been a long-standing objective for China's economic development. In reality, however, China's development model has consistently placed more emphasis on investment spending that increases supply rather than taking actions to stimulate consumer demand. Capital investment, especially in real estate and infrastructure, has driven much of China's economic growth. Household income accounts for a much lower share of gross domestic product (GDP) than in other major economies. These same households save heavily in part to compensate for inadequate welfare, health and pension provision. None of these issues is easy to change. The ambition is long-standing; the execution has been slow at best.

Second, Xi talks of the need to "optimize and stabilize production and supply chains". He calls for supply chains that are "independently controllable" and says that the imperative is to "safeguard industrial and national security". China must "increase the levels of science and technology innovation and import substitution" and "enhance our superiority across the entire production chain in sectors such as high-speed rail, electric power equipment, new energy and communications equipment". These are long-standing ambitions for technological leadership. The emphasis on control, stabilization and security is new – or, at least, more pronounced and more explicit than before – and mixed in with the economic.

Xi goes on to describe the key aspects of China's domestic development. What matters here is the list of topics; whether or not they are badged under an umbrella slogan of Dual Circulation is unimportant.

Digitization is an important part of Xi's vision for China's development. He talks of China as the world's leading online economy and the continuing need to accelerate the construction of the digital economy, digital society and digital government. The 14th Five-Year Plan for National Informatization, published in December 2021, describes a wide range of initiatives across all aspects of Chinese society.[5] "Informatization" (信息化; *xìnxīhuà*) is seen as providing the basis for the future productivity gains that are necessary for increased living standards. It also encompasses improved governance and stronger oversight of activity across all of society. In the economic sphere, the Stanford Cyber Policy Center's DigiChina project outlines how China explicitly recognizes data as a "factor of production". In a country with a party- or state-driven industrial strategy, this has the direct implication that data need to be managed and structured for the benefit of the nation rather than left to companies alone.[6] Such thinking underpins China's regulatory efforts to define and implement laws and regulations on data access, data protection and information-sharing. For some companies, this had a dramatic, immediate and negative impact on their business model and profitability from 2021 onwards. Yet the regulatory actions taken are much less surprising when the central role of "informatization" in China's future development is considered.

Xi goes on to highlight the importance of state-owned enterprises. He argues that they are "an important pillar and supporting force of the Party's governance and rejuvenation of the nation" and that they "must be made stronger, better and larger". The relative role of state-owned enterprises and private business in the Chinese economy is another recurring theme in policy debates. It is private business that accounts for the bulk of employment and economic output, yet in recent years it is state-owned enterprises whose lynchpin role is most consistently emphasized in policy speeches.

Xi identifies urbanization as the third key area of focus. The Chinese government has announced ambitious plans to create five major city clusters by 2035. These are the Jing–Jin–Ji cluster in the north, including

Beijing; the Yangtze River Delta cluster (east); the Pearl River Delta cluster (south); the Cheng–Yu cluster (west); and the Yangtze River Middle Reaches cluster in central China. Combined, these areas may end up generating about half the nation's GDP and account for half its urban population. To connect the clusters, China aims to complete a grid of 16 new high-speed railway lines.[7] This is all consistent with further investment in real estate and infrastructure, a continuation of China's investment-driven growth model and the thesis that city-dwellers will in turn become a consuming middle class. Xi details the need for "ecological and liveable" "suburban new towns" that control population density, with "city–industry integration", "jobs–housing balance" and "services such as childcare, eldercare, housekeeping, education and health care". The vision is specific, prescriptive, systemic and managed, to be implemented through the efforts of local governments.

As a fourth topic, Xi stresses the need to adjust and optimize the structure of science and technology inputs. He picks out here as research priorities heredity, genetics, virology and immunology. He talks of the need to combine industry, universities and research institutions, letting "enterprises play the main role and government play an overall planning role". These are all good ambitions, but the challenge is in the execution if they are to be anything more than fine words.

The fifth topic again stretches the definition of economic development in a broad way. It is framed as the "harmonious coexistence of people and nature". This stands in contrast to China's historic development experience, with its heavy urbanization focus and extensive environmental damage. Xi argues for the need to protect nature and to build an "ecological civilization" with a "balance of ecosystems". In this speech he covers a hotchpotch of topics, including the impact of the Covid-19 epidemic, biodiversity, wild animal trading, green production and "healthy living". For his final theme, in a time of Covid-19, Xi returns to questions of public health, in particular the need to strengthen the public health system.

XI AND COMMON PROSPERITY

Xi's speech "Making solid progress towards Common Prosperity" is quite different in nature. Although the speech concludes by listing a series of policy directions, the first section is more interesting. Xi lays out four principles for Common Prosperity, which address the role of the individual and what can or cannot be expected from the party-state. At times Xi's words sound more like those of a Western conservative or free-market political leader than those of a Marxist-Leninist.

He starts by stating that, since 2012, policy emphasis has been on "giving greater weight" to "gradually achieving the goal of prosperity for all", or even "happiness for all". This is a shift from the previous main focus on the single measure of the annual GDP growth rate. Xi places his argument in a global context: many countries have seen increasing wealth and income inequality, which has in turn spurred "social division, political polarization and a surge of populism". He talks also of the impact of technological change, saying that, although it is positive for economic development, it has affected employment and income distribution. These are all familiar themes outside China too. How to tax the wealth of billionaire entrepreneurs and how to regulate uncertain work conditions in the "gig economy" are themes in the United States as much as in China.

After speaking of "happiness", Xi quickly returns to economic fundamentals by anchoring what he says directly in the need to improve the productivity of the Chinese people. This is to happen by improving the calibre of Chinese workers. He outlines four principles.

The first is that the individual takes responsibility for his or her own prosperity: "Pursue prosperity through innovation and hard work." A happy life is to be achieved through hard work. The government will create inclusive and equitable conditions for self-development. Xi talks of upward social mobility, but this is equality of opportunity, not of outcome. Indeed, the words would sit well in conservative and free-market manifestos around the world, even though Xi's beliefs in terms of freedom of speech, the role of the individual in society and human rights are starkly different. Xi further inveighs against recent trends in Chinese society whereby individuals are less committed to self-development and to the development of China. He references the new words "involution" and "lying flat". "Involution" (内卷; *nèi juàn*) describes the burnout that many young Chinese feel from the intense competitive pressure to achieve – a sense that they are working harder and harder for little benefit. Their response has been "lying flat" (躺平; *tǎng píng*). This means doing the minimum necessary to get by and rejecting the long working hours that many Chinese companies expect. Xi argues that everyone must participate actively in society. This reflects his desire to shape the ideology and values of the younger generation in a way consistent with the fighting spirit and struggles of the past. He recalls the revolutionary commitment of CPC members in a less wealthy China. Such views are, nonetheless, not dissimilar to a Western conservative view that people need to "try harder", albeit in a very different type of society.

The second principle, "upholding our basic economic system", is one of stability rather than change despite this focus on Common Prosperity. Once again, the argument is that the state sector should retain its "predominance". Xi talks too of the healthy growth of the non-state sector. While "allowing some people to get prosperous first", there should be "more stress on pushing these people to give a helping hand to those following in their wake". The questions left unanswered here are how forceful the "push" will be and how large the "helping hand" is expected to be.

Xi's third principle again recalls the words of Western conservative leaders such as the former British prime minister, Margaret Thatcher: "We should do our utmost while working within our means" and must not make "promises that we are not able to keep." Indeed, "the government cannot take on everything". And, to be even clearer, Xi states: "Even in the future, we must not ... go overboard with social security, and [must] steer clear of the idleness-breeding trap of welfarism." The long-standing though limited role of government welfare provision is set to continue. Common Prosperity is not a plan for a welfare state. Self-reliance is for the individual as well as for China as a nation.

The fourth and final principle is also a consistent guiding light for Chinese policy: "Pursue incremental progress." Common Prosperity requires the same experimentation, learning and adaptation at the local level that has underpinned China's development over the past 40 years. Xi speaks of Zhejiang province as a demonstration zone and encourages other areas to explore "effective paths tailored to their own conditions".[8] Zhejiang is far from typical of China, however. It is one of China's richest and most entrepreneurial provinces, ranking fifth out of 31 provinces in GDP per capita. Common Prosperity may be more elusive in other provinces.

With these four principles, Xi lays out a framework for Common Prosperity without detailing any real specifics. He calls for the proper balancing of the relationship between equity and efficiency. Yet determining this balance lies at the very heart of the matter, and he leaves it unaddressed. What he does say places the responsibility on the individual as much as the state. He goes on to describe six areas of focus for implementation. There is little new here from previous economic policy discussions. Interestingly, there is a more detailed plan to expand the middle-income group, which reads much like a pro-business manifesto. It emphasizes training and skill development, the importance of entrepreneurs and the need for improvements and tax incentives in the business environment. Small businesses and the self-employed are an "important group for building wealth through entrepreneurship".

Xi goes on to tackle the question of high incomes, but, again, he does not address specifics. Policy will "regulate excessively high income in a reasonable manner and standardize the management of capital gains". He continues, "We will rectify abnormalities such as increasing executive incomes under the guise of reform [and] oppose the disorderly expansion of capital." But what is "reasonable"? What is "excessively high"? When is the expansion of capital "orderly" and when is it "disorderly"? So much is in the eye of the beholder – or, in this case, in the eyes of Xi Jinping and the broader Chinese leadership. Some might call an income of US$100,000 year excessive; others might set the level at US$1,000,000 or higher. It is this ambiguity combined with the blunt forcefulness of sudden regulatory moves that has caused uncertainty for business. Paradoxically, Xi talks of the need to "clear up confusion [about Common Prosperity] among people with a lack of solid understanding". Indeed; but how? He talks of the "guiding role of core socialist values, and [the need to] strengthen education on patriotism, collectivism, and socialism". Adding this ideological component may add to uncertainty rather than reduce it. What exactly do "core socialist values" say with regard to income levels?

Ultimately, Common Prosperity is a goal with which it is hard to argue. What remains unclear is where the priority falls between the "common" and the "prosperity", between policies that redistribute wealth and those that create wealth. In Western societies, the political parameters of these debates are reasonably well defined. Should there be a wealth tax? How should employment law apply to Uber drivers? In China, the range of potential policy goals and desired outcomes appears much more uncertain. In large part, it is the sharply shifting political conditions in China over the past 60 years that account for this: Mao's strongly egalitarian and uniform society with its communal ownership is a not so distant memory. Xi leaves the impression that wealth creation is still the priority – not least because of China's relatively low average incomes – and that opportunities for this must be made more widely available across China. But changing the economic fortunes of regional economies is tough in any country. And ambiguous "Common Prosperity" rhetoric combined with sharp regulatory changes have created a more uncertain environment for business.

PUTTING SPEECHES IN CONTEXT

Although the important personal impact of Xi Jinping's experience, judgement and beliefs on China's economic direction is undisputed, assessing what Xi "really wants" or "really believes" remains challenging. Assembling information from diverse sources, including his speeches and writings, and considering Xi's actions at critical junctures do yield some insights. The two speeches analysed here show a level of logic, nuance and focus beneath the headline soundbites. They help clarify the relevance of CPC initiatives for business and make the remaining open questions more explicit. As new speeches are made and policy evolves, these new speeches will repay reading too.

Important too is a critical understanding of Xi's own life history and experience. This includes the fact that he is a "princeling", the son of Xi Zhongxun, one of the Eight Elders or Immortals, senior Chinese leaders who formed the first and second generations of Chinese leadership. Xi Zhongxun was Mao's chief of propaganda and a vice-premier. During the Cultural Revolution he was purged and persecuted before being rehabilitated and assuming leadership roles in Guangdong province. There he led efforts to liberalize the economy after Mao's death. Two books authored by Kerry Brown profile Xi's life and experiences: *CEO, China: The Rise of Xi Jinping*[9] and, more recently, *Xi: A Study in Power*.[10] What Xi's speeches and writings do not do, however, is describe the full extent of the challenges and opportunities facing China at home and abroad, the choices available and what this all means for Dual Circulation Strategy. This is the topic of Part II.

Three questions for global business

5

How will China's internal business
environment develop?

In 2020 over 22,000 new semiconductor companies were registered in
China. A new gold rush had started as entrepreneurs and businesses –
from the private and state sectors alike – charged in to make money and
reduce China's dependence on imported semiconductors. "Here's a new
way to tell whether a Chinese company is a major player: ask the CEO
if the firm is designing its own microchips," wrote Zeyi Yang, a jour-
nalist for Protocol.[1] The money poured in – from both state and private
capital. For some, such as home appliance companies Gree, Midea, TCL
and Haier, chips played an important role in product manufacturing.
Huawei had made an early start. In 2004 it had established a separate
company, HiSilicon, to focus on chip-making. For others, there was no
clear link. They lacked the business need and had little experience but
were committed to "making it big" and keen to access government or
private funding on offer. And, alongside the 20,000 new companies,
stood SMIC, Semiconductor Manufacturing International Corporation.
Founded in 2000 as a wholly foreign-owned company, by 2020 SMIC's
main shareholders were state-owned yet it was also publicly listed.
SMIC had not lived up to hopes that it would challenge Taiwan's TSMC
(Taiwan Semiconductor Manufacturing Company) as a global semiconductor leader. Would this mix of state and private capital, policy priority,
entrepreneurialism and intense competition lead to success this time?

Semiconductors are but one sector of the Chinese economy, albeit
one at the centre of China's ambitions and the push and pull of US–
China relations. Away from the abstractions of economic theory, the
realities of China's economic growth recipe are messy and seemingly
contradictory, yet historically effective in aggregate: state ownership

and private; giant corporations *and* small businesses; competition, coordination *and* coercion.

It was ever thus. In 2007 the then premier, Wen Jiabao, described China's economy as unstable, unbalanced, uncoordinated and unsustainable. His concerns were overinvestment, reckless lending, excessive liquidity, unbalanced foreign trade, inequality between cities and the countryside, inefficient energy use, wasteful allocation of resources and environmental ruin. Xi's concerns are not so different. Chinese policy-makers have diagnosed the challenges but have been less successful at resolving them.

Yet in 2021 China's economy was nearly three times larger than in 2007.[2] China's high-speed rail network did not exist in 2007. By 2021 it extended to 40,000 km. In 2003 Huawei considered selling itself to Motorola. Now it is the world leader in 5G and holds more 5G patents than any other company. China's internet platform companies have pioneered new business models and led in the use of electronic payments. In electric vehicles (EVs) China accounts for over a half of the world market, with EVs accounting for 29 per cent of the China market in early 2022. China is also the world leader in solar, wind and hydropower, accounting for 40 per cent of global investment in renewable energy between 2012 and 2021.[3] The economy may still be unbalanced, uncoordinated and unstable, but growth has continued apace. Until the Covid-19 pandemic China's economic dynamism had proved remarkably resilient, despite increasing doubts about the sustainability of its real-estate-intensive, debt-financed growth model. Businesspeople and government officials alike found ways to manage through problems.

China's economy now faces increasing headwinds, at a time when new challenges are being added to previous ones. Stringent enforcement of a zero-Covid-19 policy, with its unpredictable lockdowns, has exacerbated this in the short term. It has reduced economic activity, hit consumer and business confidence and reminded all, especially wealthier Chinese, of the sometimes-arbitrary enforcement power of the party-state. Summer 2022 also brought record heatwaves, with direct economic consequences as power shortages led to factory shutdowns. Moreover, beyond the singular clarity of a GDP growth target, Xi Jinping has set broader policy ambitions for Common Prosperity, national security and ideology. He seeks to mould the contours of internal circulation into something distinctive and different. Will business, government and Party find ways of adapting to these new contours that result in the better outcomes "for all" that Xi promises? Indeed, can the very focus on "circulation" contribute to improved living standards? Or does this herald a "perfect storm" of competing ambitions that will damp down China's previous dynamism and lead to stagnation? Uncertainty about the answers to these questions is the defining factor of China's business environment.

TWO CONSIDERATIONS FOR THE BUSINESS ENVIRONMENT

For business, what matters in the end is the size and growth of the market, together with the ability to earn (and keep) a profit at manageable risk. Barring an economic and societal meltdown, China, with its population of 1.4 billion, will remain the world's second largest economy and market. Indeed, adjusting for different price levels between countries, China is already the world's largest economy on a purchasing power parity (PPP) basis. What is less clear is how quickly productivity, living standards and the overall economy will grow – and what profit potential and risks China will present to companies, both Chinese and foreign. This chapter focuses on the domestic environment that companies may face, the "terms of doing business in China". Later chapters will consider what this means for multinationals – whether or not they will find the terms attractive or acceptable.

In looking at the environment that companies face doing business in China, two aspects need to be considered. The first is how successful the country's leadership is at deciding on and implementing policies that address China's long-standing growth and productivity challenges. This policy agenda covers many areas, but the role afforded to the business sector will play a critical role in determining success. When policy recognizes this fact, companies are more likely to enjoy a supportive business environment in which they can earn and keep profits. The second aspect is the extent to which other policy priorities – relating to redistribution, security and ideology – either constrain or reinforce efforts to raise productivity and living standards. When national security becomes the overriding priority in a time of war, commercial objectives understandably take a back seat. Short of war, however, the need to review every commercial activity for security risks (real or perceived) adds cost. Government officials have an incentive to be cautious on any security implications and can block commercial initiatives on sometimes spurious national security grounds. A plan for Common Prosperity that emphasizes redistributing current wealth rather than creating new wealth may mean high tax rates or stringent regulations. These actions reduce profits and choke off innovation. And, when ideology stresses the primacy of the state sector, there is a risk that companies earn profits only to find they need to make additional payments at the behest of government and Party officials. Is "getting rich" still glorious – or are the risks now more than just financial?

THE OUTLOOK FOR GROWTH FUNDAMENTALS

Economic assessments turn quickly to numbers, and here some caveats are in order. Quantitative observations on China's economy rely inherently on statistics, which are necessarily imperfect, subject to dispute and not directly comparable with statistics from the Western economies.[4] Some economists argue that Chinese statistics overstate true economic growth. Most famously, former premier Li Keqiang described GDP statistics as "man-made" and unreliable when he was Party secretary in Liaoning province in 2007. Others, especially in the business sector, have found market demand to be greater than they expected based on official statistics. Despite these issues, it is helpful to review China's economic performance based on the best efforts of China's National Bureau of Statistics, the World Bank and the International Monetary Fund (IMF).

China's economic growth has slowed markedly since the heady and at times excessive levels of the noughties. Growth then did not fall below 8 per cent. In 2007 it went as high as 14 per cent. In 2012 growth fell below 8 per cent, and it stayed there until 2021, when growth hit 8.1 per cent after reaching only 2.3 per cent in Covid-19-hit 2020. Covid-19 returned to hit growth again in 2022, putting China's official 5.5 per cent growth target out of reach. Now, even when Covid-19 is past, prospects are for significantly slower growth on a sustained basis. Estimates of 3 to 5 per cent annual GDP growth may be optimistic. There are two facets to consider in judging growth prospects: looking at how productive capacity (or "supply") might grow and at which sources of demand might drive growth.

An economy's productive capacity (supply) grows from the combination of a larger, more capable working population, a greater capital stock to support them and higher effectiveness in putting people and capital together to create output (productivity, or, more precisely, total factor productivity: TFP). IMF analysis concluded that until 2015 increases in capital investment accounted for around a half of China's growth; a larger workforce contributed around 15 per cent; and the rest came from TFP growth.

Considering these three factors in turn highlights the slower growth ahead for China. The working-age population has peaked and is now starting to decline, although education levels are rising. The hopes here need to rest on increasing the "quality" of China's workforce – hence Xi's call to improve the "calibre" of the Chinese working population in his "Common Prosperity" speech. The absence of an adequate pension system for the rapidly ageing population means that many will also work for longer. From 2017 to 2037 the number of those over 65 years old will rise from 10 to 20 per cent of the population.[5] Capital investment remains high, accounting for 44 per cent of GDP in 2020, the highest level in the world.[6] Yet this investment is generating increasingly lower returns. Investment remains skewed towards real estate of all kinds and to large-scale infrastructure projects, some of which have brought significant benefits but often not yielded commercial returns. In 2021 real estate and infrastructure investments each accounted for around 25 per cent of investment, with manufacturing accounting for one-third.[7] Investment has been mostly debt-financed, resulting in high leverage across the economy. This leaves productivity as the main driver for future growth, but this too has been declining. A World Bank report concluded that China's annual TFP growth fell from just over 3 per cent in the 1980s and 1990s to only 0.7 per cent from 2009 to 2018.[8] More recent analysis found that aggregate TFP growth has slowed from 3.1 per cent (2000–09) to 1.1 per cent (2010–19).[9] Without significant changes to how the economy functions, the prospects for increasing productivity are poor.

In his book *Red Flags: Why Xi's China Is In Jeopardy*, economist George Magnus explores China's growth challenges in rigorous detail. He describes four "traps" facing China: the need to address high debt levels, especially in real estate and infrastructure; the structural weakness of the renminbi as a currency in light of strict capital controls; the need for China to break through the so-called "middle income trap"[10] through upgrading and innovation to the next level of economic development; and the challenges of an ageing population and shrinking workforce. Magnus argues that the increasing centralization and authoritarianism under Xi are incompatible with the flexibility and adjustments needed to escape the four traps and secure economic growth.

The second approach is to see which sources of demand might "drive" China's growth by looking at the importance of consumption, investment and trade in total GDP and applying the technique of growth accounting. This approach breaks down each year's growth in GDP to understand how much is accounted for by growth in consumption, growth in investment and growth in net exports (defined as the difference between exports and imports).

Xi Jinping argues that the domestic economy should become the "mainstay". Before Covid-19 this was in fact already the case. China's growth has long since stopped being "export-led". From 1978 onwards exports played a crucial role in China's economic development. At that time, exports of goods and services amounted to just 5 per cent of GDP. By 1990 this share had reached 14 per cent of a larger economy, and by 2000 the figure had grown to 21 per cent. Following China's 2001 accession to the WTO export share rocketed, to reach a peak of 36 per cent in 2006. Since then, however, China's domestic demand has grown more rapidly than its exports. Exports accounted for 18 per cent of GDP in 2020, below the pre-WTO-accession level. This share is similar to that in other large economies. In Japan exports account for 16 per cent of GDP, and for the European Union extra-EU trade amounts to 21 per cent of GDP. This export ratio may yet have further to fall. Exports account for only 10 per cent of US GDP.

From a growth accounting perspective, net exports contributed several percentage points of growth each year between 2004 and 2006, at a time when the Chinese economy was growing at more than 10 per cent annually.[11] Throughout the global financial crisis net exports were a drag on China's growth. To offset this, the government deployed a massive investment programme, financed mainly by the banking system. Since then the contribution of exports to Chinese growth was around zero until 2019. In fact, after the high investment levels from 2008 to 2010, it was domestic consumption that accounted for a half of the growth in GDP – and sometimes more – until Covid-19 hit.[12]

In 2020 this changed. Net exports accounted for just over a quarter of China's economic growth and domestic consumption shrank. Mostly, this simply reflected the macroeconomic impact of the Covid-19 pandemic. In 2021 China's exports increased by 30 per cent over the previous year, while the whole economy grew 8.1 per cent. Export strength continued in 2022, with July exports 18 per cent higher than a year previously and a record trade surplus.[13] The domestic economy was much weaker. Gavekal Dragonomics, an economics research firm, reported that in July 2022 industrial value added grew 3.8 per cent year on year, fixed asset investment 3.5 per cent and retail sales 2.5 per cent, while property sales fell 29 per cent and construction starts declined 45 per cent.[14] China's zero-Covid-19 policy, with its uncertain, repeated lockdowns, bore much of the blame. A deepening real estate crisis with government intervention to tighten funding played an important role too.

Prospectively, however, export markets are unlikely to be a sustainable source of demand growth for China. Protectionist pressures and widespread concerns about increasing dependence on China mean that there are limits to the willingness of the rest of the world to absorb Chinese exports. Countries such as Vietnam and Bangladesh are also pursuing export-led growth. The growing low- and middle-income economies in Africa, Latin America and Asia provide potential but remain much smaller markets for China than the United States and Europe. In 2021 China's exports to the United States and European Union were, in total, over eight times higher than exports to Africa.

China's sheer size makes it inevitable that internal circulation needs to play the greater role in future growth and so should offer greater opportunities.

DUAL CIRCULATION AS A NEW MODEL FOR ECONOMIC GROWTH

There is little disagreement that China's growth model needs to change. To achieve higher living standards, China needs to increase productivity across the economy. When Xi Jinping announced Dual Circulation Strategy in 2020, he placed more emphasis on the "dual" than on the "circulation". The strategic focus on internal circulation as the mainstay was clear, but – prior to Covid-19 – it had already been achieved. McKinsey had found this too in 2019, by calculating a China–World Exposure Index based on trade, technology and capital linkages.[15] China's exposure to the rest of the world fell from 80 per cent of the average level for the world's seven largest economies in 2000 to 60 per cent of the average in 2017. In other words, internal circulation was more important for China than for other countries – and became more so over the period. By contrast, the exposure of the rest of the world to China over the same period rose by a factor of three. Ironically, weakness in the Chinese economy meant that this was changing – at least, temporarily – just as Xi was speaking.

Xi did talk in effusive terms of the benefits of "smooth economic flow [that] will lead to increased material products, greater social wealth, improved wellbeing among the people, and enhanced national strength, giving rise to an upward spiral of development".[16] But, as Part I explored, this was Dual Circulation as framework and slogan. New policy specifics were lacking. Xi identified the "most important task" as "maintaining effective and smooth operations on the supply side". He went on to link this directly to the pre-existing initiative of supply-side structural reform, which required "the priority tasks of cutting overcapacity, reducing excess inventory, deleveraging, lowering costs, and strengthening areas of weakness".[17] The priorities for internal circulation were in two areas: to develop domestic consumption as the driving source of demand; and to develop China's technological capabilities. An explicit focus on the "circulation" within Dual Circulation came only in April 2022, with the announcement of the "national unified market".

Consumption, not investment

For Xi, a critical aspect of Dual Circulation Strategy is increasing consumption at the expense of investment. Xi has also declared that "houses are for living in, not for speculation". There should be less real estate investment. As Chapter 2 showed, this has been a long-standing ambition of

Chinese economic policy, yet little has changed. The framework of "circulation" sheds little light on how to achieve this. As long as household income has a share of only 55 per cent in China's GDP (compared to 70–80 per cent in Western economies), it will be hard to establish household consumption as the main, reliable driver of growth.[18] Such a change requires higher wages or government transfers and lower profits, especially in the state-owned sector. Household saving is also high, given limited pension and welfare support and the often catastrophic financial impact of needing to pay for major health treatment directly out of savings.

Weighty political interests stand in the way of the shifts in power and wealth resulting from such policy changes. Real estate sales remain a critical source of local government financing. Reduced real estate development means finding another way to fund local governments. The pivotal role of real estate places government officials in positions of power and influence with local commercial interests, from which they seek to benefit. Those who have invested heavily into real estate resist both the burden of property taxation and the increased transparency of ownership that taxation might bring. Dual Circulation does not help with any of this. Instead, judgement is needed on which political interests are worth taking on when and which are not important. Moreover, major policy changes in a complex economy always bring unforeseen consequences. Such unpredictability is not welcomed by a Party leadership focused on stability. This all has shades of St Augustine, declaring "Oh God! Please make me good, but not yet."

Nonetheless, without a shift to greater consumption, China's domestic economy remains reliant on investment spending in real estate and infrastructure. Although the investments required to address climate change may justify some massive new infrastructure projects, there is overall a shortage of attractive investment opportunities that result in improved productivity and living standards.

Technology as enabler of productivity growth

Xi Jinping holds out the promise of productivity growth based on Chinese innovation leadership in technologies of the future such as quantum computing and AI. Chinese policy has long emphasized the role of "informatization", which "pursues the introduction of digital technologies into all significant areas of economic and social life, as well as the functioning of government, in order to further the Party's development aims".[19] This fits well in this age of technology, yet the effectiveness of technology rests ultimately on the capabilities of the institutions and people using it. As Peking University professor Michael Pettis has observed, institutional development is more important than technology in raising living standards.[20] Deploying technology can help, but breakthrough innovations in AI, semiconductors and quantum computing will do little to increase living standards for most of China's population. If successful, Xi's prioritization of advanced technologies may reduce China's dependence on overseas suppliers, but it will have limited benefits for growth across the whole economy.

In parallel with pursuing technology leadership, China needs to raise average living standards at a humbler level: China ranks only 81st in the world in terms of per capita income. GDP per capita in Beijing, Shanghai and Jiangsu is around four times higher than in the poorest provinces of Guangxi, Heilongjiang and Gansu. In the framing of development economics, the "catch-up potential" remains enormous. Changing this requires continued economic growth across all provinces. It means improvements in agriculture and basic industries and services from quite low levels of productivity in comparison with developed economies. Specific regional policies can help; the "Data in the East; manage in the West" policy (东数西算; *dōng shù xī suàn*), for example, encourages locating data centres in poorer, energy-rich regions such as Gansu and Ningxia. Success in developing China's leadership in advanced technologies can therefore play a part. But it does not have a broad enough impact across the whole economy to make the difference on its own. It is some form of "catch-up" growth through the strengthening of institutions that will allow living standards to rise across China.

The national unified market

The "circulation" aspect of Dual Circulation in the domestic economy became clearer in 2022. In April the CPC Central Committee and the State Council jointly released the *Opinions on Accelerating the Construction of the National Unified Market,* a focus prefigured in the 14th Five-Year Plan, published the previous year. The aim of such a unified market was to "break down local protectionism and market segmentation, break open key blockages restricting the economic cycle, and promote the smooth flow of factors of production on a wider scale" while seeking to "accelerate the construction of a nation-wide unified market that is efficient, standardized, open, and promotes fair competition". Initiatives include intellectual property rights protection, a harmonized approach to market access and China's corporate social credit system (a system that assesses corporate trustworthiness), regulating unfair market competition, promoting fair and unified market supervision, building a unified energy market, optimizing digital and logistics networks and unifying goods and services markets.

Several points stand out from this laundry list of topics. First, these policy areas are all consistent with improving smooth economic flow, the true sense of improving circulation. Improvements are to come from harmonized rules and regulations and also from improved connectivity, a long-standing feature of China's infrastructure-driven economic policy. If realized, they do hold out the promise of improved productivity. There are parallels to the creation of the European Union's Single Market. Second, it is striking that such a policy is still required, that the one country of China is still characterized by extensive regional protectionism, barriers and differing standards. This comes in part from China's sheer scale and from the strong competitive dynamic between provinces and cities that has driven much of China's growth. Local governments back local companies and want to strengthen their own locality. Covid-19 has reinforced local differences and incompatibilities. Covid-19 health codes became critical in order to travel between provinces, yet there was no standard health code across China. Third, although the vocabulary is that of the "market", some observers have highlighted instead the centralizing force inherent in such unification. They see the announcement as a step back towards a centrally planned economy. This debate was significant enough for the government to issue an explanatory rebuttal.[21] These observers are right, however, to see a power dimension in the standardization of market regulations. Xiconomics is inherently a mix of economics and power. Finally, as for every policy proposal, the unified market is not so new. In a May 2022 announcement, the State Council itself reported that a work plan had been announced in 2013 to build a "unified and open market system" and that "gradual steps have been taken toward achieving the goal".[22]

As ever, it is the implementation that matters. And implementation is tough. Zhu Rongji's ambitious and persistent state-owned enterprise reforms made remarkable progress: in his first four years, employment in the state sector fell by 34 million people. Yet here too, as fears of instability grew, the pace of SOE reform slowed.[23] The pattern of ambitious plans and delayed or aborted implementation, at lower levels of ambition, is a recurrent one. In 2020 the Chinese government unveiled "three red lines" to set boundaries on the level of debt financing in the real estate sector. But, as real estate company Evergrande and other developers hit problems, the red lines were relaxed. Property taxation has been mooted repeatedly over the years, but in 2022 even a pilot was deemed not feasible. This represents policy pragmatism and judgement as to which risks are worth taking and which are not, but also shows the limits to reform.

THE ROLE OF BUSINESS IN INTERNAL CIRCULATION

Strong economic growth and attractive levels of profit for business are likely to go hand in hand. China's economic success since 1978 is the result of a mix of top-down guidance and policies and intense competition. State-owned, private and foreign companies, together with governments, at national, provincial and local levels, have all played a role in China's economic growth. But the role of the private sector has been particularly important. The former vice-premier, Liu He, has stated that China's private sector accounted for 70 per cent of innovation and 90 per cent of new jobs and firms.[24] Competition and the pursuit of commercial objectives – by private or by state-owned enterprises – both generate profits and increased productivity in the economy.

In his 2014 book *Markets over Mao: The Rise of Private Business in China*, Nicholas Lardy describes how private companies drove innovation, job creation and value creation in China's development. This is not a classic tale of free-market competition, however. After an era of state-directed economic activity, Chinese policy-makers needed to build the "market" itself. In addition, the Chinese government steered a state-owned banking system that financed high levels of infrastructure and capital investment. They negotiated to grant foreign companies market access in exchange for technology and know-how. In 2020 China was the world's top destination for foreign direct investment (FDI), and in 2021 foreign companies accounted for more than one-third of China's exports.

By the time that Lardy's book was published, the state had already taken on a stronger role. State-owned enterprises and government-related entities became more prominent following China's 2008 stimulus initiative. In the phrase of that time, "the state moves in; the private sector retreats" (国进民退; *guó jìn mín tuì*).[25] Lardy's subsequent 2019 book came with the title *The State Strikes Back: The End of Economic Reform in China?* Exactly how far the private sector has "retreated" remains a matter of debate. Company-level analysis by the Peterson Institute suggests that the private sector continues to prosper.[26] From 2010 to 2020 the private sector increased its share of revenues within the top 500 Chinese companies from 3.8 per cent to 19 per cent. But these numbers belie a private sector that faces greater regulatory interventions, policy uncertainty and political rhetoric that consistently supports the role of state-owned enterprises.

The past few years have heightened uncertainty about the priorities that Xi is pursuing and whether this jeopardizes the economic dynamism of the Chinese economy. The Third Plenum of the 18th Central Committee in 2013 fuelled expectations of further market-based reform, with its announcement that markets would play "a decisive role" in resource allocation – a recipe for renewed productivity growth. But the announcement also stated that "we must unswervingly consolidate and develop the public economy, adhere to the dominant position of state ownership. The public economy needs to play a leading role, and the vitality, controlling ability and influence of public economy needs to be constantly enhanced."[27] In 2020 the Fifth Plenum expressed the ambition to "give full play to the decisive role of the market in allocating resources" through actions to "further develop the role of government and promote a better combination of efficient markets and effective governments".[28] Throughout this time the creation of new firms has increased sharply, in line with the policy to increase "mass entrepreneurship" during the period of the 14th Five-Year Plan (2021–25).[29]

This is a quest for a "Goldilocks" model of the economy, neither too "market" nor too "state", each playing a valuable role under the leadership of the CPC. "Grand steerage" is the term coined by Professor Barry Naughton of the University of California – San Diego to describe this, "the Chinese government's use of massive resources to drive a market-based economy towards a visionary outcome".[30]

Government policy and regulations set the terms on which businesses compete and are able to make a profit. Although some sectors are over-regulated, many entrepreneurial businesses have also succeeded in a context of weak regulation or through too cosy relationships with government officials. China's internet platform companies and technology start-ups have benefited from a lack of regulation and had unregulated access to consumer data. Effective regulation needs to strike a balance between rewarding commercial endeavour and risk-taking, on the one hand, and protecting against monopolistic and predatory behaviour towards customers, employees and competitors, on the other. Striking the right balance unlocks productivity gains for the economy. Getting it wrong either stifles business activity or leads to monopoly businesses extracting excess profits from employees, customers and suppliers. A pragmatic, adaptive approach, rather than fixed ideology, is what has underpinned China's economic success over the past few decades. Under Xi Jinping, decision-making has become more centralized, with less open space for debate on which policies are working and which are not. Many fear that course corrections will not happen quickly enough if policies have unintended outcomes.

In 2021 sudden regulatory interventions in China's largest internet platform companies, such as Alibaba and Tencent, led to fines, reduced profits and sent share prices tumbling. At the same time companies made "tertiary contributions" out of profits – effectively, state-mandated philanthropic payments. Alibaba pledged RMB 100 billion to a "Common Prosperity drive".[31] Chinese regulators justified the actions as needed to address abusive market behaviour. Regulators did indeed ban specific instances of monopolistic behaviour, such as Alibaba's and Tencent's policy of "pick one from two" (二选一; *èr xuǎn yī*). Under this policy smaller merchants were forced into exclusivity agreements with one of the two giants.[32] Regulatory intervention benefited smaller companies at the expense of the excess profits of "big tech".

The suddenness of the actions had the smack of "shock and awe" tactics. Indeed, Chinese regulators often refer to the Chinese proverb of "killing the chicken to scare the monkey" (杀鸡儆猴; *shā jī jìng hóu*): they take very strong action against one company so that all the others get the message. Nevertheless, the actions also left the impression that the investigations were as much motivated by politics and an assertion of power over key individual entrepreneurs as by economic considerations. Some entrepreneurs started to question whether they were still welcome or whether they should "fade away", as Wu Xiaoping, a self-described financial industry veteran, had suggested in 2018.[33]

Alibaba's founder, Jack Ma, disappeared from the public eye and rumours circulated as to whether he was under political investigation or simply keeping a low profile. When Ma first resurfaced, he was shown addressing rural teachers on behalf of his charitable foundation – a clear signal of commitment to Xi's Common Prosperity. Since then regulators have also signalled a more measured approach to new regulations. Chinese leaders have repeatedly stated the importance of entrepreneurs, private business and technology companies. In this case, policy tone has adjusted, while leaving in place a new regulatory framework. It is hard to restore certainty and communicate this credibly, however, after such dramatic actions beforehand.

Government intervention is by no means simply a matter of central government action. Local government and Party officials affect the business environment through their actions. Local governments need to secure new revenue streams to replace declining real estate sales (the main source of revenue) and (in 2022) to finance the cost of intensive Covid-19-testing campaigns. They often turn to business to pay. *Caixin*, China's leading business magazine, reported in 2022 that "arbitrary fines and fees are resurfacing" and that there was a need to "protect market entities from excessive fines and irregular charges as the foundation for stabilizing the economy".[34]

MORE THAN "JUST BUSINESS" – BUT HOW MUCH MORE?

Although business competition and market reform can increase productivity and living standards, economic growth alone is no longer enough in today's China. The talk is of prosperity for all and a comprehensive approach to national security in a society where the Party leads everything. Security, resilience, ideology and values have become more intertwined with economics and business.

This intertwining of economics, security and values is not unique to China. All governments face the question of how to address inequalities and increase inclusion. Adopting a broader definition of national security that includes economic considerations has become a commonplace in the United States and Europe. What marks China out is the overarching role of the Party and the variability in how the Party has exercised its power over business since the founding of the People's Republic in 1949.

The impact on the business environment depends on how far non-commercial objectives override profit considerations – and where they create new opportunities in, for example, national-security-related fields or growing consumer markets resulting from a more equal income distribution. Common Prosperity can mean both growing profits from a larger market and shrinking profits as companies are pressured to make "tertiary contributions". There is a big difference between an economy in which extensive redistribution is the main focus, or every major business transaction is reviewed for security risks, and one in which these factors are in the background. What matters for business – and for China's future economic prosperity – is where these different aspects reinforce one another, where they are in conflict. And there is always the question: if they do conflict, which takes priority?

This is a matter of both substance and perception. When Chinese companies "buy local" as a result of government guidance rather than independent, commercial decision-making, this step towards self-reliance has an economic cost, at least in the short term. It is a choice to "buy" self-reliance at the expense of economic wealth. How high the price is in the longer term depends ultimately on how successful Chinese companies become in advanced technologies: Does this short-term cost represent an investment with a subsequent commercial pay-off as local suppliers become competitive? Or is it, rather, a price paid for the supposed security benefits of self-reliance? Whether Chinese companies succeed in becoming competitive depends on the effectiveness of the approach taken and, also, a degree of luck. To date

China's success has been limited in those sectors, such as aerospace and semiconductors, where government has been most directly involved. Maintaining intense, domestic competition between many aspiring companies will be an important part of the recipe for success. Equally, the state will not be completely absent. China's new policy of supporting the development of thousands of "little giant" companies in advanced technologies may strike a balance between state guidance and market competition that works for China.[35]

Substance matters on questions of ideology too. In 2019 China's most downloaded app was the "Study the Great Nation" (学习强国; *xuéxí qiángguó*) app, which supports the study of Xi Jinping Thought. University students and employees in government and in state-owned enterprises were expected to spend time on the app, although some found ways to game the system and avoid the time commitment.[36] Unless this app-based study increases productivity or team cohesion in some mysterious way, it represents a direct trade-off between economic and ideological goals. Time spent on the app is time not spent studying or working.

On a much broader level, Party officials are becoming more actively engaged in private business, both in domestic and foreign companies. In 2020 the CPC issued the *Opinion on Strengthening the United Front Work of the Private Economy,* calling for increased ideological work and influence in the private sector. It called on companies to "improve their corporate governance structure and explore the establishment of a modern enterprise system with Chinese characteristics".[37] Xi had previously explained "Chinese characteristics" as meaning "integrating the Party's leadership into all aspects of corporate governance".[38] The impact of this Party involvement varies widely between different companies and different regions. Seen positively, it helps company management navigate an uncertain business environment more effectively and bring together commercial aims with Party priorities. It may, however, lead to excessive influence in business decisions for those with strong ideological priorities and little commercial experience, so harming competitiveness and profits.

Although substance is critical, perceptions are not to be discounted. Viewed with a sufficiently sceptical eye, everything and everyone can be seen as a security risk. Regulators deemed the potential transfer overseas of ride-sharing data, collected by Didi, China's equivalent of Uber, to represent a security risk. Paul Gillis of Peking University observes that "China has a very expansive definition of state secrets such that basically any transaction with a state-owned enterprise in China is considered to be a state secret ... [F]or example, my mobile phone bill is technically a state secret."[39]

Uncertainty and second-guessing caused by differences in perceptions impose significant costs on the economy. Early in 2022 Zhou Jiangyong, the former Party secretary of Hangzhou, was charged with "colluding with capital and backing the disorderly expansion of capital".[40] Xi has inveighed against the "disorderly expansion of capital"[41] and the "need to strengthen anti-monopoly regulation".[42] But what do these words mean? And what personal risk does someone bear if he or she interprets them in the wrong way? Some interpret the charge of "colluding with capital" as penalizing officials for supporting business. Others see it as a legitimate move to stop corrupt practices. Research by MacroPolo has shown how China's anti-corruption efforts are now focused on "disentangling business and politics".[43]

Deciphering what is actually happening, and for what reasons, is a challenge, bringing yet more uncertainty to business. In Lewis Carroll's *Through the Looking-Glass*, Humpty Dumpty says, "When I use a word, it means just what I choose it to mean – neither more nor less." Alice responds, "The question is whether you can make words mean so many different things." Humpty Dumpty replies in conclusion, "The question is which is to be master – that's all."[44] And, in today's China, it is clear who the master is. Everyone – Chinese and foreigner alike – ends up spending time and energy reading the runes of what policy measures will come next. This is unlikely to change.

FUTURE PROSPECTS FOR BUSINESS

The business environment in China will remain more politicized and more securitized than in the years before Xi Jinping. Economic growth will also be slower. The priority given to questions of security and ideology over economics acts in effect as a tax or burden on economic productivity and growth. The size of this "tax" depends on political choices made both for domestic reasons in China and in response to the global environment, especially US–China relations.

The policy emphasis between commercial profit maximization, redistribution, security and values will continue to shift. In part, this represents shifting judgements by the Chinese leadership on short-term and longer-term priorities. A weakening economy in 2022 seemed to lessen the prominence given to Common Prosperity. But the pursuit of a zero-Covid-19 policy trumped short-term economic performance. Although self-reliance remained important for key technologies, a weak domestic economy meant that demand growth abroad was to be welcomed. Exports boomed. External events and decisions will also shift the balance. Energy and food security have become more important in the wake of the Russian invasion of Ukraine. A new US president with a more confrontational approach to China would probably strengthen China's focus on security and self-reliance and give a boost to Chinese nationalism.

The pace of economic growth rests also on the skill with which the party-state implements and adjusts economic policy interventions to advance "reform", whether under the rubric of "Dual Circulation", "High-Quality Development" or some other phrasing. Good policy needs to incorporate learning and adjustment. Many assessments of Chinese policy-making veer to one of two extremes. They presume either a fixed approach that takes little account of policy impact or an omniscient competence that means that all outcomes were intended. Neither extreme is true. Certainly, Chinese leaders and regulators have room to improve in how they implement and communicate, and this can thereby reduce business uncertainty.

Change does continue; much of it is of the kind proposed under the national unified market, with its multitude of regulatory and institutional adjustments to market functioning. The Rhodium Group and Asia Society tracked progress on China's reform agenda from 2013 to 2021 across ten dimensions: labour, land, fiscal affairs, innovation, cross-border investment, competition, trade, state-owned enterprises, environment and the financial system.[45] Reforms have generally been halted when they led to instability, which is most of the time. Rhodium found progress in the areas of the environment, fiscal affairs, innovation and cross-border investment. Elsewhere they judged reform to have "run backwards (or stalled)", especially in labour, land and state-owned enterprises.

In fact, the most noteworthy recent progress may be the continued opening up to foreign business. In 2018 China switched from a "positive list" (listing sectors open to foreign business) to a "negative list" approach, whereby all sectors were open except those on the negative list. Each year since has seen the negative list shrink in length.[46] Ownership limits and the requirements for joint ventures have been removed in sectors such as automotive and financial services. Since 2013 China has established 21 free trade zones (FTZs) across the country, starting with Shanghai, where specific, looser regulations and targeted incentives apply. These are of varying value to foreign companies. Notably, Tesla opened its Gigafactory 3 in the Shanghai FTZ in 2019.

Overall, though, progress on implementation has been slow. Maybe it would be hard for it to be otherwise in such a large and complex economy. But change in the 1990s and early 2000s was much more marked. There has been no appetite for large-scale, step-change reform, with its attendant uncertainties but also its potential benefits. In fact, priorities appear to have been elsewhere in recent years.

The overall outlook for economic growth, productivity and rising living standards is not promising. Looking forward, Bert Hofman, director of the East Asian Institute at the National University of Singapore and former World Bank country director for China, has laid out a range of scenarios for whether and when China will overtake the United States as the world's largest economy at market exchange rates. As ever, the answer rests crucially on the pace and impact of economic reforms. Comprehensive reform would see China overtake the United States in the early 2030s rather than a base case of the late 2030s. In the face of limited reforms or a debt crisis, the United States would remain the world's largest economy even in 2050.[47]

What role will China play in the world of external circulation?

Beijing 2015: Li Xiaolin, chair of the Chinese People's Association for Friendship with Foreign Countries, declares that Andorra is a particularly valued partner of China. Andorra La Vella 2017: Andorra Telecom announces that it will work exclusively with Huawei to upgrade its high-speed internet access and to provide public Wi-Fi access across Andorra's capital. In 2019 China and Andorra celebrate 25 years of bilateral relations. Li's mention of Andorra, with a population of 77,000, was to make a point. China takes an interest and sees opportunity in every corner of the world.

In 2017 Xi Jinping announced to the 19th Party Congress that China was ready to enter the centre stage of global affairs. In the economic sphere, China is now the leading trading partner of 120 countries – more than any other country.[1] China led the world as a source of outbound foreign direct investment in 2020, even excluding FDI flows out of Hong Kong.[2] Although China's recent arrival to the world of outbound investment means that its total stock of overseas investments lags behind the United States, it already ranks at the level of Japan, Germany and the United Kingdom.[3]

Over the past 20 years multinationals have seen China's economic presence in the rest of the world grow rapidly. First, imports from China offered competition in markets around the world as well as providing new sourcing opportunities for foreign companies themselves. Then, at the exhortation of Zhu Rongji in the 1990s, Chinese companies started to "go out" themselves, to establish operations overseas, invest and make acquisitions. From 2005 to 2017 acquisition activity intensified as Chinese companies bought foreign companies, so as to secure access to resources and advanced technologies or simply to capitalize on business opportunities. From 2013 onwards China's Belt and Road Initiative heralded a drive to increase infrastructure links and trade, supported by extensive lending from Chinese state-owned banks.

Just as many Western companies have struggled to succeed in China, however, so Chinese companies have often struggled in foreign markets. In 2020 Zhou Lihong, chairwoman of the China Chamber of Commerce to the European Union, said that the Chinese business community would like to see less "red tape" and fewer regulatory barriers in doing business in the European Union.[4] These are familiar issues for European companies in China. Chinese companies, especially state-owned enterprises, have often found greater opportunities in the markets of Africa, Asia and Latin America than the United States and Europe. In recent years geopolitical tensions have strengthened this skew. In 2022 there were reports that the China National Offshore Oil Corporation (CNOOC) planned to withdraw from the United States, United Kingdom and Canada, describing its business there as "marginal and hard to manage".[5] CNOOC subsequently denied that such plans were under consideration, but the logic was sound. This was a marked change from 2005, when CNOOC had launched a US$18.4 billion bid to acquire US oil producer Unocal, only to withdraw in face of opposition from the US government.[6] Others, however, have had better success. TikTok, a subsidiary of China's Bytedance, was the most downloaded app in the United States in 2021,[7] one year after President Trump had threatened to ban it. And it is not all plain sailing for Chinese companies in lower-income countries. They have faced pushback on contract terms and labour relations and often struggle to navigate local politics. In contrast with the United States, India implemented a ban on TikTok in 2020.

For China, where the Party "leads everything", the world of external circulation has one defining difference: it lies beyond the direct control of the Party and of China's leadership. It is a world of trade and investment flows, international trade, labour and financial regulation agreements and shared technology standards. It is a world of established multilateral organizations and agreements that, for the most part, have their origins in decisions made by the largest Western economies in the wake of the Second World War.[8] It is a world of the US dollar, even within Asia and even for China. Around 80 per cent of Asian exports are invoiced in US dollars and only 20 per cent of China's trade is settled in renminbi.[9] And it is a world of bilateral economic relationships, of which the US–China relationship is the most prominent and the EU–China trade relationship now the largest. These economic relationships unfold in a broader diplomatic context, shaped by history, domestic politics, values and security concerns on both sides. Although China has its own clear ambitions and national interests, so too do other countries. China can seek to shape and channel economic circulation beyond its borders but it will not do so unchallenged or unimpeded.

CHINA'S NEW ROLE IN EXTERNAL CIRCULATION

In its very formulation, Dual Circulation Strategy recognizes this difference between the internal and the external environments. It does not envisage a China cut off from the world, however. Liu He, vice-premier and China's most senior economic policy advisor until early 2023, has written that one "core mission" of Dual Circulation is to "drive higher levels of external opening, and deepen integration with the global economy … China will drive the establishment of a common human collective and form a tighter and more stable global economic circulatory system."[10] This reference to "a common human collective" echoes Xi Jinping's call for a "community of common destiny for all of mankind" (民运共同体; *mínyùn gòngtóngtǐ*).[11] The nature and form of such a "community" remains ambiguous and ill defined. It does illustrate China's aspirations to articulate and shape some form of global order beyond its own borders, however. Wei Jiangguo, a vice-chairman of the China Center for International Economic Exchanges (CCIEE), a Chinese think tank, argues that "Dual Circulation will lay the foundation for the country's upcoming higher level of opening up which will lead the new trend of globalization" and that "historical experience shows that isolating oneself from the world will only lead to backwardness, and opening to the outside world is a correct historical decision".[12]

Since China's opening up started in 1978, China has engaged in the world economy by signing up to and working within existing institutions, norms and regulations. Reform and opening up brought large benefits for China's economic development. In particular, China's accession to the World Trade Organization in 2001 laid the basis for a dramatic expansion in manufacturing exports, culminating in China's current position as the world's largest manufacturing exporter. China has taken the structure of external circulation as a given and determined where and how to best engage for its own advantage.

Recent years have seen major changes in how China and other countries view the terms on which external circulation operates. The years of liberalizing trade and investment flows prefigured Xi Jinping's Dual Circulation arguments that "smooth economic flow will lead to increased material products, greater social wealth, improved wellbeing among the people, and enhanced national strength, giving rise to an upward spiral of development".[13] But countries around the world are looking anew at the balance of benefits and costs that globalization has brought. In particular, protectionist pressures have grown in the United States in response to concerns that imports – especially from China – have caused job losses and lowered wages. US trade representative Katherine Tai has expressed particular dissatisfaction with Chinese policy: "For too long, China's lack of adherence to global trading norms has undercut the prosperity of Americans and others around the world."[14] At the same time, China's ability and willingness to reshape the global system of external circulation to its own advantage has increased. China is economically stronger and has developed clearer views of what it likes and does not like in the way that the world economy operates.

To adopt and adapt the language of economics, China has moved from being a "system-taker", which accepts external circulation as it is, to having the potential to be a "system-shaper", which reshapes that world. When China accounted for only 4 per cent of the world economy and needed access to foreign capital, know-how and markets, its best – indeed, only – strategy was to accept (to "take") the global system as it was. Now, as the world's second largest economy and – in many years – largest source of global growth, China has more options – or, at least, believes that it does. Whether these options become reality still depends on the willingness or acquiescence of other countries to go along with alternative approaches and on China's capacity to put in the effort needed to make these changes stick.

It is unsurprising that China, with its different economic structure, governance and history, has its own perspectives on how the global economy should operate. For example, state-owned enterprises and government subsidies play a more central role in the Chinese economy than in most developed economies. This has been a bone of contention in the negotiation of trade agreements, including China's accession to the WTO in 2001. Julian Gewirtz, in his article "The Chinese reassessment of interdependence", notes that "interdependence across economic networks – of trade, finance, and digital communications, among others – produces mutual economic gains due to 'comparative advantage', but it is also defined by asymmetries in power, with some countries' key positions in such networks allowing them immense opportunities for coercion".[15] This is a matter of logic, not CPC ideology. The choice rests in how and when such positions are used. Any initiative by China to shape the way the global economy operates would thus have one of three aims: first, to enhance China's own position, by ensuring that the rules are appropriate to its own situation; second, to mitigate dependences that China may have on the rest of the world; and, third, to increase dependences that the rest of the world has on China. This is a marked shift from a China that takes binary decisions on whether or not to engage with already established and mostly Western-designed institutions and norms. Now, additionally, come the questions of whether, where and how China can or should seek to change, replace or compete with this same system. In the language of international relations, is or should China be a "revisionist" power, or even a revolutionary one – a power that changes the world order? And, if so, can it succeed?

CHOOSING WHERE AND HOW TO DEPLOY LIMITED RESOURCES

Having the option to pursue different strategies is not the same as choosing to actually do so or succeeding. It takes massive effort to create new institutions and rules. It requires the agreement or acquiescence of other countries, which is not straightforward to secure. There is little appeal for China in a radical overhaul of multilateral arrangements that already work at least reasonably well. Diplomatic resources are limited, as is the appetite to spend time on foreign matters when domestic challenges are more pressing. Indeed, although a faltering Chinese economy might increase nationalist rhetoric, it would limit further the resources for substantive, large-scale initiatives abroad.

Shaping external circulation is also a competitive endeavour. Just as Xi Jinping seeks a balance favourable to China, so too the United States makes its intent clear in its Indo-Pacific strategy: "Our objective is not to change the PRC, but to shape the strategic environment in which it operates, building a balance of influence in the world that is maximally favourable to the United States, our allies and partners, and the interests and values we share."[16] Competition in the shaping of norms and the provision of global governance has increased.

For China, this is all ultimately a question of (perceived) costs and benefits. The current system has brought many benefits, in particular in the areas of trade and finance through the WTO, World Bank and IMF. The efforts and resources required to maintain these existing institutions are less than those required to establish new ones. China is strongly engaged in existing multilateral institutions, providing talented individuals to staff key positions, arguing its case and lobbying for support. Through its economic weight and its willingness to dedicate time and effort, China is well placed to have influence and to effect change. Chinese nationals head four of the United Nations' (UN's) 15 agencies: the Food and Agriculture Organization (FAO), the International Telecommunication Union (ITU), the United Nations Industrial Development Organization (UNIDO) and the International Civil Aviation Organization (ICAO).[17]

At the same time, China has also launched new organizations and new initiatives. There are new development finance institutions in the form of the New Development Bank (NDB) and the Asian Infrastructure Investment Bank (AIIB), established in 2014 and 2016 respectively. Initiatives include the Belt and Road Initiative, the Global Development Initiative and the Global Initiative on Data Security, all with the purpose of projecting China's leadership role in shaping different domains.

This logic for China's role in the world has parallels to the arguments advanced by Rush Doshi, China director on President Biden's National Security Council and former Brookings Institution scholar. In his book *The Long Game: China's Grand Strategy to Displace American Order*, Doshi draws on Chinese materials to show how China has adapted its approach to international engagement over time based on its capabilities and options relative to an assessment of the US position.[18] He argues that this has spurred China to adopt a series of "strategies of displacement" to offset US influence in the regional and global order. This started with a "blunting strategy" in the 1990s, to limit US economic influence at a time when China was relatively weak. In the wake of the global financial crisis, Doshi argues that a "building strategy" emerged as China's confidence and relative economic strength grew. China increased its efforts to shape economic links with other countries through moves such as the AIIB and the BRI. Doshi's third and final strategy, one of "expansion", is the least defined and most debated. Doshi argues that China is seeking to "project leadership over global governance and international institutions and to advance autocratic norms" and to "seize the commanding heights of the Fourth Industrial Revolution".

Doshi goes on to describe three levers available to China – and, indeed, available to the United States and other countries – in pursuing these three strategies, namely coercive control, incentivization and appeals to legitimacy. Of these, incentivization is the most likely to be effective. By definition, it forces a focus on how all parties benefit from changes that also bring benefit to China. Despite many problems, Belt and Road projects have often brought needed infrastructure investment to African countries. Exercising coercive control has a directness to it, based as it is on an assertion of power. But it can rapidly spark a backlash. Indeed, the very exercise of coercion leads many to "stand up for themselves", even at some economic cost. Countries take mitigating action, be it in their trade relations or by renegotiating contracts for Belt and Road projects. Finally, appeals to legitimacy can be powerful. The challenge here is to establish that legitimacy through deeds. This is an area in which China is relatively weak. Although China has increasingly drawn on its development success to build credibility with lower-income countries, its appeal to a "community of common destiny" has had little substance to date.

THREE (ECONOMIC) PRIORITIES FOR CHINA

A look at the balance between potential benefits and effort required suggests where China's priorities in shaping the economy of external circulation may lie. In this time of "great changes, unseen in a century", reducing the risks of dependence trumps creating new growth options – although those are welcome too. It is also common sense to focus on those areas where change is likely to meet less resistance. Often this will be in newer fields, where there are no legacy standards and structures, and in areas where other major powers (especially the United States and Europe) are less active.

This logic suggests three priorities for China. First, reducing China's reliance on shared global "infrastructure" (in the broadest sense), where access to that infrastructure is effectively in the gift of the United States currently and so China risks exclusion. The role of the US dollar in the global payments system stands out. Second, shaping standards and structures in critical, emerging domains where standards have not yet been established or need to be updated. This applies to all aspects of technology, including internet, 5G/6G and AI. It could also take in areas such as biotech and genetic engineering. Third, China gains great benefit from its integration into global trading system; participating in and helping shape new trade agreements makes sense amid the protectionist pressures of the day.

Reducing reliance on the United States: the "problem" of the US dollar

China has already taken a number of steps to reduce or eliminate its dependence on shared physical infrastructure that is under actual or effective US control. It has developed its own global positioning system, Beidou, and has plans for its own low Earth orbit satellite internet network.[19] China is emerging as a leading provider and owner of subsea cables, which carry 95 per cent of international internet data.[20] From China's perspective, its military expansion in the South China Sea is in part to ensure sea lanes remain open for its vessels in all circumstances, rather than subject to US influence.

Much more challenging than building physical infrastructure is creating alternatives to the US dollar in global finance. Three elements matter to China: the predominant role of the US dollar in global payments; the fact that all US dollar clearing happens under US jurisdiction; and the central role of SWIFT,[21] the dominant secure messaging system for global payments in all currencies. SWIFT is a multi-stakeholder cooperative, but is nonetheless under effective US and European control when it comes to determining which countries have access. In practice, this means that the United States can restrict access to US dollar payments and dollar holdings as an economic sanction to force compliance with specific behaviours globally. When the United States imposed sanctions on Hong Kong's political leaders, even Chinese state-owned banks felt the need to comply. Huang Qifan, a vice-chairman of the CCIEE think tank, bemoaned the ability of the United States to "exercise hegemony and carry out long-arm jurisdiction" through SWIFT.[22] Western sanctions on Russia following the Ukraine invasion have made this risk all the more salient for China. Once again, Chinese financial institutions have complied.

Although there may be a long-term ambition for the renminbi to rival or replace the US dollar just as the US dollar replaced the British pound, the immediate priority is much narrower in scope. It is to mitigate the impact on China of the United States' ability to wield the US dollar as an instrument of power. Beyond the extremes of sanctions, there is a point of economic realpolitik too. During the global financial crisis Chinese and other Asian exporters struggled to access the trade finance that they needed as US dollar funding dried up. They were simply lower down the priority order for liquidity-strapped banks.

For this reason, in 2015 China launched its own international payment system for renminbi payments: CIPS (Cross-Border International Payment System). For the most part, however, CIPS payments still need to use SWIFT for secure messaging. Network economics make it hard to replace the established provider; it takes time to build scale. Nonetheless, an imperfect alternative is better than none at all when it comes to self-reliance.

More recently, China's lead in digital money has been touted as a new avenue for China to reduce reliance on the US dollar. Central bank digital currencies (CBDCs) are equivalent to digital banknotes, liabilities issued by a country's central bank. At the end of 2021 China's CBDC – known as the e-renminbi or e-CNY – had 261 million users.[23] Although the e-CNY's immediate focus is primarily domestic, the PBOC has declared it "ready for cross-border use". China has a pilot under way working with the United Arab Emirates, Hong Kong and Thailand on the cross-border use of CBDCs. Such cross-border use would allow direct bilateral digital trade payments without using the US dollar, reducing the dollar's critical role.

In sum, China's focus for now is relatively limited: to create workable alternatives to the US-led payments systems so as to reduce its dependence on the US dollar in extreme circumstances. This is quite different from a grand ambition to replace the US dollar as a reserve currency. Such a transition is a matter of decades rather than years. It would require policies that China is not ready to pursue. These include capital account opening and running a persistent trade deficit to create a large pool of renminbi that can be held globally.

Staking out positions in technology standards and governance

The potential of digital currencies is just one small, uncertain opportunity on the much larger canvas of digital data and technology. Governance models and norms for these newly emerging areas are much less established than in the physical world. This, together with China's scale and growing technological prowess, opens up the opportunity for China to play a shaping role. An extensive report by the National Bureau for Asian Research summarizes the situation as follows: "China intends to define this digital architecture by building its physical infrastructure and corresponding virtual networks and platforms, setting the technical standards that govern them, and shaping the emerging global digital governance regime. In doing so, it is cementing Chinese control over the international flow of data – and, as a result, resources."[24]

Technology standards play a critical role. "Third-tier companies make products, second-tier companies design technology, and first-tier companies set standards." So runs a mantra commonly quoted in China. Standards are rarely purely technical in their impact. They generate an economic return to those who own the patents underlying the standards, a reward for successful innovation efforts. But the real significance is that those who set standards are able to shape future development.

The specific standards chosen can shape a sector's competitive structure and industry economics. Across many fields, China has announced expansive ambitions to set standards domestically and then have these serve as international standards under its China Standards 2035 initiative. China is increasingly active in the technical committees of global standards-setting organizations. In 2020 Xi Jinping announced the country's Global Initiative on Data Security (全球数据安全倡议; *quánqiú shùjù ānquán chàngyì*), a proposed framework for dealing with security in data storage and digital commerce.

For China's plans to succeed, however, the reality is that all parties need to agree that these standards are indeed mutually beneficial. Corporate innovation (whether state-guided or private sector) and market success mostly determines which standards win out. Where the focus of China's standards push is based on tangible technical superiority and economic benefits, success is more likely. Throughout the Huawei 5G controversies, a common, global approach to 5G standards has remained in place. The United States amended its Huawei ban to allow US companies to cooperate on standards. When proposed standards raise issues of national economic competitiveness, security and even values, however, it is attractive for large countries to pursue a separation into competing standards, if a mutually acceptable consensus cannot be reached. China will struggle to impose its will, just as would the United States. Incentivization beats coercion. Such divergence in standards is also not unmanageable. Before the emergence of a shared global 3G mobile phone standard, phone manufacturers produced dual- and tri-band phones or travellers rented a local phone upon arriving at the airport.

Perhaps the most critical standards relate to the architecture and associated governance of the internet. Here China has a clear position on a different approach for the future. Internet governance today takes the form of a multi-stakeholder model with many different elements and participants, including public bodies, private companies and non-profit organizations – some with national standing, some (often in the United States) with global reach, and others of international standing.[25] China, together with Russia and others, has instead long argued for an intergovernmental model of governance. The International Telecommunication Union (ITU) has issued papers discussing the so-called New IP (internet protocol), the technical architecture of a next-generation internet design for 2030, with particular input from Huawei.[26] This new China-advanced design proposal is centralized and top-down. The stronger role that it would afford national governments fits with China's stance on cyber-sovereignty, first advanced in a 2010 internet White Paper.[27] For China, unwanted influence in a country's "information space" should be banned.[28] In 2022 China announced that its annual "World Internet Conference", which promotes its model of internet governance, had transformed into an "international organization".[29]

How the very structure of the internet evolves will rest on more than technical considerations. Questions of national security and societal values will play an important role. The defining issue remains whether, all things considered, countries can agree on a single best architecture for the next-generation internet, or whether the compromises involved are deemed too great, so that two parallel architectures emerge, each under their own governance structure. In 2018 Eric Schmidt, former CEO of Google, predicted that such a "splinternet" of two systems would indeed emerge. Such a change would mark a significant reshaping of external circulation. It would also prompt the question of whether and how the two systems connect.

Maintaining and shaping a central position in trading networks

In November 2020, despite the travails of the Covid-19 pandemic, the then premier, Li Keqiang, joined 14 other Asian leaders by video link to sign a new trade agreement. RCEP, the Regional Comprehensive Economic Partnership, is the world's largest free trade area, comprising China, the ten Association of Southeast Asian Nations (ASEAN) nations, South Korea, Japan, Australia and New Zealand. Although trade may no longer be the driving force of China's economic growth, it remains of critical importance. China wishes both to continue exporting ever more sophisticated products and, increasingly, to import lower value-added products such as textiles, in which it will struggle to stay competitive. Agricultural imports will also remain important despite efforts to become more self-sufficient. RCEP is the next step in the liberalization of the trade flows that have formed the foundation for Asia's economic growth. At the same time, its terms allow for a greater accommodation of national differences than agreements in which the United States has played a shaping role. Although it eliminates tariffs on over 90 per cent of trade, RCEP does not contain major commitments on labour, the environment, intellectual property, state-owned enterprises and other areas. These issues have often been sticking points for China in trade negotiations.

China has also applied for membership in two other Asia-centred trade agreements that incorporate more stringent terms on liberalization and market opening. In 2021 China applied to join CPTTP, the Comprehensive and Progressive Agreement for Trans-Pacific Partnership. This is the successor to the Trans-Pacific Partnership proposed by the United States but from which President Trump withdrew. The remaining 11 countries[30] signed the CPTTP in 2018. Although Xi Jinping has spoken of China's commitment to make the necessary reforms, there is debate about whether China truly intends to liberalize in line with CPTPP membership requirements – those very issues that RCEP did not contain. If Xi chooses, CPTPP can serve as a lever for domestic reform in the same way that WTO accession did. Alternatively, accession negotiations could be a long-drawn-out process, with particular concerns held by Australia and Japan. In any event, the application creates options for China. The United States has not applied to join.

Also in 2021 China applied to join DEPA, the Digital Economy Partnership Agreement, signed between Singapore, New Zealand and Chile.[31] DEPA lays out common rules guiding data transfers, digital payments, financial technology and the public use of government data. Participation puts China in the midst of negotiations on the standards for digital trade, an increasingly important but as yet ill-defined area.

Trade also lies at the heart of the Belt and Road Initiative (see Chapter 3), which is more often seen as an infrastructure initiative. In addition to infrastructure, the BRI takes in questions such as customs facilitation, trade and finance. It provides an example of how China seeks to shape the world of external circulation. Bruno Maçães, a former Portuguese government minister, explored the potential impact of the BRI in his 2018 book *Belt and Road: A Chinese World Order*. He argues that, "instead of integrating into the existing world order, China could be creating a separate economic bloc, with different dominant companies and technologies, and governed by rules, institutions, and trade patterns dictated by Beijing".[32]

There are now a range of mediation and arbitration approaches to resolve BRI-related disputes in addition to already established international arbitration methods.[33] China has established its own China International Commercial Court (CICC), with two offices in Shenzhen and Xi'an, to adjudicate on disputes. The CICC is a permanent body under the Supreme People's Court (SPC), the highest court in China. There is no separate "rule of law" independent of the CPC in China, and so the CICC is ultimately subordinate to the CPC. In an analogous way to technical standards, contracting parties will choose CICC jurisdiction based on how effectively and impartially the court reaches its judgements in practice and on whether they see other benefits, such as more attractive contract terms, given the potential politicization of any decisions.

STRENGTHENING CHINA'S "DISCOURSE POWER": A FOURTH PRIORITY?

Of Doshi's three levers for influence – coercion, incentivization and appeals to legitimacy – China has struggled most with the third. In 1990 Harvard professor Joseph Nye coined the term "soft power" to describe the ability to influence others through mechanisms such as culture and political values rather than coercion. Nye saw the United States as the global leader in this regard. President Hu Jintao identified China's relative weakness. In 2007 Hu stated: "We must enhance culture as part of the soft power of our country." In 2014 Xi Jinping remarked: "We should increase China's soft power, give a good Chinese narrative, and better communicate China's messages to the world."[34] Addressing these issues has both instrumental and intrinsic value. Enhanced legitimacy and appeal would enable China to influence others more effectively. It would also be a natural element of the "Great Rejuvenation of the Chinese people". Xi Jinping has spoken of the need to make China a more "loveable" (可爱; *kě'ài*) country[35] and "tell China's story".[36]

More broadly, China's leadership wants to strengthen what it describes as "discourse power" (话语权; *huàyǔquán*). It argues that the very terms of the "global conversation" are set by Western norms and need to be challenged. Foreign perspectives on China should "converge" with those of the Party.[37] China argues for its own definition of democracy, superior to Western democracy, rather than describing its governance system as non-democratic. Both the United States and China voice support for the multilateral rules-based order but have different interpretations of what that means. China wants its perspective to be more prominent in global discourse.[38]

This is a matter both of the message ("China's story") and the messenger, or media. China has invested in expanding the global presence of CGTN, its global television broadcaster, to compete with Western media organizations. The CPC's United Front Work Department (UWFD) is responsible for organizing outreach to key Chinese interest groups, including ethnic Chinese abroad, and representing and influencing them. Much has been written about how the UFWD has both supported Chinese overseas communities and sought to influence political debates in countries such as Australia and New Zealand.[39] Suffice to say here that the perspectives, messages and structures of the Chinese party-state will increasingly be a feature of discourse around the world. This all reshapes external circulation.

China's intent to shape the world economy to its advantage will not pass global business by. In technology, trade and data, China's role in setting norms and standards will grow, especially in Asia and in developing economies. The perspectives and narratives of the Chinese government will become more prominent in these countries too. But many multilateral institutions, regulations and norms will remain relatively unaffected. How successful China is in its ambitions will depend on the efforts that it can commit to them – based in part on how its own economy fares – and the skill with which it persuades other countries of the benefits of its approach. Coercion and appeals to a not yet established legitimacy will be much less successful. And China's success will also depend on what efforts other countries commit to alternative approaches. Will there be competing or even contradictory sets of trade rules? Will the world split into two or more different systems for payments, data and technology standards? All these elements, influenced by China, matter to global companies as they conduct their business outside China, regardless of the corporate "China strategy".

7

How will the internal and the external connect?

"If Dual Circulation can be pictured as a number eight, then the Hainan Free Trade Port (FTP) is the intersection of the two circles (of internal and external circulation)," declared regional Party secretary Shen Xiaoming in December 2020.[1] As so often in China, an intangible concept (the linkages between the external and the internal) is made tangible in a physical location. Hainan's development as a free trade port is touted as the physical embodiment of how China would like to structure these links. Operational since June 2020, Hainan FTP is the most open region in China for foreign investment. Customs procedures are split into two stages: the requirements on imports from the rest of the world ("first-line procedures"), which will be increasingly relaxed by 2025; and a second line of checks, on exports from the zone to the rest of China. The declared main aim of the Hainan FTP is to use external circulation to serve internal circulation. Offshore duty-free shops allow Chinese consumers the benefits of duty-free shopping while the revenues are still earned in China. A further ambition is to attract foreign education and health providers and so remove the need for Chinese to travel overseas in order to gain access. Beyond this, there is a plan to attract high-technology companies, for example in the seeds, deep-sea and aerospace sectors, in order to accelerate capability-building in Chinese companies. Most foreign investment interest has come from large multinationals such as Tesla, GE and Itochu. Foreign companies are once again gaining access to China's market while building capabilities in China that, directly or indirectly, benefit Chinese companies too.

China's plan is that internal and external circulation will "mutually reinforce one another", according to Han Wenxiu, deputy director of the Office of the Central Economic and Financial Affairs Commission.[2]

The imagery is of virtuous cycles of mutual benefit. Yet, after decades of increasing connectivity between China and the rest of the world, the Covid-19 pandemic cut links. It brought into sharp relief divergent approaches between China and most Western economies. Stark separation between the internal and external suddenly seemed a better description of the world. Was Covid-19 accelerating the much-discussed decoupling between China and the West? China's strict lockdown and continued zero-Covid-19 policy stood in contrast to looser policies and a shift to "living with Covid-19" in the United States and across Europe. In 2020 China remained open for business internally while many Western countries were in lockdown. In 2022, as these same countries opened up, China locked down in the face of the omicron variant. The constant throughout was a Chinese economy separated from the rest of the world by quarantines, testing regimes and flight bans. The impact of lockdowns on port capacity and stricter Covid-19-related customs controls delayed trade shipments. Xi Jinping spoke of supply problems caused by Covid-19 as one motivating force behind the focus on internal circulation and the need to reduce China's dependence on the rest of the world.

Covid-19 saw a steep fall in the numbers of people moving between China and the rest of the world. From 2000 to 2019 the annual number of outbound border crossings by Chinese travellers grew from 10 million to 170 million. Covid-19 restrictions cut this to fewer than 20 million in 2020 and to 8.5 million in 2021, below the level of 2000.[3] Travel inbound to China effectively ceased. At the start of 2022 international flight arrivals into China stood at 2 per cent of the level in 2019. The foreign expatriate population in cities such as Shanghai and Beijing fell, with more planning to leave in the wake of the spring 2022 Shanghai lockdown. The "number of foreigners in China has halved since the pandemic began and could halve again ... ", said Jörg Wuttke, president of the European Chamber of Commerce in China, in April 2022.[4] As Covid-19 restrictions ease, international travel will return, but most doubt that numbers will return to pre-pandemic levels.

And so Covid-19 appeared to foreshadow one model of the future Dual Circulation world: distinct economic landscapes, separated by hard-to-penetrate barriers – a version of One World, Two Systems, in which China and the West pursue different, decoupled paths with

limited overlaps and linkages. All this is a long way from the previous decades of opening up and ever easier cross-border travel and
business dealings.

But impressions easily mislead. The cross-border movement of
people is but one linkage between China and the rest of the world.
And, even for this, communication by Zoom is at least a partial
replacement. Trade in goods and services, investment and financial
flows, flows of data, information and intellectual property are all
important ways in which China has remained connected with the
rest of the world throughout Covid-19. In fact, it has become more
connected: 2021 saw China's trade with the world boom. The result
was a record trade surplus of US$676 billion, reflecting 30 per cent
growth in both exports and imports.[5] Foreign direct investment into
China also hit a record high in 2021, growing 20 per cent from the
previous year.[6] China continued to open up its economy to foreign
capital while also becoming the world's largest source of outbound
investment.[7] Trade and investment flows found a way despite Covid-19
and US–China tensions. Foreign business in China was hit heavily by
the 2022 lockdowns, but so too was Chinese business.

The picture was more mixed in the financial sector. Facing regulatory and political pressures in both the United States and China, large
Chinese companies such as Alibaba and JD.com that had listed on US
stock markets added a second listing in Hong Kong.[8] Others, such as
Kuaishou, chose Hong Kong over the United States, contributing to
Hong Kong's position as the second largest market for IPOs in 2020. With
parallels to the ambitions for Hainan, Hong Kong was a further physical
embodiment of the internal and the external intersecting on Chinese
terms and on Chinese territory: a financial offshore market with its own
currency, pegged to the US dollar and with its own regulators, yet part of
China. At the same time, however, US portfolio investment into Chinese
bonds and equities boomed,[9] before reversing sharply as stock markets
fell and the economy slowed in the face of Covid-19 restrictions and
concerns grew about the direction of Xi's economic leadership. Foreign
portfolio investment flows out of China continued in 2022. Meanwhile,
Wall Street's largest financial institutions announced expansion plans
in China to take advantage of deregulation and the lifting of limits on
foreign ownership.

Maybe more surprisingly, China's connectivity with the world also stood out in terms of cross-border data flows. *Nikkei Asia* analysis found that China (including Hong Kong) originated or received more cross-border data than any other country in the world in 2019.[10] China accounted for 23 per cent of all flows, about twice the US share. Payment for cross-border flows of technology and innovation also continued to grow. China's payments for its use of foreign intellectual property reached US$38 billion in 2020, up from US$22 billion five years earlier.[11] At the same time, China received payments from overseas for its own intellectual property of over US$8 billion in 2020, up from US$1 billion in 2015 – a measure of China's increasing innovation capability.[12]

For all the talk of decoupling, economic linkages had, in aggregate, grown rather than receded despite the frictions of quarantine, inspections and reduced travel. This is all consistent with the declared ambitions of Dual Circulation to keep strong connections between the internal and the external. But how these links develop depends not just on what China wants. Those on the other side of the connection have a critical say in the matter too.

THE VIEW FROM CHINA

China seeks "mutual reinforcement"[13] between the cycle of internal and external circulation. But what does this really mean? "Mutual" is used here in a particular sense. It points to how the external can strengthen the internal and vice versa – for China. It does not address the cost–benefit equation for countries other than China.

From China's perspective, linkages are to help China achieve its goals of self-reliance, higher living standards and increased productivity and technological capability, so enabling a stronger leadership role on the global stage. This would be a true rejuvenation of the Chinese people. In addition to securing prosperity, the aim is to reduce China's dependence on the rest of the world and, when possible, to increase the dependence of the rest of the world on China. In April 2020 Xi spoke of the need to "sustain and enhance our superiority across the entire production chain in sectors such as high-speed rail, electric power equipment, new energy, and communications equipment, and improve industrial quality". He went on to argue that China "must tighten international production chains' dependence on China, forming powerful countermeasures and deterrent capabilities based on artificially cutting off supply to foreigners".[14] For Xi, the emphasis is on deterrence and countermeasures: that China should have the capability to respond if and when the United States or others restrict critical exports to China.

For China, the internal can strengthen the external ...

A stronger domestic economy clearly reinforces China's position in the rest of the world. The internal can strengthen the external. When Chinese companies become leaders in new technologies and higher valued-added goods and services, they will export these and expand their operations around the world. As explored in the previous chapter, China will be in a better position to shape and influence standards and norms globally, further strengthening its competitive position. Exports, outbound investment, technological innovation, standards-setting: success at home in China will bring benefits in the global arena.

Such success would make China an even more important and influential counterpart in bilateral international relations across the whole spectrum of issues. A more capable, technologically advanced China will be less dependent on key imports and in a position to increase the dependence of the rest of the world on China. It would put China in a similar position to the United States today, where the United States can determine which countries receive which key technology exports. It would strengthen China's ability to conduct "coercive diplomacy". To date, China has used restrictions on access to its market to show its displeasure at the behaviour of other countries. In future it might withhold exports or technology access.

China's transition to higher value-added production also entails relocating more basic sectors such as textiles and simpler engineering assembly and processing activities to lower-income countries. Such plans feature in bilateral agreements with Pakistan, Ethiopia and other countries under the Belt and Road Initiative. Chinese companies would establish themselves as the lead companies at the head of regionally distributed value chains, orchestrating activities across multiple countries. This mirrors the development of Western, Japanese and South Korean companies, which have historically occupied the lead position in these value chains, with Chinese companies relegated to the role of suppliers to the lead company. Finally, China will rely on imports of resources and food for the foreseeable future, however much it is able to increase domestic production. The ideal, again, is for China to ensure that it is not, in practice, dependent but, rather, that it can exercise control over the supply of such imports. Chinese policy-makers see the need to strengthen the influence of Chinese agricultural companies internationally. Du Ying, former deputy head of the National Development and Reform Commission, has argued for Chinese companies to learn from major global grain traders such as ADM and Bunge to gain influence in meat, milk, soybeans and corn globally.[15]

None of these ambitions envisages cutting China off from the world. They presage instead a larger, more sophisticated and influential role that meets the standard of the "Great Rejuvenation of the Chinese people". But this dynamic – of the internal strengthening the external – can become established only from a position of strength and dynamism in the domestic economy. If not, it is simply a wish list. The first challenge is to get to this stronger position, or at least to take significant steps along the path. And here it is the potential of the external to strengthen the internal that matters for China.

... the external should strengthen the internal

Certainly, a country of the scale and talent of China can make – and has made – massive strides in innovating on its own. In 2015 China ranked 29th globally in the Global Innovation Index published by the World Intellectual Property Organization. By 2021 China ranked 12th, and was first among middle-income countries.[16] A report by Harvard's Belfer Center describes China as a "full-spectrum peer competitor" to the United States in artificial intelligence while lagging the United States in semiconductors and biotech.[17] A report from a Peking University institute finds that "China has taken the lead in some small areas, but also obviously lagged behind in others, which are in a vacuum and have hit a bottleneck".[18]

China has made this progress both through its own efforts and through continued collaboration with those overseas. Chinese scientists and researchers innovate independently and work as equal contributors with Western researchers in many areas. Between 2018 and 2020 Chinese researchers produced more of the top 1 per cent of most-cited scientific papers than any other country, including the United States.[19] China's progress will be faster and easier, however, if it can continue to access what the rest of the world can offer in terms of technology, management practices and ideas. What is hard to disentangle is how great are the spill-over benefits – to all involved – of cooperation rather than decoupled, separate efforts. How much slower is "self-reliance" as the path to future self-reliance? IMF analysis on the potential impact of technological decoupling provides some indication. Self-reliance is a slower path, but not radically so: IMF researchers have concluded that foreign knowledge spill-overs increased Chinese labour productivity by just under 0.4 per cent annually in the period from 2010 to 2013.[20]

In the field of technology, China benefits from global engagement on two levels. First, there are benefits in basic research and the commercialization of technologies such as semiconductors, biotechnology and seeds. Here, Chinese companies have made overseas acquisitions to accelerate technological development. ChemChina's US$43 billion purchase in 2017 of Syngenta, a major Swiss agrochemicals and seeds company, was the largest overseas Chinese acquisition to date.

Second, engagement brings benefits in the broader sense of technology as processes, methods, structures and systems. This includes, for example, the development of efficient and resilient financial markets and effective governance. As Chapter 5 examined, China's future productivity growth will come at least as much from institutional and market strengthening as from breakthrough technologies. Institutional improvements need to fit China's own situation, but competitive pressure and experience from overseas help too. China's continued opening up and welcome for major global corporations in China is a testament to this. In the field of electric vehicles, Tesla was the first foreign automotive company permitted to establish a wholly owned China operation, in part to provide stronger competition for China's home-grown EV companies such as NIO and Xpeng. In finance, the Chinese government has deregulated and opened up a range of subsectors to full foreign ownership. Companies such as JP Morgan, Goldman Sachs, Schroders, Allianz and HSBC continue to expand and invest. These are all critical links from the external to the internal. Even more crudely, China imported US$432 billion in semiconductors in 2021, an increase of nearly a quarter on the prior year. Unless and until China is able to replace all these imports with domestic production, the external linkage of imports remains indispensable.

Other linkages also remain important for China. Chinese students and academics who study and research abroad gain knowledge and understanding, not least about how the rest of the world operates. Students overwhelmingly return to China after study abroad, seeing greater opportunities at home and often unconvinced that the way other countries are governed is better than China's. In the area of trade, China's accession to the World Trade Organization provided a rationale and impetus for market reforms in the country. Today, too, Chinese leaders talk of their willingness to reform in order to help China's application to join the CPTPP trade agreement, as discussed in the previous chapter. The external is used in an instrumental way for China's benefit; it remains for the Party leadership to decide whether or not to pursue this lever for reform.

Overseas financial markets have been a valuable support to Chinese development. The listing of Chinese companies in Hong Kong and New York – both for large state-owned enterprises and for internet and technology companies – had benefits far beyond the financial sums raised. Listing requirements provided a helpful lever to reform corporate governance and management practices, at least part of the way towards Western standards. Listing on Western markets allowed the early granting of stock option incentive schemes to attract talent into tech companies. These benefits are now less critical: China's own financial markets have grown in scale, both in the mainland and in Hong Kong, and the CPC's stronger role means that Western corporate governance standards are less relevant. Nonetheless, China's willingness to negotiate so as to ensure continued listings on US stock exchanges shows that access to global (especially US) financial markets continues to have value.[21] China reached agreement with US regulators to allow the inspection of Chinese audit documents, which it had previously resisted. This agreement was concluded even though China had suspended other dialogue with the United States on military matters and climate change in the wake of the visit by Nancy Pelosi, Speaker of the US House of Representatives, to Taiwan in August 2022.

THE VIEW FROM OUTSIDE CHINA

What China would like to gain from its interactions with the rest of world is clear. Such links are, by their very nature, at least a two-way street, however. Success requires another form of "mutual reinforcement": not between the internal and the external, but between the interests and ambitions of China and those of other countries. Certainly, any country or company can replay Xi Jinping's words and argue that they want the same for themselves. They too want the benefits of engaging with China without the risks of dependence, and – ideally – China would be more dependent on them than they are on China, so as to deter any potentially coercive action by China. China will secure the benefits that it seeks only when others see similar benefits – and limited risks – from engaging with China. The outlook for this form of mutual reinforcement is not good.

Historically, the economic benefits of engaging with China have been clear. Governments and companies have enthusiastically pursued the commercial opportunities that the Chinese market offers. Exports create jobs at home while in-country operations in China contribute to the profitability, growth and competitiveness of global multinationals. Consumers around the world benefit from the lower prices that Chinese manufacturers have been able to offer. Chinese outbound investment has financed infrastructure and rescued businesses in trouble.

Where China can be a source of expertise and innovation, this would be of interest too. Although innovation flows out of China have been limited so far, the opportunity is growing as Chinese innovation gets stronger. In areas such as mobility solutions, online finance and some aspects of artificial intelligence, China is already at the forefront of innovation. What is unclear is where and how Chinese policy will allow the export of such leading technology. China's broad definition of national security suggests that the most advanced expertise will not flow freely overseas. Now that China's CATL, the world's largest battery maker, wishes to expand in the United States, some US analysts are suggesting that the United States make technology transfer a condition of CATL's access to the US market, in the same way that China previously linked market access and technology transfer together.[22]

In recent years the political climate and policy debate have both changed sharply in the United States, Europe, Japan and India. Previously many in Europe saw China as economically important but politically irrelevant – and, in any event, geographically remote. In a 2022 paper, the German Institute for International and Security Affairs called these "misperceptions".[23] China's "no-limits partnership" with Russia, declared just before Russia's invasion of Ukraine, has brought China closer to home for many European countries, even if China's support to Russia has in practice had many limits. Xi Jinping has developed a prominent profile on the world stage. There has been increasing reporting (some accurate, some not) of both the CPC's role in China and the influence and activities overseas of the United Front Work Department. The focus for many countries now is on the intertwined challenges and risks posed by China in terms of economic prosperity, national security and democratic values.

China's rhetoric and behaviour in using its commercial relations for broader diplomatic aims have increased concerns of dependence on China. The Chinese government placed bans on Australian wine and coal imports after Australia called for an independent investigation into the origins of Covid-19 and delisted Lithuania from the Chinese customs system after Lithuania allowed Taiwan to open a representative office in its capital, Vilnius. Governments are increasingly concerned when a large number of jobs at home depend on decisions made in Beijing or when Chinese companies are the dominant suppliers for certain key goods. One analysis has found that the Five Eyes intelligence alliance countries[24] are dependent on China for 831 categories of imports, of which 260 are important for critical national infrastructure.[25] Policy debates about the risks and benefits of Huawei's involvement in building 5G networks around the world brought these matters to a head, with bans being announced in the United States, United Kingdom, Canada, Japan, Australia and other countries. Concern is also mounting about China's strong position in key minerals and rare earth elements that are critical to electric vehicle and battery production. China accounts for 73 per cent of cobalt processing and refining worldwide. The figure for lithium is 59 per cent.[26] In 2021 President Biden launched an initiative to review US supply chains with the aim of ensuring "resilient, diverse and secure supply chains to ensure our economic prosperity and national security".[27] The words could be those of Xi Jinping explaining his Dual Circulation Strategy. In June 2022 the United States announced a Minerals Security Partnership with the United Kingdom, France, Germany, Japan and others to bolster critical mineral supply chains.[28]

The question of technology transfer into China is even more salient. Although forced technology transfer is illegal under WTO rules, companies have long had formal agreements or informal understandings that such transfer was part of the deal in gaining access to the Chinese market. As Chinese capability has grown, multinationals have felt more intense competitive pressure from Chinese companies. For companies, the impact of strengthening future competitors through technology transfer has become more tangible and much less attractive. Increasingly as well, technology development is framed as a competition between countries and not just companies. As a result, fewer and fewer governments are sanguine about foreign acquirers buying up emerging technology leaders. The United Kingdom, India and Japan have strengthened the national security screening of deals in specified sectors, in the way that CFIUS[29] has long done in the United States. The European Union too has sought agreement between member states to strengthen investment screening and increase investment in Europe's own technology base. The United States has imposed export bans on key technologies to China, especially in the area of advanced semiconductors. The Inflation Reduction Act and the CHIPS and Science Act both link the offer of investment subsidies in key technologies to limits on certain overseas investments in markets such as China. Further restrictions may follow.

Research cooperation agreements with individual academics and between universities and institutes in the West and China are also under the spotlight. China's Thousand Talents plan (千人计划; *qiān rén jìhuà*), a Chinese government programme to attract scientists and engineers launched in 2008, has recruited thousands of researchers into China.[30] It can be difficult to disentangle legitimate competition for talent from inappropriate activity that threatens national security. Individual scientists have been the subject of allegations regarding illegal or unethical behaviour, some with good reason and some with no good reason at all. As it becomes harder to delineate commercial and national security considerations, scrutiny increases.

Importantly for policy-makers in democracies, public opinion towards China has also become more negative. In part, this is a result of Covid-19. But the concerns are much broader. In 2021 Pew Research found that 70 per cent of Americans wanted to "try to promote human rights in China even if it harms economic relations with China". Negative views of China were held by 76 per cent of the US population, 71 per cent in Germany, 63 per cent in the United Kingdom and 88 per cent in Japan.[31] A 2021 study showed that only one-fifth of British people supported any form of UK–China economic relationship.[32] The 2022 update of the same study found that 14 per cent of the population identified China as the principal security threat facing the United Kingdom (versus 26 per cent for Russia) and that 45 per cent viewed China and Russia as equal threats.[33] Support was strongest for challenging China on its human rights record (40 per cent of those surveyed) and second strongest for cooperation on climate, although the 33 per cent support level was down from 38 per cent in 2021.

Human rights concerns are playing a larger role in government legislation alongside the focus on national security. Under the Uyghur Forced Labor Prevention Act of 2021, the United States has banned imports from Xinjiang unless it can be proved that no forced labour was used in their production. The same year the United States sanctioned SenseTime, a Chinese facial recognition software company, citing "abuse enabled by the malign use of technology" in Xinjiang.[34] The European Parliament has stated that it will not ratify the long-negotiated Comprehensive Agreement on Investment (CAI) between the European Union and China so long as China maintains sanctions on parliamentary members, sanctions that were imposed in response to European sanctioning of Chinese officials for actions in Xinjiang.[35] There is also increasing debate about both the geopolitical risk and the ethics of Western institutional investors investing in Chinese financial assets.

All these perspectives apply with greatest force in the world's developed economies. For many lower-income economies the context can be quite different. Across Africa, Latin America and parts of Asia, China has been one of the primary sources of finance and development know-how. China's rapid and recent economic development offers parallels that seem more relevant than the Western experience. This is especially the case for countries with authoritarian, one-party governments. China has started to talk of a "China model" or a "China solution", and it offers a different vision of international development.[36] For some, such as Cambodia, China's offer of debt-financed infrastructure, combined with political support, is attractive. For others, such as Malaysia and Thailand, there are other options on offer, and the political aspects are not attractive. The constant across all countries is that governments want to secure the benefits and mitigate the risks of engaging with China, as with any country.

"CONDITIONAL CONNECTIVITY" RATHER THAN "MUTUAL REINFORCEMENT"

How, then, do these views from outside China and from within come together? For Thomas Friedman in 2005, *The World Is Flat*.[37] Or, rather, was. Now barriers are back. In the United States, Japan, the European Union, India and elsewhere, governments are pursuing policies with many similarities to China's Dual Circulation. Political sentiment increasingly supports measures to limit engagement with China and to manage the terms of such engagement with more precision and force. Countries in the European Union seek to develop "strategic autonomy",[38] pursue comprehensive and distinct regulatory frameworks in technology and data that differ from the United States' and build up their technological capabilities. For the United States, building its own capabilities is now the priority, and new trade deals that offer improved access to the US market remain off the table. Policy-makers emphasize protecting and then enhancing America's own technological leadership. For the European Union, China is a "partner for cooperation and negotiation, an economic competitor and a systemic rival".[39] For the United States, China is a strategic competitor, with an approach that is "competitive when it should be, collaborative when it can be, and adversarial when it must be".[40] Beneath the overall still-strong trade and investment flows, decoupling is happening in many distinct, often less visible ways.

Against this backdrop, how links between China and the rest of the world develop will depend on all sides seeing the benefits – which are still very real – and managing the risks. No one side gets it all its own way. There is a spectrum of the possible outcomes. At one end of this spectrum is the "flat" or borderless world of frictionless globalization, which now seems a bygone age. At the other end, as a maybe not so distant dystopia, is the world of complete separation and autarky – although even North Korea has trading relations beyond its borders (mainly with China).

For developed economies, interactions with China have become more conditional, more measured and more managed. All likely outcomes include a marked decoupling compared with the recent past, especially in technology. But the economic case for trade and cross-border investments remains strong. In Asia, China is an active and welcome participant in new trade agreements and a critical trading partner. Analysis also suggests that the risks of economic dependence on China are overestimated, at least in circumstances short of war. One report, "Empty threats? Policymaking amidst Chinese pressure", concludes that "foreign countries rarely suffer for long – or not as deeply as some suggest – when they anger the CPC, for the reason that China is in need of foreign knowledge. Even when thrown into the diplomatic doghouse by the CPC, trade between a scolded country and the PRC often continues to grow or is replaced by trade with other countries."[41] The risk of war has now also become part of the calculus, however, in the wake of Russia's invasion of Ukraine and with ramped-up tensions over Taiwan. Security considerations again feature alongside the economic.

The pivotal role that technology plays is the true flashpoint. China wants to develop advanced technologies as rapidly as it can. The United States along with some other countries believe that it is both in their best interests and within their control to prevent or slow this, as a means to maintain their own technological leadership. Hence technological decoupling. IMF analysis suggests that such decoupling could reduce China's GDP by 2 to 5 per cent and that of the United States by 1 to 3 per cent in the long term.[42] These numbers, if robust to assumption changes, are significant, but less than one year's economic growth. Some policy-makers and political leaders may argue that this is a small price to pay for security or the protection of values; others would argue that the likely impact on economic growth from second- and third-order effects will in fact be much higher than this. Indeed, China's decision in 2021 not to license foreign mRNA Covid-19 vaccines can be seen as a form of voluntary self-reliance or technological decoupling. This then contributed to the far-reaching impact of China's prolonged zero-Covid-19 policy.

This newly conditional connectivity is inherently fragile. It takes just one side to have concerns about the deal that it is getting, and so act to limit engagement, for the relationship to worsen. One country may introduce sanctions or tariffs on another – for whatever reason, be it genuine security concerns or to score political points domestically. This action creates its own reaction as the other country responds. The to-and-fro between the European Parliament and China on Xinjiang, sanctions and trade is but one example. Closer, more open relationships need both sides engaged to make them work. Covid-19 travel bans and increasingly divergent media messaging in China and the West have made it even more difficult to discuss matters based on a shared view of the world. Better relationships come from a clear understanding of differences rather than multiple misinterpretations based on miscommunication. Geopolitics becomes a form of dynamic game, in which the moves and outcomes shift as both facts and fears change. It is difficult to shift the dynamics from negative to positive, however. In the area of technology, it is especially hard to see how China will gain all that it wants from other countries at a time of competition rather than cooperation.

Nonetheless, China remains deeply entangled with the global economy as a critical supplier and as a market. The costs of a complete, sudden severing would be massive and highly disruptive to all economies. China's integration into the world economy was a process extending over decades. This very fact demonstrates that large-scale shifts are possible, but that they also take time, unless compelled by external factors such as war. Even Covid-19 has driven change only at the margin. A messy, evolving patchwork of agreements, controls and conditions is more desirable for all sides than a sharp, clean severing.

By their nature, multinationals have a key role to play in how internal and external circulation link together. China's continued interest in attracting foreign companies and know-how in order to strengthen the Chinese economy and Chinese companies is clear. Nevertheless, increasing regulation, introduced for reasons of national security or values, means tighter constraints than previously. The business climate has changed. The risk–return judgements that companies need to make are now much more heavily influenced by assessments of policy risk – both at home and in China – and by reactions of investors, employees and key customers. Extreme situations can also force sudden shifts. Although China's position in the global economy is many times larger and more complex than Russia's, the swift Western sanctions response to the invasion of Ukraine jolted long-held views. Jörg Wuttke, president of the European Chamber of Commerce in China, observed: "The leaders in Beijing don't realize that Western companies are grappling with the scenario that they would have to leave China ... if China tried to forcibly integrate Taiwan."[43] Part III explores what all this means in practice for companies.

Implications for global business

Multinationals and China

In October 1978, at the very start of China's reform and opening up, Deng Xiaoping visited Japan. Among those he met was Konosuke Matsushita, founder of Matsushita Electric (later renamed Panasonic). Although he continued to talk of China's self-reliance, Deng asked Matsushita to help with foreign technology and investment: "China will embark on a modernization drive. While mainly relying on ourselves, China is considering drawing on foreign technology and investment. Can you give a little help to our modernization efforts?" Matsushita replied, "I will do everything to help".[1] In the early 1980s Matsushita exported manufacturing equipment to China and transferred technology in over 150 projects, including televisions, refrigerators, washing machines, air conditioners, compressors and motors. Forty years later, to the month, Tesla came to a transformed China to buy a plot of land in Shanghai for US$140 million and build a factory to serve China's booming EV market.

HOW MULTINATIONAL BUSINESS DEVELOPED IN CHINA

From 1979 onwards China offered multinationals the promise of a new low-cost manufacturing location. Special economic zones such as Shenzhen, Zhuhai and Xiamen were established in the southern and eastern provinces of Guangdong and Fujian. These led the way in offering favourable regulations, tax incentives and other policies to attract foreign investment.[2] Depending on the region and the industry sector, foreign-invested enterprises enjoyed preferential treatment over Chinese companies. The benefits included tax reductions, reduced customs duties, simplified procedures for enterprise registrations and visa provisions and streamlined entry and exit provisions. In the automotive sector, Volkswagen (VW) was among the first foreign multinationals to emphasize China. Volkswagen first entered China in 1978, and in 1984 it signed a joint venture agreement to manufacture engines and Santana cars. Although the planned engine production was mostly for export, the cars were to be sold to government buyers and for use as taxis. But in 1984 Volkswagen saw only limited local market potential. Asked about the prospects for China as a major automotive market, the VW chairman stated, "We're convinced this will not happen in the next twenty-four years."[3] Twenty-four years later China was the world's second largest market in terms of units, and in 2009 it overtook the United States to become the world's largest market in volume terms.[4]

From 1992 onwards foreign investment into China accelerated as the country started to carve out a position as the "world's factory". Investment grew further when China entered the WTO in 2001. From the mid-1990s, as China's market potential became clear, multinationals also started investing in marketing, sales and distribution capabilities to meet the increasing local demand. Coca-Cola, Unilever, GM and other consumer companies expanded rapidly. In January 1999 Starbucks opened its first store in China in the World Trade Building in Beijing, in order to sell its coffee to the tea-drinking people of China.

The greatest opportunities for foreign business came in those sectors that the Chinese government did not regard as strategically important or in which it had to rely on foreign technologies: sectors such as consumer goods, pharmaceuticals, capital equipment, high technology and automobiles. By contrast, energy, defence, transportation, finance and telecommunications services remained relatively, though not completely, closed. From 2000 to 2017 the China subsidiaries of US multinationals were some of the fastest-growing country operations globally. In 2017 these China subsidiaries sold 82 per cent of their China production directly to Chinese customers.[5]

From the early 2000s multinational companies began to establish research and development (R&D) facilities in China, and they have continued to do so. This allowed them to develop products tailored to the Chinese market and access high-quality talent, especially in technology and engineering, while gaining favour with Chinese policy-makers, who were keen to upgrade China's economy. Microsoft was one of the earliest to do so, opening its first China R&D facility in 1995, and expanding significantly from 2008 onwards. Smaller companies did so too. In 2014 Kärcher, a German cleaning equipment firm, opened a China R&D centre. By 2017 the China R&D activity of US multinationals was over six times higher than in 2001. China was the fourth largest destination for overseas American R&D spending.[6] Despite geopolitical tensions, cooperation on research and development has continued. In 2022 Daimler Greater China Investment, a Mercedes-Benz Group subsidiary, signed an agreement with Tencent Cloud Computing to collaborate on innovations in autonomous driving.

As China integrated into the world economy, so too the China operations of many multinational companies became an integral part of their global organizational network. In 2006 IBM CEO Sam Palmisano wrote of the "globally integrated enterprise",[7] with the integration of production and value delivery worldwide. In 2010 GE trumpeted the opportunity for "reverse innovation",[8] whereby China and India would originate innovations for the rest of the world.

At the same time, Chinese companies have emerged as capable competitors in sector after sector. In construction equipment, Caterpillar and Komatsu found themselves losing customers to Sany, LiuGong, Zoomlion and others. Huawei continues to outcompete Ericsson on technical superiority and price in 5G. China's BYD outsells Tesla in electric vehicles. Chinese sporting goods companies Li-Ning and Anta have developed ever stronger and more appealing brands for Chinese consumers, who had previously aspired only to Adidas and Nike. Even General Mills' subsidiary, Häagen-Dazs, has found its premium position in ice cream under attack from the so-called "ice cream assassins" (雪糕刺客; *xuěgāo cìkè*). Zhong Xue Gao (钟薛高), known as Chicecream in English, the so-called "Hermes of ice cream",[9] justifies high prices for its ice cream as it does not melt at high temperatures.[10]

THE IMPORTANCE OF CHINA AND MULTINATIONAL BUSINESS TO ONE ANOTHER

Foreign companies have played an important role in enabling China's economic growth over the past 25 years. From the largest to the smallest, there are many foreign companies operating in China (in 2020 more than 100,000[11]), although they account for only 3 per cent of employment.[12] These companies continue to play an important if declining role in China's economy as Chinese companies become more capable.

Foreign companies introduced new product categories and the business systems required to support them. Procter & Gamble introduced disposable nappies and, together with the government, built and financed networks of suppliers and distributors. Foreign companies have nurtured Chinese talent, which has gone on to found and lead Chinese companies. Chinese suppliers have upgraded their capabilities in order to meet the demands of their foreign corporate customers. Maersk, a Danish shipping company, worked extensively with several Chinese shipyards from 1996 onwards, transferring expertise and knowledge in shipbuilding, especially in the development of product and chemical tankers. Between 1998 and 2001 Maersk accounted for nearly half the orders of Chinese shipyards for these tankers. From 2008 to 2013, however, Maersk accounted for less than 3 per cent of orders as the local shipyards grew and secured new customers.[13]

In 1996 foreign-invested enterprises in China accounted for just over 30 per cent of exports, according to Gavekal, a macroeconomic research firm.[14] By 2006 – the peak year for exports as a share of the economy – this figure had grown to over one-half. As Chinese private companies flourished and improved, their share of exports grew from almost nothing in the mid-1990s to 20 per cent or so by 2006 and 50 per cent today. In 2020 foreign-invested enterprises accounted for 36 per cent of China's exports.[15]

In 2019 China was the world's second largest recipient of foreign investment, second only to the United States. In 2020 the total stock of foreign investment was equivalent to 13 per cent of China's GDP, up from 10 per cent in 2010, though down from 16 per cent in 2000, before China's domestic investment levels ramped up. Foreign investment plays a much more limited role than in the German or US economy, but a greater role than in Japan. In 2020 the foreign capital stock was equivalent to 29 per cent of GDP in Germany, 52 per cent in the United States and 5 per cent in Japan.

China's importance to Western businesses varies widely between companies and sectors and is hard to assess precisely given limited corporate reporting.[16] From a revenue perspective, China's contribution is, on average, quite limited. A 2020 Goldman Sachs report states that revenues "specifically from Greater China"[17] accounted for 2 per cent of the total revenues of the S&P 500 in 2019, equivalent to US$240 billion.[18] Boston Consulting Group (BCG) estimates suggest a higher number: 5 per cent of the revenues of US companies, equivalent to US$410 billion. BCG does, however, estimate that China business accounted for 15 per cent of market capitalization for US companies.[19] For the 1,765 German companies identified with China revenues, China accounted for 8.4 per cent of overseas (not total) revenues in 2019, down slightly from 9 per cent in 2016.[20] Stewart Paterson, a Hinrich Foundation researcher, notes that "the lobbying efforts of these companies create the impression that China is more significant to foreign corporations than is the case".[21] The historic need for joint ventures in sectors such as automotive also skews the picture, as "a car sold in China is only half a car sold by a particular foreign automaker" when sold by a 50–50 joint venture.[22]

For some, however, the China market is of major importance. Four sectors – electronics, automobiles, chemicals and general machinery – account for around a half of the assets, revenues and profits of foreign companies in China.[23] China accounts for around one-fifth of Apple revenues, with sales in Greater China increasing by 70 per cent from 2020 to 2021. Qualcomm derives two-thirds of its revenue from China. For Nike the proportion is just under a fifth; for Intel just over a quarter; and for Procter & Gamble one-tenth.[24] Among German companies, China accounted for 38 per cent of Infineon's sales in 2021,[25] and the percentages for VW, BMW and Adidas were 13 per cent, 21 per cent and 23 per cent respectively.[26]

China is now the world's largest or second largest market for a whole series of products and services – for automotive, for steel, for cement, for fashion, for smartphones, for many other consumer items and for e-commerce of all kinds. In most years China has accounted for a larger share of global market growth than any other country. So long as a particular sector is not closed to multinationals, China's market size will attract multinational interest. CEOs continue to describe China as a "priority" or a "must-win" market. It is not a matter of sales revenue alone. Deciding not to compete in China cedes the opportunity to build scale to those competitors that do remain present in the China market, and especially to emerging Chinese companies. Success depends on the ability to outcompete these increasingly capable Chinese competitors on their home turf. As Wuttke has put it, "China is a fitness centre for firms."[27] This calculus, persuasive as it is, loses relevance when commercial success in China becomes effectively unattainable as a result of policy decisions either in China, back at headquarters or in other major economies. In 5G, Ericsson has scaled down its China activity, just as Huawei has had to do in Europe and the United States.

China's position as the world's largest manufacturing exporter makes China critical in a second way: as a source of supply. For many companies that have no operations on the ground and no China export business of their own, China remains important. Directly or indirectly (via other suppliers), Chinese companies supply important components or items for sale that keep so-called "local" businesses in business thousands of miles away from China. These can be retailers sourcing products from China or pharmaceutical manufacturers relying on APIs (active pharmaceutical ingredients), for which China accounts for 40 per cent of global production by volume and 68 per cent by value.[28]

Finally, in a number of sectors, China is now the breeding ground for new innovations and new competitors. China moved towards a "cashless society" well ahead of Western economies through the success of WeChatPay and AliPay. Chinese automotive manufacturers are at the forefront of integrating digital technology and social media into electric vehicles, leaving Western competitors behind. Chinese car buyers expect seamless in-car payment and social media connectivity, and even karaoke systems. In sheer volume terms, China accounts for half the global electric vehicle market. Multinationals that are absent from the China market risk missing out on learning and innovation. They also risk missing out on capable, creative talent that will help innovate in new technologies.

FOUR STRATEGIES FOR CHINA

At the simplest level, foreign companies can pursue four different strategies for China. They can be Localizers, Sourcers, Exporters or Separators. Figure 8.1 shows a two-by-two matrix that distinguishes between China as a market and China as a base of operations.[29] Serving

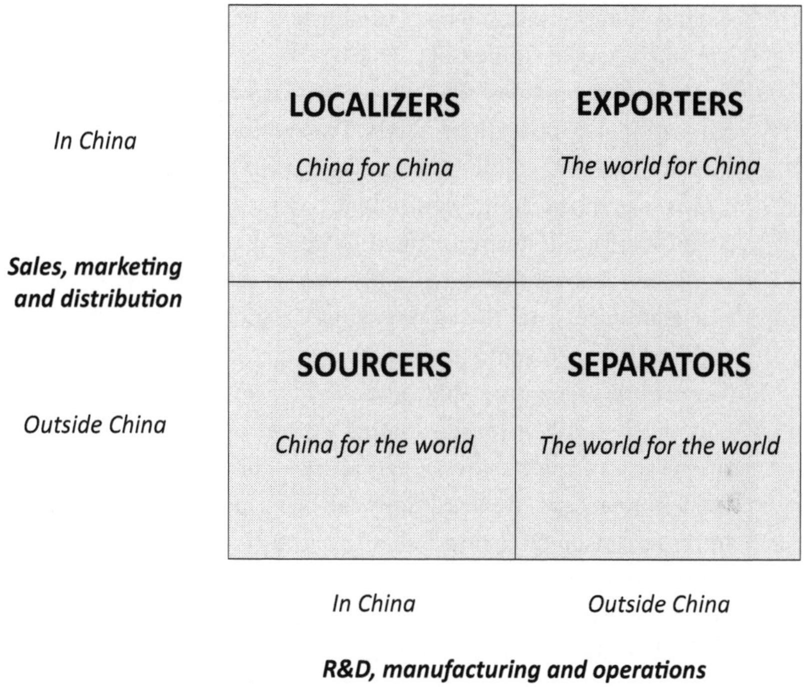

	LOCALIZERS	EXPORTERS
In China	**LOCALIZERS** *China for China*	**EXPORTERS** *The world for China*
Sales, marketing and distribution		
Outside China	**SOURCERS** *China for the world*	**SEPARATORS** *The world for the world*
	In China	*Outside China*

R&D, manufacturing and operations

Figure 8.1 Four strategies for China

China as a market usually requires some form of marketing, sales and distribution. Choosing China as a base of operations necessitates some mix of manufacturing or other operations and (increasingly) R&D facilities. The four strategies follow from this.

1. *Localizers*: companies that develop and produce products and services in China for the China market. As their business in China has grown and the market has become more competitive and differentiated, these companies have often increasingly localized their operations. Examples include Coca-Cola, VW, Starbucks, Philips, Apple.
2. *Sourcers*: companies that produce in China for the global market. These companies initially moved manufacturing to China to benefit from China's low-cost position – a position that is increasingly under threat. Examples include Apple (through its suppliers), Techtronic Industries (power tools) and, in the service sector,

Fidelity International, which established back-office operations for north Asia in China.

3. *Exporters*: companies that export to China but do not establish significant operations there. The rationales for this strategy include business volumes too low to justify separate facilities in China (e.g. niche capital equipment companies from the German Mittelstand); the desire or need to keep proprietary technology or process knowledge outside China (e.g. semiconductors, medical equipment); or the inherent national characteristics of the product (Chanel, Scottish whisky).

4. *Separators*: companies that have decided to keep their business completely separate (or "decoupled") from China. This may reflect the nature of the business (e.g. defence contractors); an unwillingness to accept the conditions for being present in China (e.g. internet censorship); or a belief that the company is simply not competitive in the China market and that other opportunities are more attractive to pursue. A complete separation is probably not achievable or desirable, however; even companies that have decided not to source or sell in China will in some way rely on direct or indirect inputs from China and may face competition from Chinese companies.

For the three business strategies that directly involve China in some way, the American Chamber of Commerce in China (AmCham China) 2022 Business Climate Survey provides one, albeit imperfect, indication of relative importance.[30] Of the 353 companies that responded, 54 per cent described their activities as equivalent to Localizers; 13 per cent were equivalent to Exporters; and 11 per cent were Sourcers. 19 per cent chose "Other" as a category. This category is likely to include those with only representative offices. These companies are most probably either preparing to become more active in China or have a watching brief on business trends in order to learn. Separators, which have chosen not to be active in China, are by definition not present in the sample.

In fact, these four strategies apply at the level of individual business units – and, indeed, even product lines – within a company. Many, if not most, multinationals pursue a mix of the four. Adidas and Nike have pursued a Localizer strategy to succeed in the China market, working with Chinese athletes for promotion and expanding into smaller towns and cities across China. In parallel, they have adopted a Sourcer strategy to serve other country markets worldwide with China-based suppliers. Both strategies now face challenge, from stronger local competitors such as Li-Ning and Anta, on the one hand, and the need to relocate some manufacturing to lower-cost locations, such as Vietnam, on the other.[31]

Medtronic, the world's largest medical devices company, also has many aspects of a Localizer: it acquired a Chinese company, Kanghui, as early as 2012. But it is also an Exporter, exporting most of its high-end equipment to China rather than manufacturing locally. At first glance, Alphabet, the parent company of Google, appears to be a Separator in its internet search business. In 2010 Google announced that it would no longer censor internet search results in China as required by the Chinese government. From mid-2014 most Google services in China were blocked, such that the Google search facility is effectively not present in China. Yet Alphabet remains active in China. It sells search-based advertising to Chinese clients, reporting revenues of US$3 billion in 2018.[32] Google is in effect exporting advertising services to China. From 2017 to 2019 Google operated an AI research centre in Beijing. Where, then, did that fit? It may be best understood as a Sourcer strategy: one that sources talent and innovation rather than low-cost manufacturing. It also created options for a future Localizer strategy.

For large multinationals, the role that China plays remains complicated and multifaceted. It also remains – mostly – profitable; in a 2021 European Chamber of Commerce survey, 79 per cent of respondents said that their China business was as profitable as or more profitable than the company average worldwide.[33] American companies have reported similar findings.[34]

DUAL CIRCULATION IN A TIME OF TURBULENCE

The public announcement in May 2020 of China's new Dual Circulation Strategy came in the middle of a turbulent time for multinational business in China. This turbulence was to become only stronger in the two years that followed. The most immediate source was Covid-19.

By May 2020 China was back at work following the suppression of the virus in the lockdowns of the first quarter. But China's borders were closed tight shut, making it almost impossible for senior executives and plant equipment maintenance engineers to come in and out of China. Meanwhile, those in headquarters and other countries were preoccupied with their own Covid-19 battles. Two years later China's borders remained shut and foreign business leaders were dealing with the impact of continuing Chinese lockdowns on both business and personal life. Day-to-day business operations in China had changed dramatically. The continued commitment to zero-Covid-19 led to extensive and repeated testing and quarantine. Unpredictable lockdowns weakened economic conditions in the near term and increased business uncertainty.

But the underlying reason was more deep-seated. Trade and technology tensions had been rising between the United States and China ever since the election of Donald Trump as US president in November 2016. The policy debate in the United States focused on the presumed benefits of "decoupling" from China: ensuring that China would not gain access to advanced US technology, reducing dependence on imports from China and preserving (or even restoring) US manufacturing jobs that had been lost as American companies relocated manufacturing to China. For US executives, access to Chinese government officials became more difficult as US–China relations worsened. Australia's call for an enquiry into the origins of Covid-19 also led to rapidly deteriorating relations with China. By November 2020 China had issued a list of 14 "grievances" that it had with Australia and that it wished Australia to "correct" if normal trade relations were to resume.[35] "Rising tensions in the US–China relationship" were cited as the top business challenge in China by AmCham members in the 2021 and 2022 surveys.[36] The concerns had ranked third behind "rising labor costs" and "inconsistent regulatory interpretation" in 2019 and 2020. In 2018 they had not ranked in the top five. Nationality and geopolitics were starting to matter much more to business.

As Chapter 2 explored, Xi's messages about Dual Circulation were not radically new. Foreign business leaders were used to hearing about China's shift to consumption and the need for technological upgrading and for self-reliance. But, against the backdrop of US–China tensions and stronger ideological messaging from the CPC, business leaders wondered what Dual Circulation would really mean for multinationals in China. Despite fine words about continued opening up, did this mark a closing to foreign companies and fresh demands to help strengthen Chinese companies? Although Dual Circulation partly mirrored decoupling pressures in the United States and Europe, it threatened to make doing business in China more complicated. Opinions split on the impact. In one survey, 44 per cent of German companies saw Dual Circulation as an opportunity, 36 per cent saw it as a challenge and 20 per cent did not know. Companies in the consumer, automotive and plastics and metals sectors viewed the prospects most positively, and those in the machinery, industrial equipment and business services most negatively.[37]

Chapter 5 described how China's business environment has become more uncertain and ambiguous. Many Chinese private sector business leaders are anxious. They are unclear about the expectations and requirements that the Party leadership now places on them in the name of Common Prosperity. A raft of new laws covering national security, data protection and foreign sanctions give some clarity in specific areas. But these laws are wide-ranging in scope and open to different interpretations. Never far from centre-stage in China, politics has become even more entwined in business decision-making. Commentators wonder how China's economy will fare as the state takes on a larger role and underlying policy challenges remain hard to address.

Yet this same period has seen continued opening up and liberalization for foreign companies. The "Phase One" trade deal signed between China and the United States in January 2020 set the stage for the much-delayed implementation of further opening of the financial sector.[38] JP Morgan and Goldman Sachs took control of their securities subsidiaries. Citigroup established the first foreign-owned custody business in China and BlackRock launched the first foreign-run mutual fund. Allianz took 100 per cent control of its life insurance joint venture. In the automotive sector, the Chinese government removed the requirement for a 50/50 joint venture structure on 1 January 2022. In electric vehicles, Tesla had already taken advantage of China's expanding free trade zones in 2018 to establish wholly owned operations in Shanghai. It continues to have ambitious expansion plans for China.

The picture is, therefore, mixed. The 2022 AmCham Business Climate Survey found that American companies were increasingly unsure about the Chinese government's commitment to further market opening: the number of those "confident" or "very confident" in the commitment fell from 61 to 47 per cent. Some 15 per cent of American companies felt that foreign businesses were "much less welcome" in 2021 than previously (up from 6 per cent in 2020), but 21 per cent still felt "much more welcome" or "slightly more welcome".[39] Nearly one-half of European companies felt that there was not a level playing field with Chinese competitors, and 31 per cent believed there never would be.[40] A British Chamber of Commerce report told a similar story. 64 per cent of respondents in 2021 felt that doing business in China had become more difficult, up from 48 per cent in 2019.[41] But nearly 70 per cent of European companies remained optimistic about the business outlook in the coming two years. They showed the lowest desire to leave China since the survey started and were making plans to onshore further manufacturing into China.[42] "Five times as many (companies) are onshoring (into China) as offshoring (out of China)," noted the European report by Roland Berger, a consulting company.[43]

The outlook turned markedly more negative in 2022 with the strict and unpredictable lockdowns in pursuit of China's zero-Covid-19 strategy, which hit consumer confidence and demand. They made manufacturing and logistics more unpredictable and expensive. Maybe more important still was the lasting psychological impact of sudden lockdowns and the scramble to secure living essentials on both expatriate and Chinese employees, who had not previously experienced such loss of control in their lives. Runology (润学; *rùnxué*), researching how to emigrate from China, became a meme on social media.

A European Chamber of Commerce survey in April 2022 provided the first signs of the impact.[44] At that time, port closures, road freight restrictions and rising sea freight costs affected over 90 per cent of companies. Although reduced revenue projections were to be expected, longer-term changes also seemed likely. A quarter of respondents were considering shifting investments out of China and three-quarters found China less attractive for future investment. A June survey of American companies had similar findings. A quarter of manufacturers were accelerating the localization of their China supply chains while moving production of global products out of the country. Only one-quarter stated that lockdowns had not affected their supply chain strategy.[45] And, in August, a US–China Business Council survey found that Covid-19 lockdowns had replaced US–China relations as the greatest challenge facing American companies in China. Over 50 per cent of those surveyed stated that China's Covid-19 policies had affected future business and investment plans for China. The top three challenges identified were intensified geopolitical risks caused by Covid-19 controls, the psychological impact on employees and reduced headquarters confidence in the China market.[46]

How, then, do the four China strategies need to change?

How Dual Circulation changes the game

> For Chinese electric vehicle buyers, "it isn't [about] handling, braking, acceleration – it's how well connected is your vehicle, and here Volkswagen is behind," says Michael Dunne of automotive consultancy ZoZoGo, an advisor on the Chinese market to large carmakers. Being run from Germany, he adds, may have put VW's China business at a disadvantage.[1]

This 2022 *Financial Times* article laid bare the decline of VW's China success story. VW had led the way in localization, with a 1984 joint venture and the launch in 1999 of a long-wheelbase model targeting the needs of the Chinese market. Now, with China's automotive market both the largest and most innovative in the world, the Localizer needed to localize more. As Herbert Diess, CEO, announced in Beijing following the first fall in car sales for 20 years, "The future of the Volkswagen Group will be decided in the Chinese market."[2] A taste of things to come in China's Dual Circulation economy?

Dual Circulation changes what foreign companies need to do. It both describes the context for business strategies that involve China and reshapes these strategies. First, the clear dividing line marked out between internal and external circulation highlights the divergent and distinct business environments between China and other markets. The much-discussed need to localize and adapt to the China context is stronger than ever. Second, the ambitions of Dual Circulation to create a technologically more capable and self-reliant China with a much larger consuming middle class change the nature of the China opportunity. In the near term, these ambitions sharpen China's policy focus on how foreign companies can help China succeed, especially in key technologies. This presents business opportunities, yet often runs counter to the China policy of governments back at headquarters. Moreover, the very aim of Dual Circulation is often to strengthen the future competitors of multinationals. In the longer term, Chinese policy success would create a much larger market, albeit one with much more capable Chinese competitors. Such success is far from a foregone conclusion, however. State intervention in technology initiatives and repeated government failure to address China's sectoral imbalances could instead lead to wasted investment, stagnant growth and a withering of entrepreneurial dynamism. The long-targeted increase in consumption's share of the Chinese economy may just never quite happen.

For now, however, China's ambitions for self-reliance place technology sectors at the centre of decisions on China strategy for multinationals. Although China wants the leading companies of the future in these sectors to be Chinese, Chinese policy welcomes support and investment by foreign companies in the interim to help achieve this aim. Multinational companies have long become accustomed to demonstrating to the Chinese government how they can support China's development priorities, while reaping commercial rewards for themselves. They have made judgements on when it is an acceptable cost of business to transfer technology to Chinese partners, which then become competitors, and when it is not. They have decided which technologies to keep out of China, both to protect their intellectual property more securely and to avoid the extra costs of manufacturing advanced products in China's less developed economy. Now they face the same considerations with a much sharper focus.

The market is larger and offers greater rewards. A 2022 survey of German firms found most planning to increase investment: 90 per cent of electronics companies, 79 per cent of automotive and 68 per cent in the plastics and metal products sector.[3] Against this, however, relations between China and the West are framed increasingly as a technological competition. Eric Schmidt, former CEO of Google, has further argued that "these are contests of values as well as investments. And it's important that American values, the things that we hold and cherish so deeply, are the winners in all of these technological areas."[4] In the United States, there is both political support and legislation to screen and limit outbound investment into China in a broadening range of technology sectors. This comes on top of export bans, such as, for example, throughout the value chain for advanced semiconductors. In addition to being legally compliant, companies need to be aware of political pressures and the potential impact on their business in the United States. When, in 2021, Intel proposed expanding semiconductor production in China, the White House stated that it was "very focused on preventing China from using US technologies, know-how and investment to develop state-of-the-art capabilities".[5] Intel did not pursue the plans.

Within China, the dynamics in priority sectors run in two different directions. First, the Chinese government welcomes as much involvement in China by foreign technology companies as it can secure. It has, for example, launched a "cross-border semiconductor work committee" platform. The aim is to facilitate collaboration between domestic companies and overseas firms such as Intel and AMD, so as to foster development hubs for software, material and manufacturing equipment.[6] Whether this is on balance an attractive – or even legally feasible – proposition for foreign companies remains to be seen. The same tensions appear wherever China is seeking to develop technologies and capabilities: semiconductors, medical technologies, financial services and agritech are of particular interest.

China's overarching policy goal is the development of Chinese company capabilities, however. This leads to preferential support for domestic companies and discrimination in procurement. Since 2014 government guidance funds (GGFs), modelled on private sector venture capital funds, have grown in scale. Total authorized funding in 2020 was RMB 11.3 trillion, equivalent to 11 per cent of total GDP.[7] Researchers estimate that China's industrial policy support amounts to 1.7 per cent of GDP annually, much more than in other major countries.[8] In semiconductors, the Chinese government is investing tens of billions of dollars into local companies through the China National Integrated Circuit Industry Investment Fund (known as the "Big Fund").[9] At the same time, Chinese auto manufacturers are investing in semiconductor manufacturers to secure supplies of the chips that they need. Industry experts report government encouragement to "buy local" even if the price/quality relationship is not competitive. Chinese auto manufacturers recognize the need to support less competitive local chip companies in their early years in the expectation that they will be preferred suppliers in future. This is by no means all productive investment. As with venture capital investment everywhere, the majority of investments will fail. Moreover, in China, corruption and investments by those without any relevant capabilities will exacerbate costs and inefficiencies. In August 2022 senior executives of the Big Fund were placed under investigation for fraud. A small number of breakthrough successes may be enough to compensate, however. The requirement is for "breakthroughs" in Chinese terms, which catch up with what foreign semiconductor companies have already found a way to do. It is not a case of inventing something completely new.

A SHIFTING, TILTING PLAYING FIELD – NOT A LEVEL ONE

None of this points to a level playing field for foreign companies. It points, rather, to a playing field that continually shifts and tilts. Companies need to judge the lie of the land and negotiate the best position for themselves, while remaining aware of the impact back at headquarters. Away from identified priority sectors, the situation is more stable. In some strategic sectors (e.g. energy, telecommunications, 5G network equipment), the opportunities for foreign companies remain limited, though by no means non-existent. In non-strategic sectors, especially consumer products and traditional automotive, policy priorities weigh less, and the playing field is more level. Customers, competitors and management capabilities determine success rather than shifting policy interventions.

There has never been a level playing field for foreign business in China, however. The notion itself may be an illusion: China's economy is shaped and guided by an interventionist party-state pursuing clear priorities for China's own economic development. The playing field was certainly not level in the first decades of opening up and reform. Then, too, it tilted in two directions at once. On the one hand, in order to attract foreign investment, the Chinese government offered significant tax, investment and regulatory incentives to foreign companies that were not available to Chinese companies. From 2005 it started reducing these incentives, and by 2019 they had been removed.[10] On the other hand, the government determined which sectors were open and on what terms, and steered the selection of joint venture partners and terms of the deals. Although market access and ownership structures were liberalized following the 2001 WTO accession, regulatory restrictions and subsidies remain.

The Chinese government repeatedly states its commitment to the equal treatment of Chinese and foreign companies, in relation, for example, to government procurement. This is equal treatment for foreign companies producing in China, however; not those importing. The reinforcement of the Dual Circulation message is clear. Reasons of national security and state secrecy also provide justification for exceptions. And, in an era of technology competition, Xi's definition of national security is wide indeed, as Chapter 3 explored. In 2022 the Chinese government again mandated that central government agencies and state-owned corporations must replace foreign-branded personal computers with Chinese models, running on Chinese operating systems, within two years.[11] This affects around 50 million PCs. It is unclear, though, whether and how this discrimination against foreign companies will be implemented. The same edict was previously issued in 2019 with a required implementation date of 2022, yet little changed.[12] Government attempts in 2014 to ban Windows 8 software on government computers also failed.[13]

Fully equal treatment – being treated in exactly the same way as Chinese businesses are treated – may also not be welcome. Party and government influence across all aspects of Chinese business has strengthened in recent years. The CPC has long asserted the right to establish Party committees in foreign companies and joint ventures, just as it does in Chinese state-owned and private businesses. This involvement is now more active. In July 2022 HSBC became the first foreign financial institution to establish a Party committee (in its Chinese investment banking subsidiary), following guidance from the Chinese securities regulator. Incorporating political considerations into certain commercial decisions is part of usual operations in Chinese companies. It is part of the context in which business leaders are operating. Fully equal treatment means this becoming more common, and potentially more directive, for foreign businesses too.

Against this backdrop, companies need to reassess and adjust their strategy for China. It means changes and adjustments in each of the four strategies. And, for some, it will mean "changing quadrant" and shifting from one strategy to another. Figure 9.1 illustrates this.

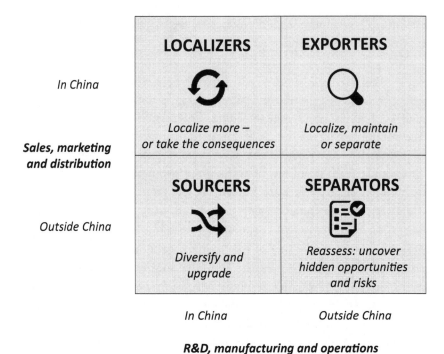

Figure 9.1 How Dual Circulation changes the four strategies

LOCALIZERS NEED TO LOCALIZE MORE – OR TAKE THE CONSEQUENCES

The localization of multinational operations in China is nothing new. "We call China our second home," announced Frans van Houten, Philips CEO, in 2013.[14] In 2010 South Korea's SK Group announced that it was "looking at China as the second home on a group level".[15] And, as early as 2006, business consultant Thomas Hout wrote that "multinationals … will increasingly treat China as a second home market".[16]

Honeywell International, an American aerospace and industrial conglomerate, has pursued a Localizer strategy with particular success. Shane Tedjarati led the China business from 2004 to 2021. China revenues grew from US$360 million to over US$6 billion in 2020, with Honeywell employing some 13,000 people in 30 cities. Honeywell's business has profited by helping Chinese companies achieve policy goals, including the development of the Comac C919 aeroplane, which aims to compete with Boeing and Airbus; the digitization of industrial manufacturing processes; and support for the Belt and Road Initiative. Tedjarati spoke in an interview of the process of localizing: "Little by little, we had this Chineseness in our bones."[17] This success has continued amid deteriorating US–China relations and while continuing to sell also to the US government.

The imperative for localization can be summarized in the phrase that "China is different" – different, at least, from the home markets of most of the world's largest multinationals. Customer needs are different. Competitors are different. Policy, politics, cultural and historical context are all different. Overall, the pace of change and decision-making in business is faster too. In multinational business there is a perennial trade-off between the benefits of commonality, standardization and scale, on the one hand, and the benefits of localization and adaptation to differences, on the other. In China, there are large benefits to differentiation (localization). And, as China grows, it offers scale on its own terms too. Increasingly, for those that succeed in building a strong market position, China's scale justifies and pays for adaptation many times over. There is in fact little trade-off. For marginal competitors that prove unable to build a strong market position, however, competing in China becomes a self-defeating struggle. Lacking scale, they find it hard and expensive to localize effectively. This weakens their position further against competitors, Chinese and foreign, which are both localized and benefiting from scale.

Dual Circulation ramps up this impetus for localization further still. Since 2020 the business context has become markedly more "different". Digitization and the way that China regulates data is one critical aspect. Data play a central role in ever more business sectors – from automotive to financial services to consumer products. China's internet ecosystem is separate from the rest of the world, behind the "Great Firewall" and with different platforms, sites and apps, such as WeChat, Alipay and Tmall. In 2021 the Chinese government significantly tightened the regulation and oversight of all data through the Data Security Law (DSL) and the Personal Information Protection Law (PIPL). Chinese-generated data must for the most part remain in China, so forcing companies to establish separate data structures and systems. Although the regulations categorize different levels of data sensitivity, interpretation remains ambiguous, especially relating to national security matters.[18] Global companies in China find themselves unable to use shared customer relationship management systems hosted in other countries or to deploy for customers in China remote equipment-monitoring systems that rely on data flowing in and out of China.

A CLEAR SHAPE TO THE LOCALIZATION MODEL

Companies that are following the localization path are finding that they need to go further and more rapidly. In effect, multinationals are mirroring Dual Circulation or decoupling, as their China operations develop more and more as stand-alone businesses. In part, this represents a natural evolution of business operations. It does also raise questions of how far multinationals can and should go in "doing whatever it takes" to succeed in China. The characteristics of an operating model for success in China alone are clear, however, with five key elements.

1. *Value chain onshoring*: implement the further – and, eventually, full – onshoring of all value chain activities for the China market into China. Often known as a "China-for-China" strategy, this entails product localization, with R&D and manufacturing facilities in China. In 2022 BMW opened a major factory extension in Shenyang and Audi announced it was building its first China electric vehicle plant. Local manufacturing plays a key role for Airbus in securing Chinese orders.[19]

2. *Digital and data*: separate technology and data systems from global systems wherever possible to ensure full compliance with strict, yet also ambiguous, Chinese data laws. Fill data protection officer roles appropriately and monitor cross-border data flows. Tesla has opened a separate data centre in Shanghai as data generated by electric and self-driving must be handled and stored in China.

3. *Sales and marketing*: adapt and develop approaches and messaging to fit China's consumer and media landscape, in terms of technology platforms, consumer habits and attitudes and government control of messaging. WeChat is much more used than

email. Media content needs to pay attention to how Chinese consumers may interpret unintentional choices: for example, Dolce & Gabbana advertising featuring an Asian woman in a lavish dress attempting to eat pizza was perceived as racist and ignorant of Chinese culture.

4. *People and organization*: further devolve decision-making authority to the China business to strengthen market responsiveness. In 2022 Volkswagen established a China board with greater autonomy in order to streamline decision-making. Continue to hire, develop and promote Chinese talent and reduce the role of expatriates even further to enable successful localized strategy and execution. This means that there is increasing competition for capable Chinese talent. At senior management levels and above, compensation packages are similar to US levels.

5. *Capital and investment*: determine whether the corporate appetite to invest in China is of the scale needed for success in a large, competitive, fast-changing market. Then decide whether to pursue a wholly owned China business or look for local partners who bring additional funding, talent, capabilities and market understanding. Western retailers such as Carrefour, Metro and Tesco have in recent years sold the majority or all of their stake to their Chinese partners. By contrast, Starbucks took full control of its China operations from its local partner in 2017.

Localization plus

However localized, multinationals remain multinationals and not Chinese companies. This is both their advantage and their handicap. From China's perspective, the China operations of a multinational will never be as "Chinese" as a Chinese company. But multinationals bring access to relationships, experience and technology from around the world and on a global scale. Companies will succeed by localizing *and* by bringing something distinctive to China.

A strong corporate presence in China should also bring benefits to operations in the rest of the world – for example, in the area of digitization or fast-cycle product development. These benefits will increase as

China's economy becomes more sophisticated but capturing them is now more challenging. Internally, communication and trust with the rest of the company becomes more difficult as the China business localizes to meet local business conditions. Covid-19-related travel restrictions and remote working made it even more difficult to build informal trusted relationships. They also made it more difficult for headquarters to maintain needed oversight of risks and opportunities.

Equally, multinationals need to decide whether to place limits on localization when it causes conflicts, costs or other concerns elsewhere in the company. This may mean accepting potentially weaker performance in China by not fully localizing. It may even lead to a decision to exit rather than meet the requirements of the China market, as Google did in its search business. Geopolitical tensions and policy divisions between the West and China have created additional complexity, uncertainty and pressure for corporate leadership. These factors all add cost (in terms of management attention, unpredictability and reputation as well as pure financials) to a localization strategy. This effort makes sense only if it is in support of a sizeable, competitive China business that aligns with corporate purpose. Localizing and separating China operations can mean duplication and extra cost in places. Companies with a smaller or currently struggling China business will find it even harder to prosper. Committing to gain the scale needed for profitability may appear too risky, leaving scale-down or exit as the sensible route.

The next two chapters explore further how a multinational's China business affects and is affected by its other global activities.

EXPORTERS NEED TO LOOK AGAIN AT BECOMING LOCALIZERS

Exporters face perhaps the most complicated situation. For many, in China's priority sectors, the pressure to become Localizers, rather than continuing to treat China simply as an export market, is large. These companies may stay as Exporters, become Localizers or – ultimately – need to accept retrenchment, diversifying to other export markets and even becoming Separators that exit China. The right answer depends on the current rationale for exporting and on how Dual Circulation evolves.

Dual Circulation promises a market that is larger but also much more challenging for Exporters, with stronger competition from companies, mostly Chinese, based in China. This suggests declining prospects for many Exporters without a change in business strategy. Alicia García Herrero at Bruegel, a Brussels-based think tank, notes that China's plans for self-reliance include much of the capital equipment, chemicals, machinery, auto parts and semiconductors that countries such as Germany, Japan and South Korea export. If these plans are successful, then Chinese competitors will substitute for China's imports of these goods. These same Chinese companies will also become more capable competitors on the global stage.[20] Exporters to China are likely to lose out even before Chinese companies have established themselves as equal competitors. In October 2021 the Chinese Ministry of Finance reiterated that foreign companies would receive equal treatment in government procurement processes.[21] This applied to foreign companies that produced in China, however. Local content is key to securing access, and pure Exporters would not qualify.[22]

Moving from Exporter to Localizer may offer a way forward for the more ambitious and capable companies. The transition is not easy, however. Building production facilities in China requires confidence that the scale of business justifies the investment. It also calls for local know-how and market understanding that Exporters may not have accumulated.

Many larger multinationals already combine Localizer and Exporter strategies. They are familiar with determining which product technologies to bring to China and which to keep offshore. For these companies it is a question of adjusting the mix. TSMC, the world's largest semiconductor manufacturer, has opened two fabrication plants in China that produce less advanced semiconductors. Given rapid demand growth, especially in the automotive sector, TSMC announced plans to double production of 28nm semiconductors in Nanjing by 2023.[23] By contrast, TSMC complied with US sanctions and stopped the export from Taiwan to Huawei in China of the more sophisticated 5nm semiconductors. From the commercial perspective alone, there is a need to balance the economics of a China plant, the ability to transfer process knowledge (which allows operation at similar productivity levels to manufacturing in Taiwan) and any risks to IP protection. But, in the current geopolitical environment, political considerations play a significant, even determining role. Some

Taiwanese politicians were concerned about TSMC's plan to expand 28nm production in China. Equally, some in Beijing called for boycott of the new production as TSMC planned to set up a plant producing 5nm in the United States but not in China. Yet TSMC needs to comply with US legislation on exporting American chip-making equipment to China, seeking licences for any such exports.[24]

There is a similar challenge in the medical devices sector. Developing Chinese capabilities in the sector is a policy priority. Historically, much of the more sophisticated equipment has been manufactured overseas and exported to China. Foreign companies have been losing market share in high-end devices such as CT, NMR imaging and X-ray tomography, however. To compete with strengthening Chinese competition, foreign companies need to determine whether to switch from Exporter to Localizer. This will require significant capital investment into a large market, in which volumes are growing rapidly, but government purchasers are aggressively driving down prices and business sentiment remains uncertain. Yet, if foreign companies choose to cede the Chinese market rather than compete, they risk facing off against the same stronger Chinese competitors in other markets in the years to come.[25] A May 2021 government announcement put an edge on the need to decide. It listed 315 items that hospitals should procure only from those companies that manufacture in China. Provincial governments followed up with their own notices to local hospitals. In 2022 Medtronic announced it would for the first time invest in core manufacturing in China by building a manufacturing plant for heart devices in the Shanghai Free Trade Zone. "Medtronic will promote localized research and development and production plans for high-end product lines in the country," said Medtronic's Gu Yushao[26] – fully in line with Dual Circulation priorities.

Many foreign companies will nevertheless choose to remain Exporters. Political and legal constraints at home or in the United States may play an influential role. Mooted US legislation to screen outbound investment in certain technology sectors in China and elsewhere would be particularly important.

Those that remain as Exporters may put greater efforts into other geographies so as to spread the risk of excess dependence on China exports. They may see declines in their China revenues as Chinese and China-based foreign companies win business. Alternatively, exports to China may still grow as Chinese demand increases or if Chinese companies fail to develop competitive products. A growing consumer market also offers the potential of continued export growth for branded products that are linked to national origin. French cheese and European designer brands are not candidates for complete localization to China. Export growth will depend crucially too on the position of China and others in multilateral trade agreements. Companies based in Asia's RCEP countries will be well placed to export more. The same applies to countries in CPTPP if China succeeds in joining that trade pact too. Whether US companies benefit will depend on the choices that the United States itself makes on membership – and on the ability of US-based multinational companies to optimize their multi-country manufacturing network to take advantage of the export opportunities that an opening China offers to others.

SOURCERS NEED TO BECOME DIVERSIFIERS AND UPGRADERS

Ever since China established itself as a leading manufacturing location, analysts have wondered how soon companies will need to move out of China as Chinese wage levels and living standards rise. In 2007 over half the respondents to Booz Allen's AmCham China Manufacturing Competitiveness survey thought China was losing its competitive edge. But manufacturing competitiveness rests on productivity rather than wage levels alone. Between 2014 and 2018 China increased its share of global manufacturing exports even as Vietnam, Taiwan and other countries gained share too.

In the short term, Dual Circulation itself has little direct impact on China as a sourcing location. The Chinese economy benefits from the export earnings and jobs created. In 2021 China announced policy measures to stabilize foreign trade, including improved export credit insurance and ensuring the availability of domestic supplies needed to manufacture exports.[27] Covid-19 lockdowns, political uncertainty, tariffs and trade tensions have brought concerns on supply chain resilience to the fore, however. Sourcers are becoming Diversifiers. In the longer term, Dual Circulation brings the prospect of greater technological capability in Chinese manufacturing. Sourcers also need to assess how they can take advantage of the upgrading in China's manufacturing capabilities: how they can become Upgraders.

Sourcers become Diversifiers

Diversification has become more important in sourcing. The 2011 disaster at the Fukushima nuclear plant in Japan highlighted the knock-on impact of random events on tightly coupled supply chains. This marked the start of many such events: Covid-19 lockdowns at different times in different countries; sudden tariff impositions and export bans (especially from the United States); trade sanctions or slowed customs processes targeted at specific countries (especially by China); the war in Ukraine. These have all put a premium on diversifying production across multiple countries to avoid supply chain disruptions. Volatility and uncertainty have led companies to focus on resilience rather than optimization, on a "just-in-case" rather than "just-in-time" approach. In 2022 China's Covid-19 lockdowns brought home forcefully the risks of over-concentration in one location.

Decisions on manufacturing location rest on factors outside China as much as inside. Companies assess the performance and risks of their global supply chain networks as a whole. China is one element, albeit a very important one. Relocation away from China presupposes that other locations are economically competitive and able to manufacture in sufficient volumes. It is not the Chinese government pushing companies to leave China. Political pressure to decouple or move away comes from Western governments, especially in the United States. Companies may also judge that China's changing business environment, explored in Chapter 5, has made it less attractive and more uncertain, at a time when other locations have become more attractive.

Companies are well versed in making these commercial decisions on how best to configure their supply chains. They want to increase supply chain resilience now to combat the increased policy uncertainty. This means examining how to reduce or minimize exposure to China within global sourcing networks so as to prepare for future scenarios of even greater geopolitical pressure. One way to do this is to reduce direct bilateral US–China sourcing flows unless the cost to do so is prohibitive. Such considerations influence new investment decisions. Expanding manufacturing in China to serve the US market has become much less attractive; but, for multinationals, pan-Asian manufacturing networks may allow the United States to be supplied from Vietnam, while China capacity serves other markets. Sourcing from China may still grow for some markets. Commercial logic will continue to be the determining factor, except when legal bans on sourcing from China are introduced. There is much greater attention now on risk and resilience, however.

Legal and ethical questions have also become more prominent, especially in terms of labour and environmental standards. Since June 2022 the Uyghur Forced Labor Prevention Act has banned the import into the United States of goods "made in whole or in part"[28] in Xinjiang, unless companies can prove that forced labour was not used. This puts the onus on thorough corporate supply chain audits, at a time when such audit access to Xinjiang has become very difficult. There are similar moves in Europe. In June 2022 the European Parliament adopted a resolution condemning crimes against humanity perpetrated against the Uyghurs in China and calling for a ban on the import of products made by forced labour. In Germany, the Supply Chain Act (Lieferkettengesetz) requires tighter corporate due diligence in supply chains from January 2023. The UK parliament has investigated forced labour in UK supply chains and legislated to ban such products from the health service. Beyond legal considerations, the increasing priority that individual and institutional investors place on environmental, social and governance (ESG) factors in investment means that further such scrutiny is likely.

Meaningful diversification away from China is easy to wish for (for some) but hard to do. Craig Allen, president of the US–China Business Council, has observed that "thinking that 'Oh, well, let's just take our supply chain and move it back to the United States' – it's just utter nonsense, for a lot of different reasons. Now, the White House is not happy to hear that. But the fact of the matter is, it's very hard to move supply chains."[29] In the same 2022 interview, Allen notes that 80 per cent of USCBC members reported not moving any segment of their supply chains from China in the last 12 months and 85 per cent of members had not paused investments in China in the last 12 months. Similar figures apply to European companies, although the number of companies pausing China investments did increase as Covid-19 lockdowns continued.

It is not easy to find immediate alternatives to China where labour, logistics, infrastructure and potential suppliers are available in large enough quantities. Gordon Hanson of the Harvard Kennedy School concluded this from his research: "Who will fill China's shoes remains something of a puzzle."[30] Vietnam, Cambodia and Bangladesh are all options, but even combined the countries are no match for China's production scale. India's manufacturing sector is developing, including growing investments by Apple, Mercedes-Benz, BMW, Hyundai and Honeywell. India may yet become a manufacturing superpower, but it might take a long time – maybe as long as it did China, at best. Nonetheless, China's own manufacturing rise over a couple of decades also demonstrates that significant shifts in manufacturing capacity are indeed achievable given favourable economic and political circumstances.

For now, many Diversifiers pursue a "China plus one" strategy, whereby China remains an important sourcing location, but some capacity – especially incremental growth – is placed in other countries. For example, in 2022 Foxconn, a Taiwanese company and one of Apple's main subcontractors, started to produce its iPhone 13 in India and shifted some iPad manufacturing from China to Vietnam. Foxconn had launched manufacturing operations in India in 2017 with the iPhone SE. Similarly, Techtronic Industries (TTI), a leader in cordless power tools and cleaning appliances, has long manufactured in China and sold to consumers in the United States and Europe under brands such as Hoover and Milwaukee. In recent years TTI has also begun to invest in Vietnamese manufacturing facilities and supplier networks.

In the longer term, China's attractiveness relative to other countries for sourcing will depend too on its participation in trade agreements – part of the strategy for external circulation explored in Chapter 6. RCEP membership is the first element. If China succeeds in joining CPTPP, with its requirements for greater trade openness, China-based manufacturers will gain further advantages in exporting to member countries as far afield as Chile and (potentially) the United Kingdom. This will, of course, not include the United States, unless it also joins CPTTP.

Sourcers become Upgraders

In the longer term, Sourcers in China need to be ready to become Upgraders and adapt their manufacturing footprint accordingly. The number and sophistication of Chinese companies is already increasing rapidly in many sectors. In robotics, for example, Shenzhen Han's Robot, founded in 2017, develops, manufactures and exports intelligent robots for industrial, healthcare, logistics, education and other applications. Dual Circulation policy success in upgrading manufacturing would mean that China becomes much less competitive in low-end products such as textiles and toys. Conversely, it would become more competitive in higher value-added products such as capital equipment, robotics and medical equipment.

For Sourcers, this upgrading poses questions of risk appetite and timing. Companies need to assess the attractiveness of moving now to upgrade their production capabilities in China – moves that would gain favour and support from the Chinese government. Alternatively, they could decide that it is better to wait for these increased capabilities to develop (or not) in other companies, and then adjust once the early work has been done. Companies need to be ready to migrate lower-end sourcing needs to other countries. Samsung Electronics is one example of a company already doing both. In 2020 Samsung ceased all mobile phone production in China; most Samsung smartphones are now manufactured in Vietnam and India. In part, this reflects the collapse of Samsung's market share in China, but it also highlights also the unfavourable manufacturing economics. At the same time, Samsung announced an expansion of its semiconductor production in China, as a Localizer, to meet China market needs.

SEPARATORS NEED TO UNCOVER HIDDEN OPPORTUNITIES AND RISKS

Against the backdrop of Dual Circulation and decoupling, it may seem paradoxical that Separators – those that do not do business in or with China – are best advised to take another look at China. But they should. First they need to reassess whether they should indeed give China a larger role in their business, looking at any new opportunities business line by business line. Then they need to examine whether they genuinely do have no exposure to or dependence on China. They should also examine how they might gain from learning more about what is happening in China even if they do not do business there.

In the near term, China's continued deregulation and opening up to foreign investment is creating new opportunities for multinationals. The removal of ownership limits across much of the financial sector has attracted new interest in pensions, wealth management, mutual funds and investment banking. Fidelity International has had a presence in China for over 20 years, developing call centre operations and technology support. Until recent deregulation, however, it had no presence in the mutual fund market.[31] In August 2021 Fidelity received approval to set up a mutual fund unit.[32] Overnight, a Separator became a Localizer in mutual funds. Those companies without any previous China presence will find such a shift difficult and risky. The change is less dramatic for those, such as Fidelity, that already have a China presence in other business lines.

For other, often smaller, companies, continued growth in income levels and technological sophistication will make China a more attractive market, either as an Exporter or through a local presence. Niche designer brands that currently find the economics and complexities of market entry unattractive may draw different conclusions when the market size has doubled. In this case, Separators become Exporters. For instance, Emma Bridgewater, a small British handmade pottery business, launched its China online presence only in 2019. Finally, as China's manufacturing capabilities become more sophisticated, engineering and technology companies with no business in China today may look to China as a new sourcing location. Separators become Sourcers.

Reassessment may, naturally, yield the same answer as before: Separator. In 2017 Google launched a confidential internal project, Project Dragonfly, to develop a censored version of its search engine that would allow the company to re-enter China. Employee resistance and potential political criticism in the United States led to the termination of the project the next year, however.[33]

China merits a second look even for those who choose to remain in the Separator quadrant. China's presence in the world economy is so pervasive that complete separation or decoupling may prove a chimera for any business. Chinese companies are increasingly a source of competition and innovation. Even Separators can benefit from a small China presence, enabling staff to observe and learn from developments in China. Separators will also encounter China's influence in other countries around the world. As Chapter 7 explored, China will play an increasing role in standard-setting, in trade negotiations and in the political environment of the many countries for which it is the largest trading partner. The overseas subsidiaries of Chinese companies can be customers too, supported by Chinese talent able to contribute local innovation and insight. Even companies that choose not to source from China may find that their suppliers do, so that they do actually rely on Chinese suppliers for key components. Alternatively, a company may sell only to non-Chinese corporate customers, but then realize that the business prospects of these customers rest in part on the Chinese market. Just as countries cannot completely decouple, so too will companies need to reckon with China in some form.

10

Ambidexterity and connectivity

"True ambidexterity is about having the people within the organization who have the mindset, skills and maturity to respond positively to different circumstances," argues Michael Fraccaro, formerly an organizational development leader in HSBC Asia-Pacific. The essence of ambidexterity is about embracing opposites. It is about transcending an either/or view and remaining flexible enough to view challenges from different perspectives.[1]

The year 1865 was a formative one for HSBC, the Hongkong & Shanghai Banking Corporation Limited. In March it opened for business in Hong Kong, helping to finance trade between Europe and Asia. In April it opened in Shanghai, and in July it was London's turn. The company was born from one simple idea: a local bank serving international needs. Ambidexterity was built in from the start. HSBC has always been committed to developing global managers, flexible enough to adapt to any culture of its 60 plus subsidiaries. Since 1865 HSBC has had a continuous presence in mainland China, albeit sharply curtailed under Japanese rule and the Mao years of the People's Republic. In 1984, as China reopened, HSBC became the first foreign bank to receive a banking licence since 1949.

Now, after decades of growth in China and globally, some are questioning again where the limits of HSBC's ambidexterity lie. In the United Kingdom, it was widely criticized for its public support of the Hong Kong National Security Law in 2020. In 2022 HSBC's largest shareholder, China's Ping An Insurance, made the case for splitting HSBC in two – separating the East from the West. Ping An argued that a split would create shareholder value through better focus on distinct markets and reduced capital requirements. It would also allow individual investors in Hong Kong to receive their valued dividends, without the risk of Bank of England intervention, as had happened during Covid-19. Some commentators saw a political agenda too: a Hong-Kong-listed HSBC Asia might be more amenable to influence from Beijing and the CPC. HSBC managers rejected the case for a split. They argued that HSBC's global connectivity brought greater value. Does HSBC need to choose between China and the West, or is much of its inherent business value based on the ambidextrous linking of the two?

HSBC is not alone. All companies operating in China face these questions of ambidexterity and connectivity. Dual Circulation means that companies must learn to operate in increasingly divergent, and sometimes contradictory, environments. They need to adapt to a changing China, but also to different conditions outside China. This leads to increasing separation and divergence within multinational structures. Those described as Localizers in Chapter 8 are especially affected. Simply manufacturing in China to serve the rest of the world also requires adapting to the Chinese context, however. Similar questions arise in terms of legal compliance, government and Party relations and the need to navigate the impact of policy uncertainties and potential diplomatic disagreements. Exporters face similar challenges shipping goods into China through in-house or third-party distribution. The impact of Dual Circulation and the potential decoupling of multinational business stretches far beyond the borders of a company's China operations.

Localization brings benefits in local market performance. But it makes more difficult the global connectivity and integration that constitute the *raison d'être* of the multinational company. Global companies need to nurture and provide oversight to a China business that may be operating in a distinct and faster-paced way – and to do this from a headquarters unused to operating in such a way. As Chapter 7 explored, connectivity itself has become more controversial and politicized. Chinese policy-makers remain as keen as ever to draw on global know-how to strengthen China's development, but they are more restrictive and cautious on data flows out of China. In the West, governments, consumers and investors increasingly express concerns about the nature of corporate involvement in China. Multinationals need to figure out both how connectivity can create value for them and then how to achieve it.

Companies also need to determine what limits, if any, they wish to place on localization. Will they simply adjust to local operating conditions whatever they may be, following the mantra of "When in Rome, do as the Romans do"? Multinational companies have long grappled with the trade-off between the benefits of differentiation to match local market conditions and the benefits of integration and commonality across global operations. The calculus is relatively straightforward when considering the different consumer tastes or dining habits that lead to different menu items in a McDonald's or Starbucks. It is much more complicated and vexed when consumers in China and Europe have completely opposing views on the appeal and ethics of products such as those containing cotton sourced from Xinjiang, or when expanding production capacity for advanced semiconductors to meet the needs of a key Chinese customer is seen as a question of national security for Western governments.

To address these issues, multinationals need to focus on two organizational capabilities in addition to deciding how to configure their China operations: *ambidexterity* – the ability to cultivate markedly different organizational models in the same company (and the limits to such ambidexterity); and *connectivity* – how and where the China organization connects with the rest of the company globally.

AMBIDEXTERITY

In 1976 Robert Duncan introduced the concept of the ambidextrous organization.[2] His article recognized that running a business as usual and creating new innovations required different ways of working and different cultures. Duncan identified how companies could use distinct, dual structures to tackle this challenge, and then link them together. Charles O'Reilly and Michael Tushman's 2004 *Harvard Business Review* article "The ambidextrous organization" had a similar focus on innovation.[3] In its most general sense, however, the term "ambidexterity" in business refers to dealing with competing demands.[4] From a strategy perspective, Boston Consulting Group describes ambidexterity as "the ability to apply multiple approaches to strategy either concurrently or successively, since many firms operate in more than one strategic environment at once".[5]

This captures well the distinction between China and Western markets today. Although successful multinationals have always recognized that China is "different", these differences have become much more marked even since 2020. The organizational solution to this increasing geographic differentiation is – at the first approximation – relatively simple: separate out the China business so that it can adapt to succeed in local market conditions. Creating this solution is a form of "structural ambidexterity",[6] analogous to setting up a separate innovation unit in a company alongside the business unit that focuses on day-to-day business. This dual structure enables a clear focus on China-specific needs while maintaining a different structure elsewhere. It is, indeed, a corporate parallel to China's own Dual Circulation, which raises the same question of how China should link with the rest of the world. This is why more multinationals have become Localizers. Nonetheless, on its own, this organizational structure weakens connectivity to global operations. It creates risk and undermines the distinct advantages that multinational operations offer.

AMBIDEXTERITY AND CONNECTIVITY

The case for multinational business rests on the ability of headquarters to create additional value for individual country operations. This comes through oversight and guidance, and from the sharing of resources and knowledge between global functions and operations in other countries. Additionally, however differently and independently the China business develops, corporate headquarters retain legal and reputational responsibility for actions taken there. The increasing volume of China-related legislation in the United States and Europe makes auditing and compliance even more pressing. The more that the China market develops in ways different from other markets, however, the harder it is for managers outside China to pass judgement on investment proposals and to provide meaningful advice. Taken to an extreme, the role of headquarters becomes similar to the central function of a financial holding company that owns a diverse range of businesses and concentrates on assessing financial performance alone. Such logic starts to make the case for spinning off the China business completely. In 2016 Yum China, the operator of KFC restaurants in China, listed on the New York Stock Exchange as a separate company from Yum Brands. This allowed Yum Brands to focus on operating as a global franchisor, freeing up capital, with Yum China as the exclusive franchisee for China, raising its own capital as needed. In 2020 Yum China launched a secondary stock market listing in Hong Kong, and in 2022 it converted this to dual primary listing with New York.

Most companies continue to pursue closer and more effective organizational connectivity that brings value for customers in China and elsewhere. In fact, in some sectors, such as trade finance, airlines and shipping, connectivity is core to the value proposition. Despite protectionism, pandemics and politics, this global connectivity continues to generate significant business value. Indeed, now that connectivity is less seamless and more politicized, those that excel at connecting may prosper even more than they did previously.

Headquarters need to continue to provide oversight and guidance for their China operations. The organizational mechanisms for doing this remain essentially unchanged: reporting lines, metrics, incentives, processes, people selection, development and career planning, and so on. The execution challenges of doing this well have become greater, however. Success in China now typically requires the China business to have more autonomy in strategy, operations and people matters. But more localized China management teams often find it harder to gain the trust of those working in the very different environment of head office. They may also be more reluctant and less suited to making career moves outside China that will build relationships and experience. Those outside China may have outdated perceptions of China and lack the humility and sensitivity to understand different perspectives. Covid-19 travel restrictions have made much more difficult the informal interactions that help build trust across cultures. The different media and information environments in China and Western countries exacerbate the challenge. One British corporate lawyer spoke of how fulfilling he found working on business deals with Chinese counterparts, but then returned home to watch the television news and hear only negatives about China. Little by little, the shared assumptions and perspectives that make cooperation and trust easier are being eroded.

This all makes oversight and the sharing of knowledge and learning more difficult. Ensuring that the rest of the company learns from China may be the greatest challenge. This is still an unfamiliar approach for many. Yet today, in a number of critical sectors, China either leads in the scaling up of innovation or offers a world-competitive alternative approach. Examples include electric vehicles, online retailing and the integration with offline, e-payments and green energy. If headquarters staff or those in other markets miss the significance of China-based innovation, then they are failing in part of their role. Here, too, incentives, structured processes, communication and leadership in a supportive culture remain the familiar tools for promoting sharing. But they are all more difficult in a world of more localized business, less travel and background geopolitical tensions.

THE LIMITS OF AMBIDEXTERITY

Ambidexterity allows multinationals to adapt successfully to different business conditions by separating competing demands. But leaving these differences unmanaged is not an option. "The left hand doesn't know what the right hand is doing" is a criticism rather than an alibi for allowing fully independent choices. Values, corporate purpose and corporate social responsibility feature prominently in corporate mission statements today. These have a direct implication for the behaviours and choices that are acceptable within the company anywhere in the world – and those that are not.

In a continuation of this chapter's opening quote, Michael Fraccaro mentioned that, in HSBC, "[people] align their behaviours to the group's core values and business principles which, above all else, are about acting with courageous integrity. This is critical when you have operations around the globe with over 300,000 employees – you want people who have a sense of empowerment, but also accountability."[7] HSBC's experience of lawsuits, fines and political controversy around the world is a testament to how challenging it is to implement such aspirations.[8]

Doing business in China has become much more difficult in this respect for foreign companies. Document 9, a Party document issued in 2013, provided a succinct summary of the CPC perspective on issues of values or, as its title proclaimed, "The current state of the ideological sphere".[9] These perspectives have consistently resurfaced in subsequent years. The document identifies the ideological situation in China as a "complicated, intense struggle". It goes on to identify a number of "false ideological trends, positions, and activities". These include promoting Western constitutional democracy; promoting "universal values" as defined by the West in areas such as "democracy, freedom, equality, justice and the rule of law"; and promoting "the West's idea of journalism".

At the same time, the topic of environmental, society and governance factors has become a prominent feature of investor and regulator interest in the United States and Europe. How ESG investing and reporting should be implemented remains a matter of debate. Environmental aspects often receive the greatest focus. China too has introduced regulations on ESG reporting and compliance, primarily focusing on green finance and decarbonization.[10] Outside China, however, the "S" and the "G" of ESG place a focus on issues of human rights, worker rights and the rule of law. China's shortcomings in these areas may become increasingly a matter of investor concern. ESG will be interpreted in different ways by China and the West. In some cases global companies will be able to comply with both definitions, but contradictions are also inevitable.

For example, cotton originating from Xinjiang has starkly different connotations to European and Chinese consumers. Many Western consumers wish to boycott Xinjiang cotton, fearing that its manufacture involves forced labour, or simply in protest at the actions of the Chinese government in Xinjiang. By contrast, Chinese consumers accuse Western companies of "spreading rumours to boycott Xinjiang cotton, while trying to make a profit in China",[11] and boycott those that do not use Xinjiang cotton. Swedish clothing company H&M faced a forceful, rapid response from Chinese consumers, companies and government when it stated that it did not source cotton from Xinjiang. H&M stated publicly its concerns on "accusations of forced labour and discrimination". As a result, H&M was removed from online retailers Taobao, JD.com and Pinduoduo. Its app was delisted, store locations were deleted from online mapping services and about 20 physical locations were shut. In the three months to May 2021 H&M sales in China fell 23 per cent year on year.[12] By contrast, Chinese sportswear companies such as Li-Ning Anta trumpeted their use of Xinjiang cotton and gained sales. Metro and

Carrefour hypermarkets in China also launched campaigns promoting Xinjiang fresh produce: Metro and Carrefour each now own only 20 per cent of their China operations, both having sold majority ownership to Chinese partners a few years previously.

There are difficult choices in entertainment too. American film companies have historically self-censored the portrayal of China in films so as to maintain access to the Chinese market.[13] When Chinese film censors requested the removal of footage of the Statue of Liberty as a condition of approving the movie *Spider-Man: No Way Home*, however, Sony Pictures refused to do this.[14] Being known for censoring the Statue of Liberty at China's insistence would have unleashed a backlash in the United States. In *Top Gun: Maverick*, Tom Cruise's jacket still bore the Taiwanese flag, despite debate that it would be removed in order to pre-empt Chinese objections.

Legal constraints on such corporate decisions are growing. Using Xinjiang cotton in the United States and Europe will increasingly fall foul of the law, whatever consumers demand, as a result of the impracticalities of certifying the cotton as free of forced labour. Western companies will still need to choose whether to use it in the China market, however, where there is consumer demand. Companies around the world – including Chinese state-owned enterprises – have long accepted the need to comply with US legislation and sanctions, which can have extraterritorial reach, applying anywhere in the world regardless of the nationality of a company. Following the Russian invasion of Ukraine, Chinese companies have been careful not to act in direct breach of sanctions imposed on Russia. What threatens to be unmanageable is where US and Chinese laws stand in direct conflict to one another. In 2021 China passed the Anti-Foreign Sanctions Law (AFSL). This broadly worded piece of legislation made it an offence to comply with sanctions imposed by another country that penalized Chinese individuals or organizations.[15] Enforced strictly, there would be many circumstances in which multinationals faced a choice between US or Chinese law. In practice, China has not yet sought to force this issue, and also delayed the AFSL's application in Hong Kong. The uncertainty does remain, though.

Beyond legal compliance, there are no easy answers as to how companies should handle these knotty questions if they want to continue doing business in China. When should they "do as Romans do in Rome" and when should they insist on "red lines" that might lead to exiting China, driven either by stakeholder pressure or because of conflicts with corporate values and mission?

In a 2022 *Harvard Business Review* article, Seth Kaplan outlines four approaches for dealing with ethical questions when doing business in China.[16]

1. *Continue and contain*: some companies try to maintain a low profile and avoid attention. Disney maintains operations such as theme parks and film and content distribution, despite a ban on its streaming service Disney+. This does not eliminate controversy, however. In 2020 Disney was criticized in the United States for filming a portion of its movie *Mulan* in Xinjiang. Such an approach can succeed within China but may bring increasing costs outside the country.

2. *Operate with opposition*: others try to speak out on allegations of abuses while continuing operations in the country. The H&M experience on Xinjiang cotton provides an example of the costs of this approach. In the second quarter of 2021 China no longer ranked in the top ten markets for H&M, even though it had previously been H&M's fifth largest market.[17] This approach will increasingly limit business success in China.

3. *Support China's standards*: foreign companies that are highly dependent on China revenues tend to make statements supportive of Chinese positions and avoid criticism. Herbert Diess, CEO of Volkswagen, declared that supply chains were compliant with German laws, refused to answer critical questions on forced labour and told the BBC that he was "not aware" of reports about detention camps in Xinjiang.[18] This approach appears increasingly unsustainable amid increasing divergence, tensions and sharper media coverage in the West.

4. *Withdraw (Separator strategy)*: companies decide that they are unwilling to adapt their ways of doing business to Chinese government requirements and so exit. This has most often been the case for businesses that were already struggling in China or of marginal significance. In 2021 both Yahoo! and Microsoft's LinkedIn business withdrew from China. Microsoft attributed its decision

to a "significantly more challenging operating environment and greater compliance requirements",[19] in particular greater pressure to censor details on LinkedIn personal profiles. Microsoft continued to operate its Bing search engine in China, however, returning censored search results – suggesting censorship was not the only concern.

Exit is also not a simple decision. Following Russia's invasion of Ukraine, multinational companies had rapidly to revisit their ties with Russia after doing business there for decades. Pressures from both consumers and investors exerted pressure while legal restrictions increased. Hundreds of companies decided to exit immediately, though Unilever and Nestlé continued operations in part. Both argued that this course of action was in line with their purpose and preferable to alternatives that would transfer operations to Russian ownership or lead to legal exposure.[20] Unilever stated, "We will continue to supply our everyday essential food and hygiene products made in Russia to people in the country. We will keep this under close review."[21] Reckitt Benckiser, active in many similar product lines, reached a different conclusion and decided to exit.

11

Resilience and agility in the face of uncertainty

Now, more than ever, doing business with China presents uncertainty. This uncertainty is not limited to China alone. How relations between the West and China will evolve is also unclear. Michael Green and Scott Kennedy of CSIS, a Washington, DC, think tank, observe that "global companies that have thrived on doing business with China are not well prepared to adapt to this new normal or to try and stem the tide". When talking with companies, Green says that he found "an unexpected combination of overconfidence and resignation in their views".[1] In fact, this may not be so unexpected. Uncertainty evokes an emotional response as often as a push for rational analysis. "Common wisdom from the psychologist's perspective is that people do not like uncertainty, especially about the future, and that it generates a negative response."[2] Psychologists call this "ambiguity aversion". Faced with uncertainty, some multinationals understandably take a "wait and see" approach to investment in their China business. For the largest investments, this makes sense in the depths of Covid-19 lockdowns. But uncertainty is not going away, and companies need to decide in order to succeed.

The track record of experts in predicting China's future is not good. "China cannot grow into an industrial giant in the 21st century. Its population is too large and its gross domestic product too small."[3] So wrote Bruce Nelan in an October 1992 edition of *Time* magazine under the title "How the world will look in 50 years". Twenty years later the situation had already changed, with China serving as the "factory of the world", providing multinational companies with low-cost manufactured goods. In 2014 distinguished Harvard professors Regina Abrami, William Kirby and Warren McFarlan could still pen an article with the title "Why China can't innovate".[4] Many still asserted that "China [was] largely a land of rule-bound rote learners"[5] that could only imitate, not innovate. The argument was based largely on an assumption that those working within the constraints of an authoritarian regime could not innovate. Eight years later China was producing technology innovations across a range of industries and is likely to move ahead in others before too long. China has done this without converging to models of free-market economics or electoral democracy and free speech. Warren Buffett famously said, "Never bet against America."[6] The maxim may extend to never betting against China – and, only then, figuring out what that means for foreign business.

In the past few decades multinational companies have benefited from reform and opening up in China. Until recently many expected the positive trajectory to continue without any major need for adaptation. The China opportunity was a large part of the "growth story" that companies pitched to their investors. The best multinationals were learning to adapt and to thrive in China's different, fast-paced business environment. Barring extreme events, China will remain strategically important for many multinational firms. BCG analysis suggests that China will account for 25 per cent of global growth in the years up to 2030. But, as Chapter 5 described, China's business environment is now changed and uncertain. Alongside uncertainty in the Chinese economy, business leaders need to deal with uncertainty in China's relations with other countries, especially the United States. Will China grow or stagnate, or even collapse? Will it continue to welcome foreign business or close off? How will critical bilateral relations develop, especially the US–China relationship? Will a US presidential election result or a Chinese move on Taiwan suddenly change all business calculations?

Although China's response to Covid-19 has posed its own challenges to business and the economy, these questions are not really new. The uncertainty, defined as the range of potential outcomes, seems larger than ever, however. "The inability to change policies is something new to me," said Jörg Wuttke, president of the European Chamber of Commerce in China, in the summer of 2022 in relation to zero-Covid. "Chinese politicians and technocrats used to be really good at getting a pragmatic policy up and running. The fact that they are now willing to take an economic hit is a new dimension to me. I'm really puzzled."[7]

In this environment, companies need more resilience and agility – in other words, the ability both to sense, assess and absorb quickly internal and external shocks and to respond rapidly, creatively and effectively to changes, small or large. Experience already gained doing business in China can help here. Companies need to apply these lessons at a global level too and incorporate geopolitical expertise, scenarios and war-gaming into strategy development, operations and contingency planning.

UNCERTAINTY IN CHINA: NOTHING NEW, BUT VERY DIFFERENT

It is hard and unwise to generalize between countries and across a population of 1.4 billion individuals, but China is indeed different. It is different both in the speed of change and in the uncertainty about what form that change will take. Between 1990 and 2019 China's GDP per capita grew by over 30 times, whereas it only tripled in the United States. Zak Dychtwald has written in the *Harvard Business Review* about the Lived Change Index. This takes the change in lifetime per capita GDP as a proxy for the scale of change that people are experiencing. China has simply experienced a much faster pace of change in recent decades than other countries.[8] This change is more than just quantitative. Growth on this scale changes life qualitatively and viscerally for individuals in terms of their knowledge, outlook, mindset and expectations.

Looking back further, older generations experienced life under Chairman Mao, and these memories live on in many of their descendants. The turbulence and extremes of Mao's Cultural Revolution (1966–76) pushed many family and friendship bonds to their limits and beyond. The period was characterized by uncertainty and threat, when local "guerrilla tactics" often replaced clear central command.[9] Survival required flexibility and adaptation. The impact persists today. Yuhua Wang of Harvard University demonstrates that those growing up in regions that experienced more violence between 1966 and 1971 are less trusting of their political leaders at all levels today.[10] Traumatic experiences during the Cultural Revolution led individuals to internalize strategies of trust or distrust as a heuristic or "rule of thumb". Once such behaviour is

161

shown to work, it persists and is applied time and again. Experience in living memory of widely differing political environments reinforces the awareness that things may again change radically. People remain all too alert to widely varying potential outcomes.

THE KEY UNCERTAINTY

There are, of course, many uncertainties in China, and new ones quickly replace any that resolve themselves. Can the government fix problems in the real estate sector? How will Chinese society operate in a world where Covid-19 is endemic? Will China become a world leader in semiconductors? There is perhaps one uncertainty above all, however. How effectively will Xi Jinping and the CPC as a whole make choices, exercise power and execute policy? This is what will ultimately determine China's economic prospects, and so the revenue, profit and risk outlook for foreign business.

Getting to grips with this question is made more difficult by the nature of policy-making in China. Richard McGregor at the Lowy Institute in Australia has written of the "radical secrecy" surrounding all aspects of Party decision-making.[11] China commentators opine on what may be happening at the Beidaihe meeting of CPC leaders each summer. Yet former China diplomat Charles Parton concludes that it is not even certain such a meeting takes place.[12] This opacity in itself breeds uncertainty, and is unlikely to change.

Xi's dominant position is all the more certain in the wake of the October 2022 20th Party Congress and the selection of a Politburo Standing Committee made up of Xi loyalists. Yet, although media messages emphasize positive, unquestioning support for Xi, there are also glimpses of tensions, problems and disagreements beneath the surface that go beyond unsubstantiated rumour. The street protests against the zero-Covid-19 policy in November 2022 brought all this vividly to life, with some protesters even calling for Xi to step down. Cai Xia, formerly a professor teaching Party officials at the Party School, wrote two detailed articles in 2020 and 2022 entitled "The party that failed"[13] and "The weakness of Xi Jinping".[14] They provide illustrations of a centralized, micro-managing style and the difficulties and personal risks for others of advocating for policy change once decisions have been made. The specifics ring true in part because they are just what one would expect in any organization with a dominant single leader.

What is clear is that decision-making is now, and will remain, highly centralized. Xi is at the heart of all key decisions. Decision-making and power are also described in a highly personalized way. Some analysts portray this as the "rise of Xi Jinping and the demise of the collective leadership system" and draw imperfect parallels with the leadership of Mao Zedong.[15] One major difference between Xi and Mao, though, is that Xi demands order and structure, while Mao stimulated and sought to benefit from disorder and chaos. Xi is not Mao.

Analogies to corporate leadership provide food for thought in considering how effective Xi's decisions and actions might be. Kerry Brown's 2016 book on Xi bears the title *China CEO: The Rise of Xi Jinping* but also notes Xi's other CEO role: leading the CPC itself. To continue the corporate analogy, the CPC can be seen as the (monopoly) supplier of governance and direction to the Chinese people. Chapter 3 quoted Xi Jinping's words that "China's success hinges on the Party". As with any CEO, Xi wishes to keep his job and then wants his company (the CPC) to survive and prosper. This does indeed mean "meeting the needs of the Chinese people", thus maintaining legitimacy. Just as companies may be tempted to profit at the expense of customers in the short term, however, so too the CPC will place its own interests first. This temptation is especially strong for monopolies. Equally, "imperial" CEOs may act in their interests rather than the long-term interests of their company. They also make mistakes when others do not feel comfortable challenging their decisions. Xi does not have the equivalent of a strong, independent "board of directors" able to hold him to account or urge change. The influence of Party elders, guiding and wielding influence on key decisions, has substantively and visibly declined; the symbolism of Hu Jintao being escorted out of the 20th Party Congress was clear even if the underlying reasons for it were not. This all means that there is an increased risk that policy mistakes are made and that they go uncorrected. It means also that Xi's declared emphasis on security, ideology and the role of the state may continue to hamper economic growth significantly.

Turning to policy execution, Xi is a CEO leading a massive transformation programme across a party of over 90 million members and a total population of 1.4 billion. He faces the change management challenges that corporate CEOs in a similar position also face – but on a much, much larger scale. In 2015 state media reported that Xi faced "unimaginably fierce resistance" to reforms.[16] In considering China under Covid-19, Wang Xiangwei, former editor of Hong Kong's *South China Morning Post*, writes of how "fragmented and chaotic the country's bureaucratic command structure still is, especially in a crisis". "Local mandarins may cower in [Xi's] presence and publicly pledge loyalty to him and the central authorities, but the truth of the matter is that regional governments often ignore or obfuscate explicit directives from Beijing."[17] Centralization and top-down edicts are positive when they help overcome resistance to change. Reaping the economic benefits of a national unified market means overcoming the resistance of provincial leaders. At other times, however, eager officials may over-interpret or misinterpret vague guidance with excessively strict implementation, for fear of the consequences if they are perceived to be weak or inadequate. This has proved to be the case with Covid-19.

True skill in leading forward China's development lies in blending together the pursuit of prosperity, security and values. And for the CPC, and for Xi, it is to do so in a way that maintains their position in power. This means leaving scope for local adaptation while pushing back on those resisting the "right" changes – whatever they may be. Whether Xi and the Party leadership can make the "right" calls on what to prioritize when, and when to push back on resistance and when to adjust, is the enduring key uncertainty – for businesses and individuals alike, and affecting decision-making for all.

RESILIENCE AND AGILITY IN CHINESE BUSINESS

Many Chinese managers handle extreme business uncertainty in China more effectively than Westerners. They have grown up in an environment of greater uncertainty and ambiguity and have a more nuanced understanding of the context in which events and announcements are occurring. Based on a few cues, these managers take a pragmatic approach to getting things done in the moment. They refine their actions once more information becomes available. Deng Xiaoping's dictum captures this: "Cross the river by feeling for stones" (摸着石头过河; *mōzhe shítou guò hé*). Rather than engage in long-term, fixed planning, an effective approach in the face of uncertainty is often to take small steps to see what works and does not, and then adjust accordingly.

Reaching back further into history, Chinese philosophy also provides an underpinning for a different mindset and approach to uncertainty. The concept of "yin and yang" thinking is known to most Chinese. The two aspects of yin and yang reflect an understanding of the world as an eternal cycle, with two opposing yet complementary elements inseparably linked in unity (e.g. heaven and earth, sun and moon, light and darkness, water and fire).[18] This lays the foundation for an approach of "dual thinking" that is more accepting of apparent contradictions. What starts out as a crisis will turn into opportunity; what is black turns white; what is difficult will become easy, and vice versa. In business relations, the yin–yang approach provides a perspective that accepts paradoxical conditions and allows for the dynamic evolution of business relationships.

Western business leaders often lack the experience or training to deal with the contradictions that arise from a high level of uncertainty. Such thinking is found most typically in individual entrepreneurs rather than in the leadership of large corporations. Western corporate business culture prefers an approach of linear, analytical thinking, following Aristotelian logic with either/or choices and clear decisions.[19] Linear thinking works well in comparatively stable environments with information transparency. It works less well in fast-changing situations of ambiguous, imperfect and often contradictory information – such as China. Multinational business leaders with a track record of success in China typically incorporate dual thinking into their leadership and decision-making approach. Such leaders talk of switching between "linear analytic thought and intuitive holistic thought"; they focus on "context and relationships" as well as "individual details and abstract categories"; they combine "intuitive and analytical" approaches to strategy.[20] This leads to what Sean Upton-McLaughlin calls "dual-culture management" (双文化管理: *shuāng wénhuà guǎnlǐ*),[21] whereby leaders simultaneously observe and respect the values and beliefs of two cultures.

165

UNCERTAINTY ON HOW CHINA'S INTERNATIONAL RELATIONS AFFECT BUSINESS

Uncertainty in the China business is no longer limited to China alone. Relations with China are now an important part of the political and policy landscape in the United States, Europe, India, Japan and elsewhere. Decisions that business leaders make on China can have repercussions on their business in the United States and other markets. Investors, customers and employees outside China may all raise questions about what the company is doing in China. Economic action by China against foreign companies in response to political disagreements or "interference in China's internal affairs" is on the rise. MERICS, a China think tank based in Berlin, has identified 123 cases between 2010 and 2022 of "economic coercion": action taken against foreign business in China. The intensity of action increased after 2018 and was concentrated in sectors of lower strategic importance to China, in particular consumer goods. Consumer boycotts featured in 56 per cent of cases, reflecting the nationalist pride of many Chinese consumers, which can be either intensified or at least not restrained by state-controlled media and government messaging. The Chinese government put in place trade and tourism restrictions in 41 per cent and 20 per cent of cases respectively. In 21 per cent of cases, empty threats were made.[22]

One of the more extreme examples is the impact on South Korea's Lotte Group when the South Korean government stationed THAAD missiles on land owned by Lotte in South Korea, and the Chinese government objected. The consequence was tax audits, regulatory challenges and consumer boycotts. In 2017 Lotte had 130 retail stores in China, and confectionery and beverages businesses, and was planning further real estate investment. From 2018 onwards Lotte withdrew from China, and by 2022 it had closed all China operations and its China headquarters.[23]

In the words of CSIS's Green and Kennedy again, "Corporations need to think about their operating environment the way geostrategists now are [doing] – which is to say that there are multiple players shaping relations with China that have weight in Washington and Beijing."[24]

ADDRESSING UNCERTAINTY THROUGH RESILIENCE

The increased uncertainty in China and the broader geopolitical environment means that companies need to build resilience. Resilience is based on the concept of absorbing external shocks and "bouncing back". The principles of risk management, derived originally from the financial sector, frame potential actions. Risks can be diversified, mitigated or accepted. For the most part, however, the risks that companies now face are hard to model using quantitative techniques alone. "Once-in-a-century" climate events appear to be happening much more frequently than once a century. And there is no meaningful probability distribution of geopolitical outcomes.

Chapter 10 explained how, in global supply chain configurations, "just-in-case" considerations have become more important than "just-in-time" performance. In such circumstances, diversifying activity across multiple locations reduces the impact of adverse changes in any one location, in terms both of revenue and of supply chain risk. In the case of China, this approach does have its limits, though. The very appeal of China is often the sheer scale of the opportunity, in terms of sales or manufacturing capacity.

Companies can also manage risk through matching revenues against costs, assets against liabilities. In fact, they are used to managing structural foreign exchange rate exposure by matching cost and revenues in the same currency. A further benefit of the Localizer or "China-for-China" strategy is a similar supply–sales matching, which partly hedges the risk of deteriorating bilateral relations. Geopolitical risk persists when diplomatic tensions lead to a company's China operations being targeted by consumers or the Chinese government based on their nationality. By contrast, Sourcer and Exporter strategies are inherently at risk from disruptions in cross-border relations, increasing protectionism or disrupted customs clearance.

Holding buffer stock is a standard operational strategy to protect against external shocks and damaging disruptions. It provides some protection at the cost of carrying stock that is not strictly necessary when all is running smoothly. It is, in other words, a form of insurance. In a riskier world, it is worth paying higher insurance premiums. The concept of "buffer stock" embraces more than physical goods. The same thinking applies to all forms of organizational redundancy or "excess capacity", in areas such as management leadership talent, supplier capacity and information systems. Such redundancy means that the organization is more able to adapt if and when key linkages are disrupted: that there is more than one way to execute a certain set of tasks. Although these actions improve resilience, they also, typically, add cost. For those companies with sizeable, profitable market positions in China, this is a manageable additional cost of doing business. For those with weaker, less competitive positions, however, these costs may tilt the decision towards exit.

AGILITY AT THE GLOBAL LEVEL

Resilience alone, with its connotations of stability and returning to the status quo ante, is not enough. The term "agility" better captures how companies need to decide and act in the face of changing conditions. One characterization of agility is "the ability of a company to keep questioning and changing its course of action strategically".[25] Strategic agility enables a firm to change and adjust quickly without losing momentum, which increases its viability in uncertain, volatile and rapidly changing environments.

Multinationals have long been familiar with a faster-paced business environment in China. The most successful have developed agile organizations that can compete effectively with strong Chinese competitors operating at "China speed". The greater volatility in international relations has heightened the need too for agility at the global level when managing China within the corporate portfolio. It may now be changes in the United States or Europe that have the biggest impact on the China business, rather than changes in China itself. Companies need to probe and see what makes most sense, continually testing conclusions. At the operating level, "agile" methodologies derived from software management methodologies have become popular.[26] A similar mindset is needed at the strategic level. At its simplest, this means regularly bringing together those with the right knowledge and experience in all aspects to assess the changing situation, evaluate options, decide and execute rapidly.

In practice, this is much more challenging in an environment of diverging geopolitical perspectives, limited information and constrained travel to China. The European Chamber of Commerce in China has concluded that "senior decision-makers from headquarters are also being deprived of first-hand China experience, which is resulting in less understanding of – and therefore less tolerance towards – China ... A shift in mindset leads managers to believe that the uncertainty of the geopolitical environment immediately cuts through to the level of company relationships."[27] Staff in headquarters start to consider alternative scenarios for the China business. If the China business leaders are *not* involved, these discussions risk missing key aspects of what is really happening on the ground. If they *are* involved, they may find it hard to communicate their own perspectives in a credible way: the lack of shared experience and shared assumptions may limit trust. Unspoken in the discussion may be the accusation that "you are saying that only because you are Chinese or because the CPC is listening". Leaders in the China business may also find such discussions demotivating and destabilizing – so much so that they may decide to leave and work elsewhere, given the competition for talent in China. The push for greater localization is bringing greater autonomy to China business leaders just when the China strategy has greater interdependencies with the rest of the global business.

Investments of time and money to build trust and connectivity between those in China and those elsewhere in the company are more important than ever. China advisory boards, made up of seasoned individuals, can provide useful guidance and judgement when they bring experience across business and government in China and of multinational business. This can help both the China business and global leadership as they navigate shifting dynamics.

Companies can also prepare better how to respond to changes in the global environment as it relates to China. Scenario planning and war-gaming techniques sensitize business leaders to the decisions they might have to take in widely varying situations. They help leaders stay alert to early warning signs that such situations requiring action are indeed developing. And they identify actions and contingency plans that leaders can take now so as to be better prepared.

What would happen if Xi Jinping were to fall under the proverbial bus, or under his personal Red Flag limousine? Or if the US government applied sanctions to doing business with China in the way that it did to Russia? Unsurprisingly, the Chinese government is reported to have analysed just such a scenario.[28] Businesses can and should apply the same techniques. In the 1970s Shell pioneered the development of scenario planning as a way to explore and prepare for uncertain future developments in the global economy. Scenarios represent alternative futures that the company may need to confront and succeed in. They are "plausible and challenging descriptions of the future landscape. They stretch our [Shell] thinking and help us to make crucial choices in times of uncertainty and transitions."[29] Pierre Wack, one of the initiators of Shell's scenario planning, observed that business forecasts tend to be wrong when they are needed most – in anticipating "major shifts in the business environment that make whole strategies obsolete".[30] The next, concluding chapter introduces some simple overall scenarios for China's relations with the world.

War-gaming also helps. The United States and China both stage repeated war games in which they envisage how China might seek to take control of Taiwan and how the United States might react. Business war games simulate a set of business conditions and then challenge executives to design successful strategies that are able to evolve with the changing nature of the environment.[31] This approach is most valuable in highly interactive, uncertain situations, when there are many stakeholders or actors, each with different objectives and different tools at their disposal and drawing on different information sources. Forced to think themselves into these different roles, managers gain a better understanding of how and why others may act. They are particularly valuable now when there are such divergent perspectives between political leaders in the United States, China and elsewhere. War games can result in unexpected outcomes and provide a way for managers to build some "muscle memory" of how to act in unfamiliar situations under pressure.

HAVING AN EXIT PLAN

The speed with which many, but not all, companies left Russia in the wake of the Ukraine invasion has highlighted how rapidly business circumstances can change. Not all decisions are a question of adjustments at the margin. Sometimes binary, rapid action is required. The need is to prepare and be ready to act in a range of different situations.

Many companies leaving Russia found there were no easy options either transferring businesses – often at a steep discount – to local partners or closing down, with resultant lay-offs. Following the 2008 financial crisis, financial regulators now require the largest banks to prepare a "living will". This "must describe the company's strategy for rapid and orderly resolution in the event of material financial distress or failure of the company, as well as include both public and confidential sections".[32] Multinationals with significant operations in China would do well to prepare their own such plan. They do need to recognize the sensitivity of such a document, however, and the potential repercussions on key relationships were it to become public.

Conclusion: navigating the contradictions in China's ambitions

For Mao Zedong, in his 1937 essay *On Contradiction*,[1] contradiction played a central role in all matters of ideology, politics and policy. Mao argued that contradiction was the source of all movement and life in universe and society. This is not contradiction in the sense of logical inconsistency. It is, instead, the coming together of opposing forces, out of which a unity or synthesis arises that allows for progress. Eighty years later, at the 19th National Congress of the CPC in October 2017, Xi Jinping stated a change in the principal contradiction facing Chinese society. "What we now face is the contradiction between unbalanced and inadequate development and the people's ever-growing needs for a better life," Xi announced. "The evolution of the principal contradiction represents a historic shift that affects the whole landscape and that creates many new demands for the work of the Party and the country."[2] By resolving and managing the tensions in this "contradiction", China is to achieve greater prosperity and strength. This is by no means an easy task, and it has not become easier in the last few years.

As outlined in Part I, Dual Circulation Strategy provides both the framework and a series of strategic choices for China's future economic development. It makes a sharp distinction between the realm of internal circulation, in which Xi Jinping and the CPC "lead everything", and the world of external circulation. Dual Circulation prioritizes the internal and lays out a vision for mutual reinforcement between the internal and external. A look back over the past 150 years described how Chinese leaders consistently grappled with the questions of how to engage with the rest of the world and the meaning of self-reliance. Dual Circulation marks an adjustment rather than a radical change, but it is still a distinct shift from the years of "reform and opening up" in a globalizing world. The economic logic of Dual Circulation is just one of many pieces in what Chapter 3 described as the China policy puzzle. The role of Xi Jinping and of the CPC makes the development of the Chinese economy more than a matter of economic concepts alone. Xiconomics adds security, ideology and control into the drive for economic prosperity. A look at two of Xi's speeches in Chapter 4 highlighted Xi's personalized observations on character and ideology, alongside more technocratic economic ambitions.

Part II explored both the promise and potential reality of Dual Circulation for China. There is the promise of a stronger, more competitive China, playing an active role overseas; a China that is self-reliant, with a burgeoning consumer economy at home. It is a China that seeks strategic autonomy and secures its citizens' prosperity without excessive reliance on other countries, while encouraging the dependence of others on China. The ambitions are clear. What is unclear is whether these ambitions will come to pass. At home, growth and productivity improvements have slowed, although China has become a much more innovative economy in emerging technologies. The broader economic climate is one of uncertainty: uncertainty about whether security and ideology matters will keep dampening economic growth or whether business can adjust – as it has so often beforehand – and will find a way to continue to prosper. There is uncertainty too about the commitment to economic reform. The latest initiative draws on the logic of circulation to argue for a "national unified market". This would bring benefits for business and for economic productivity, but implementation requires sustained commitment and the focused exercise of power to overcome institutional resistance. Finally, it is unclear how quickly consumer and business confidence will recover from both the physical and psychological constraints of the zero-Covid-19 policy, with its repeated and sudden lockdowns. Yet, despite booming exports in the short term, it is indeed internal circulation that must power future Chinese growth on a sustainable basis, however weak domestic demand is as a result of Covid-19 lockdowns and a declining real estate market.

Dual Circulation is by no means a closing off from the world: China will remain active overseas. China's influence will increase through engagement in finance, technology and trade, although the extent of this engagement will rest too on a strong economy at home. Dual Circulation is clear on the benefits that China seeks to reap from the rest of the world, in terms of know-how, technology and export markets. What is much less clear is whether others will be happy to continue providing such benefits – or on what terms.

Although Xi emphasizes his new principal contradiction, its focus is on the forces within Chinese society alone. Indeed, the vision of Dual Circulation is centred squarely on what China wants and what China will do. As such, it neglects the interests and ambitions of other countries. There are in fact two additional contradictions that will be critical in determining success or failure.

TWO CONTRADICTIONS

Xi's formulation of the principal contradiction makes no mention of two more fundamental contradictions that China will need to address if it is to succeed. The first is the contradiction between separation and connection or between self-reliance and openness. The second is between what China is seeking and the fact that other countries seek similar influence and autonomy. For Dual Circulation to yield its intended benefits, China's political and business leaders need to address both contradictions. As a reminder, these contradictions are not meant as insuperable logical inconsistencies that make success impossible. Instead, they should spur a focus on creative ways to address them. Such contradictions are well known in the corporate world. Multinational companies have long faced the contradiction between being global and being local. The word "glocal" was coined to capture the ambition of being both at the same time. Realizing the ambition takes imagination, effort and practical application; it is not an impossibility.

The opposition between separation and connection may be the easier of the two to resolve. It is indeed false to argue that China must be either "open" or "closed". The aspiration to reap the benefits of openness and global integration together with the benefits and control of autonomy is a natural and worthy one. It is also one that other countries have in their sights. But finding ways to do this, issue by issue and sector by sector, takes a lot of work. Chapter 2 examined different approaches that China's leaders have taken to this perennial question in previous decades. There are parallels here with the question as to how developed the "rule of law" is in an economy. The rule of law, which allows for the enforcement of property rights, has been found to play an important role in economic development. Yet, in China, legal decisions are subordinate to the decisions of the CPC, and so ultimately subject to political influence – and the economy has boomed. Political scientist Francis Fukuyama has written of the need for a rule of law that is "good enough" for the protection of certain economic and individual rights rather than pursuing perfection.[3] Can self-reliance and openness both be simultaneously "good enough" in China? Or does an absolutist approach to self-reliance thwart openness? Finding some way to manage this tension should be feasible.

The bigger contradiction is that what China wants is also what other countries want. For example, Japan is debating how it can achieve strategic autonomy and strategic indispensability.[4] Like China, Japan has identified semiconductors and cloud services as areas in which it wants to build its own capabilities. The European Union talks of gaining "strategic autonomy". And the United States seeks to preserve its strategic indispensability and ability to influence and coerce other nations. A simplistic but costly way in which all can achieve autonomy is through decoupling and autarky. For China, and others, such a choice brings self-reliance but not openness and integration. It is likely to have exorbitant economic costs. It also precludes the achievement of strategic indispensability on a global level. It is choosing one side of the contradiction rather than finding a resolution.

If each country is to some extent indispensable for the others, then the world remains one of interdependence. In fact, this may be the best description of today's world. The challenge is for no one side to abuse the influence that it has over others. Doing so makes the risk of dependence more tangible and sparks a reaction. When Russia switches off the Nord Stream gas pipeline, European countries rethink their energy strategy. When the United States uses the US dollar as a tool of sanction and coercion, so countries, China included, look for alternatives. So too, when China uses market access or its export capacity as a tool of economic coercion, other countries look to do business elsewhere. For most countries, it is unimaginable to sever economic ties with China completely.

Significant adjustment is possible over a longer time frame, however. The rapid rise of China, and now of Vietnam, demonstrates this. What is up for debate currently is the extent of trading and investment relations with China, especially in the area of technology. For China and others too, success means finding a balance whereby all parties to an agreement or business deal see genuine advantage for themselves. Such an approach will be needed if China is to have a significant role in shaping external circulation. If China is to "make the foreign serve China", then China will need to serve the foreign, too.

Managing through and resolving the two contradictions outlined above, as well as the many lesser ones, requires creativity, adaptability, persistence and engagement with others. The actions of other global leaders are important, in particular those of the US president, whoever holds power in Washington. But, for China, ultimately it is Chinese leadership that matters. In 2021 Xinhua published a video documentary, *Xi Jinping as Crisis Manager.* It highlights the many crises that Xi has dealt with, citing corruption, poverty alleviation, environmental problems and Covid-19. By 2022 Xi's record on Covid-19 was subject to much more criticism at home and abroad.

Whether China is successful in its ambitions rests in large part on the choices made at the very top: on which priorities are chosen in matters of economics, security and ideology or values. In Xi's work report to the 20th Party Congress, Marxist-Leninism, Party-building and, in the broadest sense, national security featured more prominently than the economy. Once again, state-owned business appeared to be more in favour than the private sector. Overall, however, the message was one of continuity in the priorities of the past few years, rather than a further change. The change from 2012, a time of absolute focus on economic growth, was nonetheless very clear.

But China's success rests too on how well the linkages between security, economy and values are understood, and how well policies are then implemented. Common Prosperity can help create a larger consuming society or it can choke off business incentives. National security can go hand in hand with technological innovation and upgrading or it can rule out attractive commercial opportunities. All this will shape how businesses, consumers and investors respond and innovate, in China and overseas.

SCENARIOS FOR THE FUTURE

What actually happens – what business landscape multinationals will face in China and globally – depends on a myriad of actions and reactions (e.g. how does China respond to new US technology controls?); on what "works" and what doesn't (e.g. how effective is China at accelerating development of its own semiconductor capabilities?); and – in the words of one-time British prime minister Harold Macmillan – on "events, dear boy, events": unexpected changes such as Covid-19 and the Ukraine war.

For business leaders, it is more important than ever to be prepared for future changes. They need to be aware of the range of possible outcomes and understand the implications for their own company. Four scenarios that outline different relations between China and other countries are presented here as a way to organize the discussion. These four scenarios both influence – and are influenced by – the critical question of how successful China is in its own economic and innovation ambitions. Success for China is to be measured both in absolute terms and in relative terms – to the United States, in particular.

Relations at the global level can be described along two dimensions (Figure C.1).

1. *Connection versus separation.* How connected and open are economic relations between China and the rest of the world? Different bilateral relations will evolve in different ways. Some countries will have much closer relations with China than others.
2. *Antagonism versus acceptance.* How antagonistic or mutually accepting are relations between China and the rest of the world? An antagonistic stance could emerge primarily from China, the United States or another country. It may or may not be viewed by others as being "justified". Again, different bilateral relations may evolve differently; the United States may be more antagonistic towards China than major Asian countries.

The first scenario, "Globalization 1.0", would represent a return to the world of 2015 and beforehand. It offers renewed economic integration based on the benefits of trade and interdependence. Multinationals know well how to succeed in such a world. There are no significant signs that such a world will return, however. Chapter 7 highlighted the

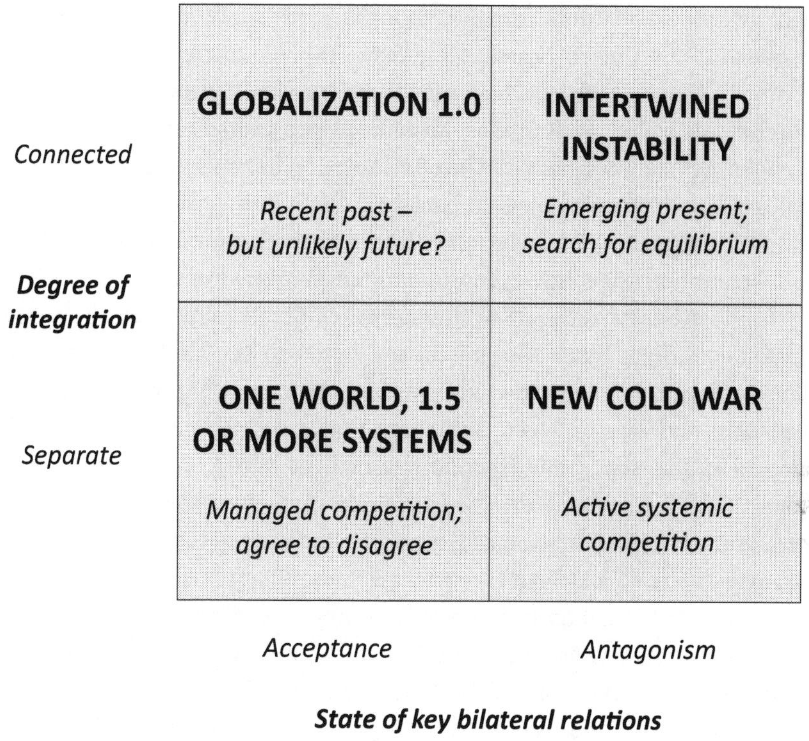

Connected	**GLOBALIZATION 1.0** *Recent past – but unlikely future?*	**INTERTWINED INSTABILITY** *Emerging present; search for equilibrium*
Degree of integration Separate	**ONE WORLD, 1.5 OR MORE SYSTEMS** *Managed competition; agree to disagree*	**NEW COLD WAR** *Active systemic competition*
	Acceptance	*Antagonism*

State of key bilateral relations

Figure C.1 Four simple scenarios

tensions and contradictions between what China wants from the rest of the world and what others seek. Nonetheless, although a reversion to the past seems unlikely today, the unexpected can sometimes occur.

A second scenario, "Intertwined instability", appears more likely. The economic benefits of integration result in continued interdependence, yet differences are expressed vocally. Each country takes policy actions to protect its own interests, with the emphasis on national security, industrial strategy (especially in technology) and protecting the nation's values. It is a "noisy" world, in two senses of the word "noisy". There are many loud and mostly rhetorical exchanges between countries, expressing their displeasure at others. It also remains hard to decode the underlying "signal" of continued integration from the "noise" of policy tweaks and changes that run counter to integration. Through this noise, trade and investment flows continue strongly. Some companies will become collateral damage, though, in the fallout from political moves in the United States, China or other countries. Lotte lost its China business. High-end US semiconductor exports to China are more tightly controlled. Paying close attention to understand what is really happening becomes critical. The contradiction between antagonism and integration leads to a constant back-and-forth in the search for equilibrium in relationships. Uncertainty is endemic. Economic reality speaks a different language, however: of continued business deals.

In the other two scenarios, there is much greater separation between major economic blocs – in particular, between the United States and China. The third scenario envisages acceptance that there are different economic systems between China and Western countries and that each should evolve separately. Technology evolves based on different technical standards. Businesses face very different regulatory and political environments. Multinational businesses need then to become ever more ambidextrous, to allow them to succeed in both systems while providing much of the connectivity between the different environments. Yet the state of mutual acceptance means that such ambidexterity and connectivity is valued and respected by stakeholders on all sides.

The phrase "One World, Two Systems" has often been used to describe this outcome. Such a clear and stark division of the world seems unlikely. It also begs the question of the geographic scope of each "system". China is unlikely to want or be able to cut itself off from the rest of the world economically. Living standards in China would suffer from such deglobalization,[5] although there may be political benefits for the CPC in certain situations. Trade and technology flows remain important, China imports much of its food, energy and semiconductors, and the export sector provides many jobs. A more likely outcome is the emergence of a "multipolar" world.[6] Each "pole" attracts activity and has certain norms and ways of operating. There is competition but no sharp dividing lines between the reach of each pole's influence. There then remains one overall system. For many countries, China and Western economies alike maintain positions of influence based on trade, investment, technology, standards, agreements and norms. Other poles also emerge, either in specific sectors or more broadly. Although the roles of the European Union and India are most discussed, even South Korea has rapidly gained a position of influence and soft power in the areas of music and entertainment. Rather than One World, Two Systems, this may be a world of 1.5 – or even three or four – systems depending on the field of activity.

For most countries in the world, China is an important – often the most important – trading partner. Bilahari Kausikan, former permanent secretary of the Singapore Foreign Ministry, has emphasized that the prospect is for competition within a single global system rather than between two different systems. Competition within a system, he argues, depends on defining and occupying a position and defending it against others: "Competition within a system is not and cannot be about one system displacing another system. It cannot even be about any vital part of the system disrupting any other vital part of the system in any way that could fundamentally damage the entire system."[7] Expressed differently, although economic relations between the United States and China are decoupling to an extent, both countries remain actively engaged economically with the rest of the world.

The fourth scenario, "New Cold War", describes a world of continued antagonism and separate systems. It is this antagonism that marks out the difference from the third scenario. Interpreted strictly, a new Cold War also seems unlikely – or, rather, the phrasing is ill suited to the more integrated global economy of today. Replicating the US–Soviet Cold War rivalry implies a massive reduction in economic relations between the United States and China. Former British diplomat and China expert Charles Parton has phrased the situation as "[n]ot Cold War, but a Values War".[8] A more likely scenario is continued antagonism – in both "noise" and "substance", that stops short of military confrontation – combined with significantly greater separation than today, especially in technology. Parton phrases this as "not decoupling but divergence". Such continuing antagonism makes life much more difficult for Western multinationals. Many stakeholders question the value and values of adapting to do business successfully in both the West and China. Continued antagonism today appears more likely than acceptance. Domestic political considerations play a role for many, as do deeply held concerns on each side about the actions of other countries. The question is, rather, how far the antagonism will go.

How the Chinese economy develops – in terms of growth, innovation and the role of private business – plays an important role too.

Fundamentally, this determines how attractive the Chinese market is for multinationals. But it also has an important impact on which geopolitical scenarios develop. It influences China's approach to integration and antagonism – though not necessarily in a simple way. Which China is more likely to be antagonistic: an economically dynamic China looking for a stronger role in the world; or an economically stagnant China still needing technology from the rest of the world, but potentially taking a more nationalist stance to compensate for economic shortcomings? An economically strong China will pursue integration on its own terms, but also seek to reshape the world economy more actively. The greater its technological strength and economic vitality, the stronger the role it will play in setting global standards, the more countries will look to China for new technologies and the greater the resources available to China to pursue a global leadership role. An economically weak China may turn inwards, reach out anew for the benefits of global integration or focus on disruptive non-economic engagement in the way that Russia has.

SUMMING IT UP FOR BUSINESS

Part III described what all this means for foreign companies active in China. Companies have pursued four different strategies for China, with many larger companies blending several of these together within their business. Localizers have concentrated on building a business in China for Chinese customers. Exporters continue to serve China from overseas. Sourcers look instead to manufacture in China for other markets. Separators decide that China is not for them. Xiconomics and Dual Circulation means that Localizers need to localize more – unless they decide that market requirements and investments needed are not commercially attractive, and they decide to leave. Many Exporters consider becoming Localizers, although this can seem a daunting move amid so much uncertainty. For others, continuing as an Exporter is feasible and appropriate, albeit likely to become increasingly difficult in the face of localization needs in China. Sourcers increasingly need to diversify away from China by adding capacity in other countries, although China will remain an important manufacturing base for years to come. Sourcers can also become Upgraders, taking advantage of China's technology upgrading and manufacture more sophisticated products in China. Separators need to re-evaluate. Some have already become Localizers as market liberalization opens up new opportunities. Others do not change their stance.

In parallel, all multinationals need to consider the linkages between their China business and the rest of their operations, especially headquarters. This requires a focus on ambidexterity and on connectivity, although Chapter 10 also highlighted the limits to ambidexterity. Values, corporate purpose, stakeholder pressures and the law all set limits here. The business context has become much more uncertain and volatile – in China and on a global level alike. This requires resilience and agility, both in terms of adaptation and risk diversification and in readiness for the need to move quickly and radically in response to extreme change in external conditions.

What, then, is the outlook for multinational business amid so much uncertainty and these divergent scenarios? The impact on individual companies differs widely based on the sector, nationality and strategy of each company. Which of the geopolitical scenarios described in Figure C.1 best describes the world also matters. Scenarios shape how much ambidexterity companies will require to succeed across divergent business environments and where it might hit limits. They determine whether the geopolitical context forces things to breaking point, so that companies need to choose which markets to exit. They also influence the value of the connectivity that multinationals can provide and the form that it takes. This is a form of Dual Circulation for multinationals. Companies aim to succeed in markedly different market contexts and then determine how "mutual reinforcement" can work between them.

Despite these uncertainties, several common observations hold

First, barring an economic and political meltdown, China remains a massive economy under any growth scenario. It both offers business potential in its own right and is an important component of global success for many multinationals. Craig Allen, president of the US–China Business Council, has expressed it as follows: "[I]f your competitors have

183

the scale of selling into China, but you don't; if your competitors are able to purchase from China, but you don't; if your competitors are allowed to have ventures in China, but you don't; you are systemically at a disadvantage not only to Europeans, Japanese, Korean, and others, but also to Chinese companies."[9] The "if"s have become much more relevant than beforehand, however. Nationality and geopolitics may simply make certain options for sales or procurement too costly, or preclude them entirely.

Second, multinational businesses can pursue a range of strategies in China, as outlined in Chapters 8 and 9. Localization to the China context is becoming more important than it ever was. This requires increasing ambidexterity in the global organization, both to ensure oversight and connectivity and to realize the full potential of a China presence. Success in China can bring new innovations that strengthen business globally.

How far and how successfully these strategies can be pursued depends in part on decisions external to the company. This mostly involves matters of national security, industrial strategy and values. However large the Chinese economy, foreign businesses now need to consider more extreme scenarios in which they need to limit, ring-fence or exit their China business as a result of policy decisions, or even military actions, taken by governments. In less extreme scenarios, companies continue to assess their commercial opportunity in the face of all these uncertainties and map out a strategy. More specifically, the outlook for foreign companies depends on four factors:

1. How much the Chinese government continues to welcome foreign involvement in specific sectors and how actively it supports Chinese competitors; how the Chinese business environment evolves, especially on issues of state intervention, values and ideology.

2. How extensively the Chinese government acts – or is perceived to act – in penalizing commercial interests of foreign companies during times of tension and disagreement with other governments.

3. How much the US government, the European Union and the government in countries where the company has its headquarters discourage, constrain or prohibit foreign company involvement in China; how strongly investors, consumers and employees outside China express critical views on the company's China strategy.

4. The company's own assessment of the overall risk–return trade-offs from operating in China and the impact on corporate ethical and reputational "red lines", relative to the other opportunities available.

Finally, beyond China, as multinationals do business around the world, they will increasingly encounter China's influence in other countries, as trading and diplomatic partner, as a standards-setter and innovator, as an investor, lender and exporter. How strong this influence is will depend on the strength of China's continued development. Multinationals need to build the right relationships and knowledge to incorporate this into their business.

The four factors listed above pose the knottiest challenges. As Chapter 11 explored, resilience and agility in the face of such uncertain, external factors is the only path forward. Success requires constant evaluation and re-evaluation of what China wants, what China says and what China does. "China" here is a shorthand for what Chinese people want as customers and employees, for competing Chinese companies, for government policy and for the direction in which Xi and the CPC take the country. The same is true for other countries where the multinational does business, too – especially the country where the corporate headquarters are based and, given their size and reach, the United States and the European Union.

The sudden decision that many Western companies made to withdraw from Russia in the wake of its 2022 invasion of Ukraine shows the need to be ready for extreme scenarios. These were mostly decisions taken by companies following their own assessment, not mandated legally by government. The Covid-19 lockdowns in China in 2022 shook foreign business perceptions on the unpredictabilities, costs and hardships of operating in China – even in Shanghai, a city that had always been seen (and saw itself) as different from, more international than, the rest of China. Suddenly more extreme options for the China business merited at least consideration and contingency planning. Equally, companies need to be ready for more positive scenarios, slim though the prospects may often appear – a China that recovers spectacularly and pursues economic reform; where foreign business continues to prosper; and where such success brings little or no opprobrium back home, at least outside the most sensitive technology sectors.

In the face of these uncertainties, foreign companies need not and must not be passive. The tempo of business runs rapidly, regardless of the political cycle. Multinational business has a valuable role to play in providing balance and sustainability in the global economy, as a by-product of its own commercial objectives. In a world of differences, there is value to the inherently cross-border, cross-cultural nature of multinational businesses and their focus on reaching agreement on deals that benefit all involved. This is different from discredited arguments of *Wandel durch Handel* (change through trade) or the long-standing American argument that China might become a democracy as a result of integration into the world economy. There is no sign at the moment that such convergence will happen. Instead, the approach accepts and respects differences and then finds mutual agreement where that is possible.

Yet the nature of the differences means that a focus on security and values is also needed. Companies have a role to play there too. Determining which transfers of technology pose a true security threat requires granular analysis. Those in government often lack the deep knowledge required to make a thorough assessment. Companies can help here, although governments need also to recognize that companies can make self-interested commercial arguments if left unchallenged. On issues of values too, companies will be called on to make tough decisions, consistent with their own purpose and the views of their key stakeholders. Overall, however, overblown rhetoric and extreme nationalism should not stand in the way of successful business engagement.

Notes

INTRODUCTION

1. "President Xi Jinping's message to the Davos Agenda in full". World Economic Forum, 17 January 2022. www.weforum.org/agenda/2022/01/address-chinese-president-xi-jinping-2022-world-economic-forum-virtual-session.
2. J. Xi, "Certain major issues for our national medium- to long-term economic and social development strategy". *Qiushi*, 1 November 2020. https://cset.georgetown.edu/wp-content/uploads/t0235_Qiushi_Xi_economy_EN-1.pdf.
3. J. Mai, "'Xiconomics': the one word set to define China's long-term agenda". *South China Morning Post*, 22 December 2017. www.scmp.com/news/china/economy/article/2125330/xiconomics-one-word-set-define-chinas-long-term-agenda.
4. Xinhua, "Xiconomics: China's vision on economic governance inspiration for global development". *China Daily*, 25 March 2022. www.chinadaily.com.cn/a/202203/25/WS623cb99ea310fd2b29e5324d.html.
5. W. Lam, "What is 'Xiconomics'?". Jamestown Foundation, 12 January 2018. https://jamestown.org/program/what-is-xiconomics.
6. C. Yu, "China's antimonopoly efforts bear fruit". *China Daily*, 13 March 2022. http://global.chinadaily.com.cn/a/202203/13/WS622dd411a310cdd39bc8c479.html.
7. China Project, "What happened at China's 19th Party Congress". 2 November 2017. https://thechinaproject.com/2017/11/02/what-happened-19th-party-congress.
8. China Leadership Monitor, "Featured excerpt from *The Long Game: China's Grand Strategy to Displace American Order*". 1 September 2021. www.prcleader.org/dashi.
9. China Media Project, "One page says it all". 19 October 2017. https://chinamediaproject.org/2017/10/19/one-page-says-it-all.

CHAPTER 1

1. Xi, "Certain major issues".
2. W. Han, "Looking forward to the 14th Five-Year Plan". Sina Finance, 30 October 2020. https://finance.sina.com.cn/review/jcgc/2020-10-30/doc-iiznctkc8527378.shtml.
3. Teller Report, "'An important meeting of overall and historical significance'". 30 October 2020. www.tellerreport.com/news/2020-10-30-%22an-important-meeting-of-overall-and-historical-significance%22-the-central-committee-of-the-communist-party-of-china-held-a-press-conference-to-interpret-the-spirit-of-the-fifth-plenary-session-of-the-19th-cpc-central-committee-.Hy8ved3tOD.html.
4. J. Y. Lin, "New structural economics: a framework for rethinking development", Policy Research Working Paper 5197 (Washington, DC: World Bank, 2013). https://openknowledge.worldbank.org/handle/10986/19919.
5. J. Y. Lin & X. Wang, "Dual Circulation: a New Structural Economics view of development". *Journal of Chinese Economic and Business Studies* 20 (4) (2022), 303–22. https://doi.org/10.1080/14765284.2021.1929793
6. *Ibid.*, p. 303.
7. *Ibid.*, p. 304.
8. *Ibid.*, p. 305.
9. A. Sheng, "Dual circulation is a strategic process, not a theory". East Asia Forum, 20 January 2021. www.eastasiaforum.org/2021/01/20/dual-circulation-is-a-strategic-process-not-a-theory.
10. J. Xi, "Understanding the new development stage, applying the new development philosophy, and creating a new development dynamic". *Qiushi*, 8 July 2021. http://en.qstheory.cn/2021-07/08/c_641137.htm.
11. Lin & Wang, "Dual circulation", p. 303.
12. J. Wang, "Choose the right long-term development strategy: a framework for 'the great international circulation' economic development strategy". *Economic Daily*, 5 January 1988.
13. Z. Wang, "In Xi's own words: what's 'dual circulation'? Why it's new development stage". Pekingnology, 6 May 2021. www.pekingnology.com/p/in-xis-own-words-whats-dual-circulation.
14. Lin & Wang, "Dual circulation", p. 304.
15. Xi, "Understanding the new development stage".
16. C. Ballentine, "US lifts ban that kept ZTE from doing business with American suppliers". *New York Times*, 13 July 2018. www.nytimes.com/2018/07/13/business/zte-ban-trump.html.
17. M. Green & S. Kennedy, "US business leaders not ready for the next US–China crisis". Center for Strategic & International Studies, 16 May 2022. www.csis.org/analysis/us-business-leaders-not-ready-next-us-china-crisis.
18. M. Schuman, "Why Biden's block on chips to China is a big deal". *The Atlantic*, 25 October 2022. www.theatlantic.com/international/archive/2022/10/biden-export-control-microchips-china/671848.

19. Lin & Wang, "Dual Circulation", p. 304.
20. Xi, "Understanding the new development stage".
21. J. Blanchette & A. Polk, "Dual circulation and China's new hedged integration strategy". Center for Strategic & International Studies, 24 August 2020. www.csis.org/analysis/dual-circulation-and-chinas-new-hedged-integration-strategy.
22. Lin & Wang, "Dual Circulation", p. 318.

CHAPTER 2

1. N. Ahrens, "Innovation and the visible hand: China, indigenous innovation, and the role of government procurement", Carnegie Papers 114 (Washington, DC: Carnegie Endowment for International Peace, 2010). https://carnegieendowment.org/files/indigenous_innovation.pdf.
2. McKinsey Global Institute, *From "Made in China" to "Sold in China": The Rise of the Chinese Urban Consumer* (Washington, DC: McKinsey Global Institute, 2006). www.mckinsey.com/~/media/mckinsey/featured%20 insights/urbanization/from%20made%20in%20china%20to%20sold%20 in%20china/mgi_rise_of_chinese_urban_consumer_full_report.pdf.
3. World Bank, "Household and final consumption expenditures 2015". https://data.worldbank.org/indicator/NE.CON.PRVT.KD?locations=CN.
4. PRC State Council, "Notice of the State Council on the publication of 'Made in China 2025'". 10 March 2022. https://cset.georgetown.edu/publication/notice-of-the-state-council-on-the-publication-of-made-in-china-2025.
5. M. Zenglein & A. Holzmann, "Evolving Made in China 2025: China's industrial policy in the quest for global tech leadership", MERICS Paper on China 8 (Berlin: Mercator Institute for China Studies, 2019). www.merics.org/en/report/evolving-made-china-2025.
6. M. Komesaroff, "Make the foreign serve China: how foreign science and technology helped China dominate global metallurgical industries", Occasional Paper 2 (Washington, DC: Center for Strategic & International Studies, 2017). https://csis-website-prod.s3.amazonaws.com/s3fs-public/publication/170301_Komesaroff_MakeForeignServeChina.pdf.
7. A.-M. Brady, *Making the Foreign Serve China: Managing Foreigners in the People's Republic* (Lanham, MD: Rowman & Littlefield, 2003).
8. J. Desjardins, "2,000 years of economic history in one chart". Visual Capitalist, 8 September 2017. www.visualcapitalist.com/2000-years-economic-history-one-chart.
9. Ch'ien Lung (Qianlong), "Letter to George III". https://marcuse.faculty.hist ory.ucsb.edu/classes/2c/texts/1792QianlongLetterGeorgeIII.htm.
10. D. Roos, "The Silk Road: 8 goods traded along the ancient network". History, 20 September 2021. www.history.com/news/silk-road-trade-goods.

11. J. Carter, "Lord Macartney, China, and the convenient lies of history". China Project, 9 September 2020. https://supchina.com/2020/09/09/lord-macartney-china-and-the-convenient-lies-of-history.

12. X. Zhou, "Chinese historian's review of past isolationist policy goes viral, reflecting unease over closed borders, lockdowns, crackdowns". *South China Morning Post*, 30 August 2022. www.scmp.com/news/china/article/3190589/chinese-historians-review-past-isolationist-policy-goes-viral-reflecting.

13. M. Cartwright, "The seven voyages of Zheng He". World History Encyclopaedia, 7 February 2019. www.worldhistory.org/article/1334/the-seven-voyages-of-zheng-he.

14. King's College History Department, "China in the 20th century". https://departments.kings.edu/history/20c/china.html.

15. W. Ernst, "The foreign trade policy of the Mao Tse-tung clique". *Chinese Economic Studies* 3 (1) (1969), 33–47.

16. N. Thomas, "Mao redux: the enduring relevance of self-reliance in China". Macro Polo, 25 April 2019. https://macropolo.org/analysis/china-self-reliance-xi-jin-ping-mao.

17. K. Mishra, "Chinese way of nation building: re interpreting the early Maoist era". *Vidyasagar University Journal of History* 7 (2018), 44–52. www.http://inet.vidyasagar.ac.in:8080/jspui/bitstream/123456789/6465/1/04_Keshav%20Mishra.pdf; Ernst, "The foreign trade policy of the Mao Tse-tung clique".

18. Thomas, "Mao redux".

19. *Ibid.*

20. The Third Plenary Session of the 11th Central Committee of the Chinese Communist Party was a pivotal meeting of the Central Committee of the Chinese Communist Party, held in Beijing from 18 to 22 December 1978, and it led to the commencement of "China's reform and opening up policy".

21. Chinese Communism Subject Archive, "Resolution on certain questions in the history of our Party since the founding of the People's Republic of China". www.marxists.org/subject/china/documents/cpc/history/01.htm.

22. Komesaroff, "Make the foreign serve China".

23. P. Lamy, "China was strong when it opened to the world", WTO director general's speech in Shanghai, 6 September 2006. www.wto.org/english/news_e/sppl_e/sppl_e.htm.

24. B. Hofman, "Reflections on forty years of China's reforms". World Bank, 1 February 2018. https://blogs.worldbank.org/eastasiapacific/reflections-on-forty-years-of-china-reforms.

CHAPTER 3

1. Xinhua, "High-quality development paves China's path toward modernization". Xinhua News, 3 June 2022. https://english.news.cn/20220306/50b9980eee4a4321aeee636a3e64a6ec/c.html.

2. China Media Project, "The CMP dictionary: core". 13 June 2022. https://chinamediaproject.org/the_ccp_dictionary/the-core.

3. Xinhua, "Xi: principal contradiction facing Chinese society has evolved in new era". 18 October 2017. http://english.www.gov.cn/news/top_news/2017/10/18/content_281475912458156.htm.

4. Xinhua, "China focus: Xi's thought enshrined in CPC constitution". 24 October 2017. www.xinhuanet.com/english/2017-10/24/c_136702802.htm.

5. Xinhua, 受权发布:中国共产党章程 ["CPC constitution"]. www.xinhuanet.com//politics/19cpcnc/2017-10/28/c_1121870794.htm.

6. Swiss Institute for Global Affairs, "Small yet influential: China's leading small groups". 1 February 2022. www.globalaffairs.ch/2022/02/01/small-yet-influential-china-s-leading-small-groups.

7. R. Huang & J. Henderson, "From fear to behavior modification: Beijing entrenches corruption fight". MacroPolo, 8 March 2022. https://macropolo.org/beijing-entrenches-corruption-fight/?rp=e.

8. W. Zheng, "China's Xi Jinping to his top leadership: 'no mercy' to fight against corruption". *South China Morning Post*, 12 January 2022. www.scmp.com/news/china/politics/article/3163016/xi-jinping-his-top-leadership-no-mercy-fight-against-corruption.

9. Huang & Henderson, "From fear to behavior modification".

10. Reuters, "China to enshrine Xi's thought into state constitution amid national 'fervor'". 19 January 2018. www.reuters.com/article/us-china-politics-idUSKBN1F812P.

11. Xinhua, 扬帆破浪再启航—以习近平同志为核心的党中央推进党和国家机构改革 纪实 ["Sail through the waves and set sail again – a documentary record of the Party Central Committee with Comrade Xi Jinping at the core promoting the reform of Party and state institutions"]. 2019. www.gov.cn/xinwen/2019-07/06/content_5406818.htm.

12. L. Li, "The muddled case against Xi Jinping's third term". London School of Economics, 31 March 2022. https://blogs.lse.ac.uk/cff/2022/03/31/the-muddled-case-against-xi-jinpings-third-term.

13. L. Shu, "A correct understanding of 'making the past serve the present'". *Chinese Studies in History* 11 (4) (1978), 42–7. www.tandfonline.com/doi/abs/10.2753/CSH0009-4633110442?journalCode=mcsh20.

14. C. Yu, "The fading legacy of Deng Xiaoping". *The Spectator*, 12 February 2022. www.spectator.co.uk/article/the-fading-legacy-of-deng-xiaoping.

15. Y. Tian, "China's Communist Party hails president Xi as 'helmsman'". Reuters, 12 November 2021. www.reuters.com/world/china/president-xi-is-helmsman-chinas-rejuvenation-says-party-official-2021-11-12

16. J. Xi, "Speech at a ceremony marking the centenary of the Communist Party of China", embassy of the PRC in Latvia. Ministry of Foreign Affairs, 1 July 2021. www.fmprc.gov.cn/ce/celv/eng/xwdt/t1889004.htm.

17. *The Economist*, "The Chinese dream: the role of Thomas Friedman". 15 August 2013. www.economist.com/analects/2013/08/15/the-role-of-thomas-friedman.

18. E. Feigenbaum, "The big bet at the heart of Xi Jinping's New Deal". Carnegie Endowment for International Peace, 27 November 2017. https:// carnegieendowment.org/2017/11/27/big-bet-at-heart-of-xi-jinping-s-new-deal-pub-74847.
19. PRC State Council, "China issues white paper on its democracy". 4 December 2021. http://english.www.gov.cn/archive/whitepaper/202112/04/content_WS61aae34fc6d0df57f98e6098.html.
20. *The Economist*, "To each according to his abilities: market reforms mean that China is becoming more unequal". 31 May 2001. www.economist.com/asia/2001/05/31/to-each-according-to-his-abilities.
21. J. Xi, "Solidly promoting Common Prosperity". *Qiushi*, 15 October 2021. www.qstheory.cn/dukan/qs/2021-10/15/c_1127959365.htm.
22. Cited in D. Roberts, "What is "common prosperity" and how will it change China and its relation with the world?". Atlantic Council, December 2021. www.atlanticcouncil.org/wp-content/uploads/2021/12/Common_Prosperity_IB_2021_1.pdf.
23. Xi, "Understanding the new development stage".
24. C. Liru, "China's period of historic opportunities". China Focus, 1 February 2018. www.chinausfocus.com/foreign-policy/chinas-period-of-historic-opportunities. R. Doshi, *The Long Game: China's Grand Strategy to Displace American Order* (Oxford: Oxford University Press, 2021).
25. Xinhua, "Xi Jinping meets with envoys attending 2017 annual conference on diplomatic envoys and delivers important speech". 28 December 2017. www.xinhuanet.com/politics/leaders/2017-12/28/c_1122181743.htm.
26. Xinhua, "Full text of remarks by Chinese President Xi Jinping at high-level meeting to commemorate 75th UN anniversary". *Qiushi*, 22 September 2020. http://en.qstheory.cn/2020-09/22/c_538079.htm.
27. Doshi, *The Long Game*.
28. J. Shi, "China says 'East is rising and West is declining', but has it been misunderstood?". *South China Morning Post*, 22 October 2021 www.scmp.com/news/china/diplomacy/article/3153379/china-says-east-rising-and-west-declining-has-it-been.
29. Xinhua, "Communiqué of the Fifth Plenum of the 19th Central Committee of the Communist Party of China". 29 October 2020. www.xinhuanet.com/politics/2020-10/29/c_1126674147.htm [hereafter "Communiqué"].
30. Xinhua, "Full text of the report to the 20th National Congress of the Communist Party of China". 25 October 2022. https://english.news.cn/20221025/8eb6f5239f984f01a2bc45b5b5db0c51/c.html.
31. J. Blanchette, "The edge of an abyss: Xi Jinping's overall national security outlook". China Leadership Monitor, 1 September 2022. www.prcleader.org/blanchette-september-2022.
32. S. Greitens, "How does China think about national security?". American Enterprise Institute, 6 September 2022. www.aei.org/articles/how-does-china-think-about-national-security.

33. J. Xi, *Xi Jinping on the Holistic Approach to National Security* [in Chinese] (Beijing: Central Party Literature Press, 2018).

34. S. Greitens, "Prepared testimony before the Senate Armed Services Committee hearing on 'The United States' strategic competition with China'". University of Texas, 8 June 2021. www.armed-services.senate.gov/imo/media/doc/06.08%20Greitens%20Testimony.pdf.

35. T. Culpan, "Didi's secrets risk China's Wall Street future". *Washington Post*, 29 November 2021. www.washingtonpost.com/business/didis-secrets-risk-chinas-wall-street-future/2021/11/28/d104ab72-50cd-11ec-83d2-d9dab0e23b7e_story.html.

36. E. Kania & L. Laskai, "Myths and realities of China's military-civil fusion strategy". Center for a New American Security, 28 January 2021. www.cnas.org/publications/reports/myths-and-realities-of-chinas-military-civil-fusion-strategy.

37. J. Nolan & W. Leutert, "Signing up or standing aside: disaggregating participation in China's Belt and Road Initiative". Brookings Institution, 5 November 2020. www.brookings.edu/articles/signing-up-or-standing-aside-disaggregating-participation-in-chinas-belt-and-road-initiative.

38. J. Hillman & M. McCalpin, "Watching Huawei's 'Safe Cities'", CSIS brief (Washington, DC: Center for Strategic and International Studies, 2019). https://csis-website-prod.s3.amazonaws.com/s3fs-public/publication/191030_HillmanMcCalpin_HuaweiSafeCity_layout_v4.pdf.

39. Lin & Wang, "Dual Circulation".

CHAPTER 4

1. Bloomberg, "Shocked investors scour Xi's old speeches to find next target". 5 August 2021. www.bloomberg.com/news/articles/2021-08-04/shocked-investors-scour-xi-s-old-speeches-to-find-next-target?sref=OYPzOH4r.

2. *Qiushi*, "Introduction to Qiushi Online". 16 June 2020. http://en.qstheory.cn/2020-06/16/c_461019.htm.

3. Xi, "Certain major issues".

4. J. Xi, "Making solid progress towards Common Prosperity". *Qiushi*, 18 January 2022. http://en.qstheory.cn/2022-01/18/c_699025.htm.

5. J. Costigan & G. Weber, "14th Five-Year Plan for national informatization", translation (Stanford, CA: Stanford Cyber Policy Center, 2022). https://digichina.stanford.edu/wp-content/uploads/2022/01/DigiChina-14th-Five-Year-Plan-for-National-Informatization.pdf.

6. Q. Chen, "China wants to put data to work as an economic resource – but how?". Stanford Cyber Policy Center, 9 February 2022. https://digichina.stanford.edu/work/china-wants-to-put-data-to-work-as-an-economic-resource-but-how.

7. L. Xin, "What's bigger than a mega-city? China's planned city clusters". *MIT Technology Review*, 28 April 2022. www.technologyreview.com/2021/04/28/1022557/china-city-cluster-urbanization-population-economy-environment.

8. Z. Ma, "Zhejiang details pilot zone for common prosperity". PRC State Council, 21 July 2021..

9. K. Brown, *CEO China: The Rise of Xi Jinping* (London: I. B. Tauris, 2016).

10. K. Brown, *Xi: A Study in Power* (London: Icon Books, 2022).

CHAPTER 5

1. Z. Yang, "Chinese companies are making their own semiconductors". Protocol, 13 March 2021. www.protocol.com/china/chinese-companies-make-own-semiconductors.

2. In inflation-adjusted US dollars: https://data.worldbank.org/country/CN.

3. N. O'Malley, "What if China saved the world and nobody noticed?". *The Age*, 20 August 2022. www.theage.com.au/environment/climate-change/what-if-china-saved-the-world-and-nobody-noticed-20220818-p5bavz.html.

4. Economic Intelligence Unit, "Recent challenges in reading China's GDP". 4 March 2021. www.eiu.com/n/recent-challenges-in-reading-chinas-gdp.

5. China Power, "Does China have an aging problem?". 15 February 2016. https://chinapower.csis.org/aging-problem.

6. World Bank, "Gross capital formation". https://data.worldbank.org/indicator/NE.GDI.TOTL.ZS.

7. S. Sheng, Y. Long & D. Wang, "Infrastructure investment has a vital role in stabilizing growth". *People's Daily*, 28 February 2022. http://en.people.cn/n3/2022/0228/c90000-9963597.html#.YhzFOsjglCY.twitter.

8. L. Brandt *et al.*, "China's productivity slowdown and future growth potential", Policy Research Working Paper 9298 (Washington, DC: World Bank, 2020). https://documents1.worldbank.org/curated/en/839401593007627879/pdf/Chinas-Productivity-Slowdown-and-Future-Growth-Potential.pdf.

9. L. Brandt *et al.*, "Recent productivity trends in China: evidence from macro- and firm-level data". *China: An International Journal* 20 (1), 93–113. https://muse.jhu.edu/article/848481/pdf.

10. The World Bank defines the "middle income trap" as a situation whereby a middle-income country fails to transition to a high-income economy because of rising costs and declining competitiveness. Few countries successfully manage the transition from low to middle to high income.

11. I. Roberts & B. Russell, "Long-term growth in China". Reserve Bank of Australia, 12 December 2019. www.rba.gov.au/publications/bulletin/2019/dec/long-term-growth-in-china.html.

12. *Ibid.*

13. E. Zhang & R. Woo, "China's exports gain steam but outlook cloudy as global growth cools". Reuters, 8 August 2022. www.reuters.com/mark ets/asia/chinas-export-growth-gains-steam-despite-weakening-global-demand-2022-08-07.
14. J. Authers, "China surprise data could spell r-e-c-e-s-s-i-o-n". Bloomberg, 16 August 2022. www.bloomberg.com/opinion/articles/2022-08-16/if-the-china-crisis-deepens-a-global-recession-will-be-much-harder-to-avoid.
15. McKinsey Global Institute, *China and the World: Inside the Dynamics of a Changing Relationship* (Washington, DC: McKinsey Global Institute, 2019). www.mckinsey.com/~/media/mckinsey/featured%20insights/china/china%20and%20the%20world%20inside%20the%20dynamics%20of%20a%20changing%20relationship/mgi-china-and-the-world-full-report-june-2019-vf.ashx.
16. Xi, "Solidly promoting Common Prosperity".
17. *Ibid.*
18. M. Pettis, "Will China's common prosperity upgrade dual circulation?". Carnegie Endowment for International Peace, 15 October 2021. https://carnegieendowment.org/chinafinancialmarkets/85571.
19. W. Qu, "China's path to informatisation", cited in R. Creemers, "China's cybersecurity regime: securing the smart state". Leiden Institute for Area Studies, 30 March 2022. https://papers.ssrn.com/sol3/papers.cfm?abstract_id=4070682.
20. M. Pettis, "China's economy needs institutional reform rather than additional capital deepening". Carnegie Endowment for International Peace, 24 July 2020. https://carnegieendowment.org/chinafinancialmark ets/82362.
21. G. Xiao, "China's national unified market". CF 40, 26 July 2022. www.cf40.com/en/news_detail/12765.html?_isa=1.
22. Xinhua, "China's unified market a vital boost for economic circulation". 17 May 2022. https://english.www.gov.cn/policies/policywatch/202205/17/content_WS628352ddc6d02e533532acba.html.
23. D. Zweig, "China's stalled 'Fifth Wave' – Zhu Rongji's reform package of 1998–2000". *Asian Survey* 41 (2), 231–47. https://library.fes.de/libalt/journ als/swetsfulltext/14218782.pdf.
24. W. Shen & Q. Li, "Vice Premier Liu He vows unwavering support for private sector". *Global Times*, 6 September 2021. www.globaltimes.cn/page/202 109/1233502.shtml.
25. P. Chovanec, "Guo Jin, Min Tui – the state advances, the private sector retreats". Seeking Alpha, 31 August 2010. https://seekingalpha.com/article/223160-guo-jin-min-tui-the-state-advances-the-private-sector-retreats.
26. R. Huang & N. Véron, "The private sector advances in China: the evolving ownership structures of the largest companies in the Xi era", Working Paper 22-3 (Washington, DC: Peterson Institute for International Economics, 2022). www.piie.com/publications/working-papers/private-sector-advances-china-evolving-ownership-structures-largest.

27. China.org, "Communiqué of the third plenary session of the 18th Central Committee of the Communist Party of China". 15 January 2014. www.china.org.cn/china/third_plenary_session/2014-01/15/content_31203056.htm.

28. J. Blanchette & S. Kennedy, "China's Fifth Plenum: reading the initial tea leaves". Center for Strategic and International Studies, 30 October 2020. www.csis.org/analysis/chinas-fifth-plenum-reading-initial-tea-leaves.

29. PRC State Council, "More actions to promote mass entrepreneurship and innovation". 25 June 2021. http://english.www.gov.cn/premier/news/202106/25/content_WS60d589a4c6d0df57f98dbddd.html.

30. B. Naughton, "Grand steerage as the new paradigm for state–economy relations", in F. Pieke & B. Hofman (eds), *CPC Futures: The New Era of Socialism with Chinese Characteristics*, 105–12 (Singapore: NUS Press, 2022). https://epress.nus.edu.sg/cpcfutures.

31. C. Lui, "Alibaba pledges $15.5 billion to 'common prosperity' drive". Bloomberg, 2 September 2021. www.bloomberg.com/news/articles/2021-09-02/alibaba-pledges-15-5-billion-to-xi-s-common-prosperity-drive#xj4y7vzkg.

32. J. Li, "'Er xuan yi': the business tactic that led to Alibaba's $2.8 billion antitrust fine". Quartz, 12 April 2021. https://qz.com/1994879/what-is-erxuanyi-which-led-to-alibabas-2-8-billion-fine.

33. *The Economist*, "A Chinese writer calls for private companies to fade away". 6 October 2018. www.economist.com/china/2018/10/06/a-chinese-writer-calls-for-private-companies-to-fade-away.

34. *Caixin*, "Editorial: local government overreach is undermining China's economic recovery". 5 September 2022. www.caixinglobal.com/2022-09-05/editorial-local-government-overreach-is-undermining-chinas-economic-recovery-101936037.html.

35. *Global Times*, "China to develop 10,000 'little giants' in push for advanced manufacturing". 5 July 2021. www.globaltimes.cn/page/202107/1227877.shtml; A. Brown, "China relies on 'little giants' and foreign partners to plug stubborn technology gaps". Mercator Institute for China Studies, 24 February 2022. https://merics.org/en/short-analysis/china-relies-little-giants-and-foreign-partners-plug-stubborn-technology-gaps.

36. P. Spence, "How to cheat at Xi Jinping Thought". Foreign Policy, 6 March 2019. https://foreignpolicy.com/2019/03/06/how-to-cheat-at-i-jinping-thought.

37. S. Livingston, "The Chinese Communist Party targets the private sector". Center for Strategic and International Studies, 8 October 2020. www.csis.org/analysis/chinese-communist-party-targets-private-sector.

38. *Ibid.*

39. D. Hoicowitz & F. McKenna, "US stock exchanges and the China problem". The Dig, 10 January 2022. https://thedig.substack.com/p/us-stock-exchanges-and-the-china?s=r.

40. *Global Times*, "Former Party chief of E.China's Hangzhou to be prosecuted for corruption". 11 April 2022. www.globaltimes.cn/page/202204/1259013.shtml.

41. Reuters, "China will prevent platform monopolies and disorderly expansion of capital, Xi says". 19 October 2021. www.reuters.com/world/china/china-will-prevent-platform-monopolies-disorderly-expansion-capital-xi-says-2021-10-19.

42. CGTN, "Xi highlights anti-monopoly regulation, anti-pollution fight, better reserve system". 30 August 2021. https://news.cgtn.com/news/2021-08-30/President-Xi-stresses-anti-monopoly-tough-fight-against-pollution-139t53pyNTa/index.html.

43. Huang & Henderson, "From fear to behavior modification".

44. L. Carroll, *Through the Looking-Glass* (London: Macmillan, 1934 [1871]), p. 205.

45. Asia Society Policy Institute, "Quarterly net assessment, winter 2021". https://chinadashboard.gist.asiasociety.org/winter-2021/page/overview.

46. PRC State Council, "China shortens negative list for foreign investment 5th year in a row". 8 January 2022. http://english.www.gov.cn/news/videos/202201/08/content_WS61d90203c6d09c94e48a3564.html.

47. B. Hofman, "A broad assessment of the growth outlook for China: will it meet Xi Jinping's goals, will China overtake the US? How will China seek to achieve this?". Harvard University, 27 April 2022. https://fairbank.fas.harvard.edu/events/critical-issues-confronting-china-series-featuring-bert-hofman.

CHAPTER 6

1. China International Import Expo, "China's booming foreign trade brings benefits to the world". 24 March 2021. www.ciie.org/zbh/en/news/exhibition/news/20210324/27370.html.

2. United Nations Conference on Trade and Development (UNCTAD), *World Investment Report 2021: Investing in Sustainable Recovery* (New York: United Nations Publications, 2021). https://unctad.org/system/files/official-document/wir2021_en.pdf.

3. Estimating the level and country origins of investment flows and capital stock is a thorny exercise. Valuation is one challenge. Investments are booked out of countries that do not correspond to the true source, for reasons of tax management or confidentiality. UNCTAD estimates that China's total overseas investments stand at just under 30 per cent of the US level (just over 50 per cent if Hong Kong's overseas investments are also included).

4. S. Stolton, "Chinese business wants less EU red tape". Euractiv, 24 September 2020. www.euractiv.com/section/economy-jobs/interview/chinese-business-wants-less-eu-red-tape.

5. Offshore Technology, "China's CNOOC plans to exit Canada, UK, and US due to sanctions concerns". 14 April 2022. www.offshore-technology.com/news/cnooc-exit-canada-sanctions.

6. M. Pottinger *et al.*, "CNOOC drops offer for Unocal, exposing US–Chinese tensions". *Wall Street Journal*, 3 August 2005. www.wsj.com/articles/SB112 295744495102393.

7. L. Forristal, "TikTok was the top app by worldwide downloads in Q1 2022". TechCrunch, 26 April 2022. https://techcrunch.com/2022/04/26/tiktok-was-the-top-app-by-worldwide-downloads-in-q1-2022.

8. The Republic of China participated in the Bretton Woods conference, was a founder member of the United Nations and was one of the original 23 signatories to GATT, the General Agreement on Trade and Tariffs, the predecessor of the World Trade Organization. This was all prior to the establishment of the People's Republic of China in 1949.

9. R. Greene, "Beijing's global ambitions for central bank digital currencies are growing clearer". Carnegie Endowment for International Peace, 6 October 2021. https://carnegieendowment.org/2021/10/06/beijing-s-global-ambitions-for-central-bank-digital-currencies-are-growing-clearer-pub-85503.

10. China Banking News, "Liu He sheds light on China's dual circulation development strategy". 26 November 2020. www.chinabankingnews.com/2020/11/26/liu-he-sheds-light-on-chinas-dual-circulation-development-strategy.

11. J. Mardell, "The 'community of destiny' in Xi Jinping's new era". The Diplomat, 25 October 2017. https://thediplomat.com/2017/10/the-community-of-common-destiny-in-xi-jinpings-new-era.

12. Xinhua, "China's 'dual circulation' powers foreign investors' development". 17 December 2020. https://en.imsilkroad.com/p/318344.html.

13. Xi, "Understanding the new development stage".

14. K. Tai, "Remarks as prepared for delivery of Ambassador Katherine Tai outlining the Biden–Harris administration's 'new approach to the US–China trade relationship". Office of the US Trade Representative, October 2021. https://ustr.gov/about-us/policy-offices/press-office/speeches-and-remarks/2021/october/remarks-prepared-delivery-ambassador-katherine-tai-outlining-biden-harris-administrations-new.

15. J. Gewirtz, "The Chinese reassessment of independence". China Leadership Monitor, 1 June 2020. www.prcleader.org/gewirtz.

16. A. Lo, "How to practice political unrealism". *South China Morning Post*, 8 March 2022. www.scmp.com/comment/opinion/article/3169729/how-practise-political-unrealism-america.

17. C.-C. Tung & A. Yang, "How China is remaking the UN in its own image". The Diplomat, 9 April 2020. https://thediplomat.com/2020/04/how-china-is-remaking-the-un-in-its-own-image.

18. Doshi, *The Long Game*.

19. A. Jones, "China is developing plans for a 13,000-satellite megaconstellation". Space News, 21 April 2021. https://spacenews.com/china-is-developing-plans-for-a-13000-satellite-communications-megaconstellation.

20. J. Hillman, "Securing the subsea network: a primer for policymakers" (Washington, DC: Center for Strategic & International Studies, 2021). https:// csis-website-prod.s3.amazonaws.com/s3fs-public/publication/210309_Hillm an_Subsea_Network_1.pdf?1c7RFgLM3w3apMi0eAPl2rPmqrNNzvwJ.
21. Society for Worldwide Interbank Financial Telecommunication. www. swift.com.
22. Bloomberg, "China banks act to comply with Trump sanctions on Hong Kong". 13 August 2020. www.bloomberg.com/news/articles/2020-08-12/ chinese-banks-move-to-comply-with-u-s-sanctions-on-hong-kong.
23. C. Feng, "China's digital currency: e-CNY wallet nearly doubles user base in two months to 261 million ahead of Winter Olympics". *South China Morning Post*, 19 January 2022. www.scmp.com/tech/tech-trends/article/3163953/ chinas-digital-currency-e-cny-wallet-nearly-doubles-user-base-two.
24. National Bureau of Asian Research, "China's digital ambitions: a global strategy to supplant the liberal order". March 2022. www.nbr.org/nbr-reports.
25. K. O'Hara & W. Hall, "Four Internets: the geopolitics of digital governance". Center for International Governance Innovation, December 2018. www.cig ionline.org/sites/default/files/documents/Paper%20no.206web.pdf.
26. Huawei United States, "Internet 2030: toward a new internet for the year 2030 and beyond" (Cupertino, CA: Huawei United States, 2018). www. itu.int/en/ITU-T/studygroups/2017-2020/13/Documents/Internet_2 030%20.pdf.
27. A. Segal, "Chinese cyber diplomacy in a new era of uncertainty", Aegis Paper 1703 (Stanford, CA: Hoover Institution, 2017). www.hoover. org/sites/default/files/research/docs/segal_chinese_cyber_diplomacy. pdf; W. Hoxtell & W. Nonhoff, "Internet governance: past, present, and future" (Berlin: Konrad-Adenauer-Stiftung, 2019). www.gppi.net/media/ Internet-Governance-Past-Present-and-Future.pdf.
28. N. Schia & L. Gjesvik, "The Chinese cyber sovereignty concept (part 1)". Asia Research Institute, University of Nottingham, 7 September 2018. https://theasiadialogue.com/2018/09/07/the-chinese-cyber-sovereignty-concept-part-1.
29. Damalion, "2022 World Internet Conference summit is coming to Wuzhen". 10 November 2022. www.damalion.com/2022/11/10/2022-world-internet-conference-summit-is-coming-to-wuzhen.
30. Australia, Brunei. Canada, Chile, Japan, Malaysia, Mexico, New Zealand, Peru, Singapore and Vietnam.
31. L. Zhou & A. Wang, "China can set the rules and counter moves on Asia-Pacific digital trade, if DEPA bid succeeds". *South China Morning Post*, 28 November 2021. www.scmp.com/news/china/diplomacy/article/3157 616/china-can-set-rules-and-counter-us-moves-asia-pacific-digital.
32. B. Maçães, *Belt and Road: A Chinese World Order* (London: Hurst, 2018).
33. A. Goh, "Framework for the resolution of disputes under the Belt and Road Initiative". *Arbitration: The International Journal of Arbitration, Mediation, & Dispute Management* 87 (2) (2021), 243–67.

34. J. Nye Jr, "Soft power". *Foreign Policy* 80 (1990), 153–71. www.wilsoncenter. org/chinas-soft-power-campign.

35. BBC, "Xi Jinping calls for more 'loveable' image for China in bid to make friends". 2 June 2021. www.bbc.co.uk/news/world-asia-china-57327177.

36. China Media Project, "Telling China's story well". 16 April 2021. https:// chinamediaproject.org/the_ccp_dictionary/telling-chinas-story-well.

37. M. Schrader, "China is weaponizing globalization". Foreign Policy, 5 June 2020. https://foreignpolicy.com/2020/06/05/china-globalization-weaponiz ing-trade-communist-party.

38. H. Jones, "China's quest for greater 'discourse power'". The Diplomat, 24 November 2021. https://thediplomat.com/2021/11/chinas-quest-for-greater- discourse-power.

39. D. van der Kley, "What should Australia do about the influence of United Front work?", policy brief (Pyrmont, NSW: China Matters, 2020). https:// chinamatters.org.au/policy-brief/policy-brief-september-2020.

CHAPTER 7

1. Cited in A. Petino, "Hainan Free Trade Port". *EURObiz: Journal of the European Chamber of Commerce in China* 61 (2021), 16.

2. CGTN, "China's dual circulation an active choice and long-term strategy: official". 30 October 2020. https://news.cgtn.com/news/2020-10- 30/China-s-dual-circulation-an-active-choice-and-long-term- strategy-V0kW26SOu4/index.html.

3. C. Madden, "Chinese outbound tourism falls below 2000 levels in 2021". DFNI Frontier, 12 January 2022. www.dfnionline.com/lead-stories/ chinese-outbound-tourism-falls-2000-levels-2021-12-01-2022.

4. E. Tham & Y. Xie, "Expats flee as Shanghai's Covid lockdowns drag". Reuters, 28 April 2022. www.reuters.com/world/china/expats-flee-shanghais-covid- lockdown-drags-2022-04-28.

5. Reuters, "China posts record trade surplus in December and 2021 on robust exports". 14 January 2022. www.reuters.com/markets/currencies/ chinas-exports-imports-grow-more-slowly-december-2022-01-14.

6. UNCTAD, "Global foreign direct investment rebounded strongly in 2021, but the recovery is highly uneven". 19 January 2022. https://unc tad.org/news/global-foreign-direct-investment-rebounded-strongly- 2021-recovery-highly-uneven.

7. CGTN, "China tops world for first time in outward foreign direct investment". 3 October 2021. https://news.cgtn.com/news/2021-09-29/ China-s-ODI-up-12-3-in-2020-13WBTGvyKCQ/index.html.

8. S. Yu, Y. Shen & J. Cheng, "Alibaba, JD.com investors boost shift to Hong Kong's market". Bloomberg, 17 January 2022. www.bloombergquint.com/ markets/alibaba-jd-com-investors-boost-shift-to-hong-kong-s-market.

9. N. Lardy, "Foreign investments into China are accelerating despite global economic tensions and restrictions". Peterson Institute for International Economics, 22 July 2021. www.piie.com/blogs/china-economic-watch/foreign-investments-china-are-accelerating-despite-global-economic.

10. *Nikkei Asia*, "Divided internet: China and US switch place as powerhouse". 26 November 2020. https://vdata.nikkei.com/en/newsgraphics/splinternet.

11. World Bank, "Charges for the use of intellectual property, payments China". https://data.worldbank.org/indicator/BM.GSR.ROYL.CD?locations=CN.

12. *Ibid.*

13. Xinhua, "Outline of the People's Republic of China 14th Five-Year Plan for national economic and social development and long-range objectives for 2035". 12 March 2021. https://cset.georgetown.edu/wp-content/uploads/t0284_14th_Five_Year_Plan_EN.pdf.

14. Xi, "Certain major issues".

15. O. Wang, "China food security: 5 major concerns". *South China Morning Post*, 6 March 2022. www.scmp.com/economy/china-economy/article/3169278/china-food-security-5-major-concerns-loss-fertile-land.

16. Global Innovation Index 2021. www.globalinnovationindex.org/Home.

17. G. Allison *et al.*, "The great tech rivalry: China vs. the US", paper (Cambridge, MA: Belfer Center, Harvard Kennedy School, 2021). www.belfercenter.org/sites/default/files/GreatTechRivalry_ChinavsUS_211207.pdf.

18. K. Lo, "Tech war: Beijing will come out of decoupling worse off than the US, say Chinese academics". *South China Morning Post*, 1 February 2022. www.scmp.com/news/china/diplomacy/article/3165435/tech-war-beijing-will-come-out-decoupling-worse-us-say-chinese.

19. L. Xin, "China beats US in most-cited science papers, moving to top of new rankings". *South China Morning Post*, 18 August 2022. www.scmp.com/news/china/science/article/3189382/china-beats-us-most-cited-science-papers-moving-top-new-rankings.

20. D. Cerdeiro *et al.*, "Sizing up the effects of technological decoupling", Working Paper 50125 (Washington, DC: IMF, 2021). www.imf.org/en/Publications/WP/Issues/2021/03/12/Sizing-Up-the-Effects-of-Technological-Decoupling-50125.

21. P. Temple-West & T. Kinder, "US and China reach landmark audit inspection deal". *Financial Times*, 26 August 2022. www.ft.com/content/a9d18d7e-1e75-49fb-842d-d8554b420553.

22. C. Chang, "Faced with CATL battery dominance, US trade experts mull a China-like tech transfer". SupChina, 30 March 2022. https://supchina.com/2022/03/30/faced-with-catl-battery-dominance-u-s-trade-experts-mull-a-china-like-tech-transfer.

23. I. Bond *et al.*, "Rebooting Europe's China strategy" (Berlin: German Institute for International and Security Affairs, 2022). www.swp-berlin.org/publications/products/sonstiges/2022_Rebooting_Europes_China_Strategy.pdf.

24. Australia, Canada, New Zealand, the United Kingdom and the United States.

25. J. Rogers *et al.*, "Breaking the China supply chain: how the 'Five Eyes' can decouple from strategic dependency". Henry Jackson Society, 14 May 2020. https://henryjacksonsociety.org/publications/breaking-the-china-supply-chain-how-the-five-eyes-can-decouple-from-strategic-dependency.

26. E. Chen, "Critical minerals, in context". The Wire China, 15 May 2022. www.thewirechina.com/2022/05/15/critical-minerals-in-context.

27. White House, "Executive order on America's supply chains". 24 February 2021. www.whitehouse.gov/briefing-room/presidential-actions/2021/02/24/executive-order-on-americas-supply-chains.

28. US Department of State, "Minerals Security Partnership", media note. 14 June 2022. www.state.gov/minerals-security-partnership.

29. Committee on Foreign Investment in the United States, Department of Treasury. https://home.treasury.gov/policy-issues/international/the-committee-on-foreign-investment-in-the-united-states-cfius.

30. Z. Yu, "The Thousand Talents plan is part of China's long quest to become the global scientific leader". The Conversation, 1 September 2020. https://theconversation.com/the-thousand-talents-plan-is-part-of-chinas-long-quest-to-become-the-global-scientific-leader-145100.

31. A. Connaughton, "Fast facts about views of China ahead of the 2022 Beijing Olympics". Pew Research Center, 1 February 2022. www.pewresearch.org/fact-tank/2022/02/01/fast-facts-about-views-of-china-ahead-of-the-2022-beijing-olympics.

32. S. Gaston & E. Aspinall, "UK public opinion on foreign policy and global affairs". British Foreign Policy Group, 16 February 2021. https://bfpg.co.uk/2021/02/2021-annual-survey.

33. S. Gaston, "UK public opinion on foreign policy and global affairs: annual survey – 2022" (London: British Foreign Policy Group, 2022). https://bfpg.wpenginepowered.com/wp-content/uploads/2022/06/BFPG-UK-Opinion-Report-June-2022.pdf.

34. J. Fromer, "US sanctions Chinese AI firm SenseTime, Xinjiang officials, citing human rights abuses". *South China Morning Post*, 11 December 2021. www.scmp.com/news/china/article/3159297/biden-administration-sanctions-chinese-ai-company-sensetime-citing-human.

35. European Parliament, "MEPs refuse any agreement with China whilst sanctions are in place", press release. 20 May 2021. www.europarl.europa.eu/news/en/press-room/20210517IPR04123/meps-refuse-any-agreement-with-china-whilst-sanctions-are-in-place.

36. M. Ferchen, "How China is reshaping international development". Carnegie Endowment for International Peace, 8 January 2022. https://carnegieendowment.org/2020/01/08/how-china-is-reshaping-international-development-pub-80703.

37. T. L. Friedman, *The World Is Flat: A Brief History of the Twenty-First Century* (New York: Farrar, Straus & Giroux, 2005).

38. European Parliament, "EU strategic autonomy 2013–2023: from concept to capacity", briefing (Luxembourg: Publications Office of the European

Union, 2022). www.europarl.europa.eu/RegData/etudes/BRIE/2022/733 589/EPRS_BRI(2022)733589_EN.pdf.

39. European Union, "EU–China relations factsheet". 1 April 2022. www.eeas. europa.eu/eeas/eu-china-relations-factsheet_en.

40. C. Li, "Biden's China strategy: coalition-driven competition or cold war-style confrontation". Brookings Institution, May 2021. www.brooki ngs.edu/research/bidens-china-strategy-coalition-driven-competition-or-cold-war-style-confrontation.

41. C. Parton, "Empty threats? Policymaking amidst Chinese pressure", Report SBIR01 (London: Council on Geostrategy, 2021), p. 3. www.geostrategy. org.uk/app/uploads/2021/07/Report-SBIR01-07072021.pdf.

42. D. Cerdeiro *et al.*, "Sizing up the effects of technological decoupling".

43. M. Dittli, "China's leadership is prisoner of its own narrative". The Market NZZ, 28 April 2022. https://themarket.ch/interview/chinas-leadership-is-prisoner-of-its-own-narrative-ld.6545.

CHAPTER 8

1. *Global Times*, "Gentlemen's agreement between Deng Xiaoping und Konosuke Matsushita". 21 July 2021. www.globaltimes.cn/page/202107/1229219.shtml.

2. World Bank, "China's special economic zones: experience gained" (Washington, DC: World Bank, 2015). www.worldbank.org/content/dam/Worldbank/Event/Africa/Investing%20in%20Africa%20Forum/2015/investing-in-africa-forum-chinas-special-economic-zone.pdf.

3. *New York Times*, "VW plans to make cars in China". 11 October 1984. www.nytimes.com/1984/10/11/business/vw-plans-to-make-cars-in-china.html.

4. *The Economist*, "Motoring ahead". 23 October 2009. www.economist.com/news/2009/10/23/motoring-ahead.

5. K. Malden & A. Listerud, "Trends in US multinational activity in China, 2000–2017" (Washington, DC: US–China Economic and Security Review Commission, 2020). www.uscc.gov/sites/default/files/2020-06/US_Multi national_Enterprise_Activity_in_China.pdf.

6. *Ibid.*

7. S. Palmisano, "The globally integrated enterprise". *Foreign Affairs*, 4 May 2006. www.foreignaffairs.com/world/globally-integrated-enterprise.

8. General Electric, "Forward in reverse: how 'reverse innovation' helps win future markets". 10 April 2012. www.ge.com/news/reports/forward-in-reverse-how-reverse-innovation-helps.

9. *South China Morning Post*, "Chinese 'Hermes of ice cream' under fire for products that do not melt". 8 July 2022. www.scmp.com/yp/disco ver/news/asia/article/3184455/chinese-hermes-ice-cream-under-fire-products-do-not-melt.

10. P. Wu, "China's market regulators take aim at 'ice cream assassins'". Sixth Tone, 21 July 2022. www.sixthtone.com/news/1010815/chinas-market-regulators-take-aim-at-ice-cream-assassins?source=channel_home#:~:text=%E2%80%9CIce%20cream%20assassins%E2%80%9D%20has%20become,ice%20creams%20from%20unknown%20brands.

11. National Bureau of Statistics of China, *Statistical Yearbook 2021* (Beijing: China Statistics Press, 2021), tab. 1-7. www.stats.gov.cn/tjsj/ndsj/2021/indexeh.htm.

12. S. Paterson, "Will MNCs survive China's dual circulation strategy?". Hinrich Foundation, 14 December 2021. www.hinrichfoundation.com/research/wp/us-china/china-dual-circulation-strategy-multinational-corporations.

13. M. Enright, *Developing China: The Remarkable Impact of Foreign Direct Investment* (Abingdon: Routledge, 2016).

14. See https://twitter.com/adam_tooze/status/1142584301260722176.

15. UNCTAD, *World Investment Report 2021*.

16. M. Zenglein, "Battered in Russia, companies need to be more transparent about risks in China". Mercator Institute for China Studies, 30 March 2022. https://merics.org/de/kommentar/battered-russia-companies-need-be-more-transparent-about-risks-china.

17. Mainland China, Hong Kong and Taiwan.

18. Goldman Sachs estimates that foreign sales accounted for 29 per cent of the US$12 trillion aggregate revenues of the S&P 500 in 2019, down from 30 per cent in 2018. Only 2 per cent of revenues came "specifically" from Greater China. See E. Bacani, "S&P 500 companies' non-US revenue share hits 10-year low". Goldman Sachs. www.spglobal.com/marketintelligence/en/news-insights/latest-news-headlines/s-p-500-companies-non-us-revenue-share-hits-10-year-low-8211-goldman-sachs-59094991.

19. US companies have US$410 billion of revenue "at risk" in China. Although that represents 5 per cent of their total revenues, its loss would translate into around 15 per cent of their market capitalization, or about US$2.5 trillion in value. The estimate of market capitalization risk is calculated on the basis of the average 2019 profit margin structure (49 per cent gross margin) for S&P 500 companies and EV/EBITDA (enterprise value/earnings before interest, taxes, depreciation and amortization) valuation multiples that historically range from 11 to 14. See R. Varadarajan *et al.*, "What's at stake if the US and China really decouple?". BCG, 20 October 2020. www.bcg.com/publications/2020/high-stakes-of-decoupling-us-and-china.

20. Deutsche Bundesbank, "Foreign affiliates statistics". www.bundesbank.de/en/statistics/external-sector/direct-investments/foreign-affiliates-statistics-fats--795240#:~:text=In%202019%2C%20the%20number%20of,with%20German%20investors%20increased%20slightly.&text=In%202019%2C%20the%20number%20of%20persons%20employed%20in%20foreign%20a%20liates,the%20%20European%20Union%20(EU).

21. Paterson, "Will MNCs survive".

22. *Ibid.*
23. National Bureau of Statistics of China, *Statistical Yearbook 2021.*
24. All data from company annual reports: Apple: https://s2.q4cdn.com/ 470004039/files/doc_financials/2021/q4/_10-K-2021-(As-Filed).pdf; Qualcomm: https://investor.qualcomm.com/financial-information/sec-filings/content/0001728949-21-000076/0001728949-21-000076.pdf; Nike: www.annreports.com/nike/nike-ar-2021.pdf; Intel: www.intc.com/filings-reports/annual-reports/content/0000050863-21-000010/0000050863-21-000010.pdf; Procter & Gamble: https://assets.ctfassets.net/oggad6svuzkv/ 4Jv0tM2D5D4uo9fpGkFINt/51f922cfc331f8cd887e86f5dca2a59f/2021_annual_report.pdf.
25. Infineon: www.infineon.com/dgdl/Infineon+Annual+Report+2021.pdf?fileId=8ac78c8b7d507352017d622b5bfb0161.
26. T. Dams & X. Martin, "Investors beware: Europe's top firms are highly exposed to China", report (The Hague: Clingendael Institute, 2022). www.clingendael.org/sites/default/files/2022-04/Report_Are_Europes_top_firms_highly_exposed_to_China.pdf.
27. J. Petring, "Danach braucht man erst mal Whiskey". *WirtschaftsWoche*, 2 May 2021. www.wiwo.de/my/politik/ausland/interview-mit-joerg-wuttke-danach-braucht-man-erst-mal-whiskey/27141836.html?ticket= ST-1180074-bnsMjTsv0l4R0dtrelOb-ap5.
28. Daxue Consulting, "The API industry in China: producing and exporting to the global market". 1 July 2020. https://daxueconsulting.com/api-industry-in-china.
29. Black and Morrison's approach has some similarities. They present a two-by-two matrix of strategies for companies that are active in China, distinguishing "upstream" and "downstream" activities, where each can be pursued with a "low" or "high" focus; see J. Black & A. Morrison, "The strategic challenges of decoupling". *Harvard Business Review* 99 (3) (2021), 49–54. https://hbr.org/ 2021/05/the-strategic-challenges-of-decoupling.
30. AmCham China, *2022 China Business Climate Survey Report* (Beijing: AmCham China, 2022). www.amchamchina.org/2022-china-business-climate-survey-report.
31. S. Shah, "As local competition grows, Nike faces a new reality in China". Modern Retail, 1 October 2021. www.modernretail.co/retailers/as-local-competition-grows-nike-faces-a-new-reality-in-china.
32. J. Song, "Google earns solid $3bn from China, despite stranded plans to re-enter the country". KrAsia, 28 February 2019. https://kr-asia.com/ google-earns-solid-3b-from-china-despite-stranded-plans-to-re-enter-the-country.
33. D. Depoux, "Despite Covid-19, European companies enjoy a resurgent market in China". Roland Berger, 9 June 2021. www.rolandberger.com/en/ Insights/Publications/Despite-COVID-19-European-companies-enjoy-a-resurgent-market-in-China.html.

34. AmCham Shanghai, "AmCham Shanghai releases 2022 China business report". 28 October 2022. www.amcham-shanghai.org/en/article/amcham-shanghai-releases-2022-china-business-report.

35. L. Niewenhuis, "The 14 sins of Australia: Beijing expands list of grievances and digs in for extended diplomatic dispute". SupChina, 18 November 2020. https://supchina.com/2020/11/18/the-14-sins-of-australia-beijing-expands-list-of-grievances-and-digs-in-for-extended-diplomatic-dispute.

36. AmCham China, *2022 China Business Climate Survey Report*.

37. Außenhandelskammer [AHK] & KPMG, *German Business in China: Business Confidence Survey 2021/2022* (Berlin: AHK, 2022). https://china.ahk.de/filehub/deliverFile/74912be3-ce50-45a8-8d33-282d4d60487b/1407744/AHK-GC_BCS_2122_web.pdf_1407744.pdf.

38. US government, "US–China agreement fact sheet". 15 January 2020. https://ustr.gov/sites/default/files/files/agreements/phase%20one%20agreement/US_China_Agreement_Fact_Sheet.pdf.

39. AmCham China, *2022 China Business Climate Survey Report*.

40. European Chamber of Commerce in China, *European Business in China: Business Confidence Survey 2021* (Beijing: European Chamber of Commerce in China, 2022), p. 31. https://europeanchamber.oss-cn-beijing.aliyuncs.com/upload/documents/documents/BCS_EN_final[917].pdf.

41. British Chamber of Commerce in China, *British Business in China Sentiment Survey 2021/22* (Beijing: British Chamber of Commerce in China, 2022). www.britishchamber.cn/wp-content/uploads/2021/12/British-Business-in-China-Sentiment-Survey-2021-2022.pdf.

42. European Chamber of Commerce in China, *European Business in China: Business Confidence Survey 2022* (Beijing: European Chamber of Commerce in China, 2022). https://europeanchamber.oss-cn-beijing.aliyuncs.com/upload/documents/documents/European_Chamber_Business_Confidence_Survey_2022[1020].pdf.

43. European Chamber of Commerce in China, *Business Confidence Survey 2021*, p. 14.

44. European Chamber of Commerce in China, *Business Confidence Survey 2022*.

45. AmCham Shanghai, "AmCham June Covid impact survey". 15 June 2022. www.amcham-shanghai.org/en/article/amcham-shanghai-june-covid-impact-survey.

46. US–China Business Council, *US–China Business Council Member Survey 2022* (Washington, DC: US–China Business Council, 2022). www.uschina.org/sites/default/files/uscbc_member_survey_2022.pdf.

CHAPTER 9

1. J. Miller, "Volkswagen and China: the risks of relying on authoritarian states". *Financial Times*, 16 March 2022. www.ft.com/content/7fe10b69-bc19-4aff-9b46-e0233e00c638.

2. Cited in J. Ehrling, "Die Zukunft von Volkswagen wird in China entschieden". *Die Welt*, 7 January 2019. www.welt.de/wirtschaft/article 186697100/Herbert-Diess-Di_e-Zukunft-von-Volkswagen-wird-in-China-entschieden.html.

3. AHK & KPMG, *German Business in China.*

4. J. Klein, "Post ex-Google CEO Eric Schmidt stresses 'urgency' in countering China on artificial intelligence as US–China tech war continues". *South China Morning Post*, 24 February 2021. www.scmp.com/news/china/arti cle/3122857/us-china-tech-war-former-google-ceo-eric-schmidt-stresses-urgency.

5. J. Leonard & I. King, "White House spurns Intel plan to boost chip production in China". Bloomberg, 13 November 2021. www.bloomberg. com/news/articles/2021-11-13/white-house-spurns-intel-plan-to-boost-chip-production-in-china.

6. D. Kaur, "China to launch chipmaking platform in collaboration with Intel, AMD". Techware Asia, 14 February 2022. https://techwireasia.com/2022/02/china-to-launch-chipmaking-platform-in-collaboration-with-intel-amd.

7. Naughton, "Grand steerage as the new paradigm".

8. G. DiPippo, I. Mazzacco & S. Kennedy, "Red ink: estimating Chinese industrial policy spending in comparative perspective". Center for International and Strategic Studies, 23 May 2022. www.csis.org/analysis/red-ink-estimating-chinese-industrial-policy-spending-comparative-pers pective.

9. W. Sheng, "China's second chip-focused 'Big Fund' raises $29 billion". Technode, 28 October 2019. https://technode.com/2019/10/28/chinas-new-chip-focused-big-fund-raises-rmb-204-billion.

10. HarrisBricken, "China's foreign investment law: not good news". 23 April 2019. https://harrisbricken.com/chinalawblog/chinas-foreign-investment-law-not-good-news.

11. Bloomberg, "China orders government, state firms to dump foreign PCs". 6 May 2022. www.bloomberg.com/news/articles/2022-05-06/china-orders-government-state-firms-to-dump-foreign-pcs.

12. D. Coldewey, "China moves to ban foreign software from state offices". TechCrunch, 9 December 2019. https://techcrunch.com/2019/12/09/china-moves-to-ban-foreign-software-and-hardware-from-state-offices.

13. K. Rawlinson, "China bans Microsoft Windows 8 on government campus". BBC News, 20 May 2014. www.bbc.co.uk/news/technology-27494650.

14. M. Steinglass, "Philips bolstered by rising demand for healthcare". *Financial Times*, 22 July 2013. www.ft.com/content/7e936c9a-f2bf-11e2-802f-00144 feabdc0.

15. *Korea Herald*, "SKT, MtekVision in talks on investment in China". 13 September 2010. www.koreaherald.com/view.php?ud=20100913000705.

16. T. Hout, "A brave new world". *Wall Street Journal*, 8 May 2006. www.wsj.com/articles/SB114703801264446079.

17. T. Moss, "Honeywell's formula for success in China". *Wall Street Journal*, 22 October 2021. www.wsj.com/articles/honeywells-formula-for-success-in-china-11634911201.

18. K. Wong, "US firms say China's 'ambiguous' data laws are creating a 'uniquely restrictive' environment". *South China Morning Post*, 21 April 2022. www.scmp.com/economy/china-economy/article/3174887/us-firms-say-chinas-ambiguous-data-laws-are-creating-uniquely.

19. *South China Morning Post*, "China still an investment hotspot for European firms despite rising geopolitical tensions". 18 August 2022. www.scmp.com/economy/china-economy/article/3189312/china-still-investment-hotspot-european-firms-despite-rising?module=perpetual_scroll_0&pgtype=article&campaign=3189312.

20. A. García Herrero, "What is behind China's dual circulation strategy?" China Leadership Monitor, 1 September 2021. www.prcleader.org/herrero.

21. H. Zhu, "China reiterates equal treatment of foreign-invested companies in government procurement". China Trade Monitor, 26 October 2021. www.chinatrademonitor.com/china-reiterates-equal-treatment-of-foreign-invested-companies-in-government-procurement.

22. US–China Business Council, "Government procurement and sales to state-owned enterprises in China". www.uschina.org/reports/government-procurement-and-sales-state-owned-enterprises-china.

23. P. Che, "TSMC says Nanjing wafer fab expansion plans on track as second quarter revenue surges 28 percent". *South China Morning Post*, 15 July 2021. www.scmp.com/tech/tech-trends/article/3141240/tsmc-says-nanjing-wafer-fab-expansion-plans-track-second-quarter.

24. *Nikkei Asia*, "TSMC gets 1-year US license for China chip expansion". 13 October 2022. https://asia.nikkei.com/Business/Tech/Semiconductors/TSMC-gets-1-year-U.S.-license-for-China-chip-expansion.

25. Deloitte, "Chinese medical device industry: How to thrive in an increasingly competitive market?" (Beijing: Deloitte China, 2021). www2.deloitte.com/content/dam/Deloitte/cn/Documents/life-sciences-health-care/deloitte-cn-lshc-medical-device-white-paper-en-210301.pdf.

26. T. Qian, "Medtronic to invest millions in core heart device production in Shanghai FTZ". Yicai Global, 14 February 2022. www.yicaiglobal.com/news/medtronic-to-invest-millions-in-core-heart-device-production-in-shanghai-ftz.

27. O. Wang, "China to roll out trade support amid 'increasing pressure' behind the scenes". *South China Morning Post*, 25 November 2021. www.scmp.com/economy/china-economy/article/3157348/china-roll-out-trade-support-amid-increasing-pressure-behind.

28. D. Brunnstrom & P. Grant, "Biden signs bill banning goods from China's Xinjiang over forced labor". Reuters, 24 December 2021. www.reuters.com/world/us/biden-signs-bill-clamp-down-products-chinas-xinjiang-2021-12-23.

29. A. Peaple, "Craig Allen on US business confidence in China". The Wire China, 27 March 2022. www.thewirechina.com/2022/03/27/craig-allen-on-u-s-business-confidence-in-china.

30. M. Bain, "If China no longer wants to be the world's factory, who will take its place?". Quartz, 9 January 2021. https://qz.com/1953026/if-china-is-no-longer-the-worlds-factory-what-will-replace-it.

31. C. Flood, "Fidelity International applies to launch China retail funds". *Financial Times*, 20 May 2020. www.ft.com/content/d4a31198-d1fb-4715-ae57-b7b1b3f0e79e.

32. Reuters, "Update-2: China allows Fidelity International to set up mutual fund unit". 6 August 2021. www.reuters.com/article/china-fidelity-unit-idUSL1N2PD0JR.

33. BBC News, "Google's Project Dragonfly 'terminated' in China". 17 July 2019. www.bbc.co.uk/news/technology-49015516.

CHAPTER 10

1. Eureka Report, "Building an ambidextrous business success". 9 November 2011. www.eurekareport.com.au/investment-news/building-an-ambidextrous-business-success/89982.

2. R. Duncan, "The ambidextrous organization: designing dual structures for innovation". *Management of Organization* 1 (1976), 167–88.

3. C. O'Reilly III & M. Tushman, "The ambidextrous organization". *Harvard Business Review* 82 (4) (2004), 74–81. https://hbr.org/2004/04/the-ambidextrous-organization.

4. C. Prange & L. Heracleous, *Agility.X: How Organizations Manage in Unpredictable Times* (Cambridge: Cambridge University Press, 2018).

5. BCG Henderson Institute, "Ambidexterity: your strategy needs a strategy". www.bcg.com/publications/collections/your-strategy-needs-strategy/ambidexterity.

6. J. Birkinshaw & C. Gibson, "Building ambidexterity into an organization". *MIT Sloan Management Review*, 15 July 2004. https://sloanreview.mit.edu/article/building-ambidexterity-into-an-organization.

7. Eureka Report, "Building an ambidextrous business success".

8. HSBC, "Violation tracker parent company HSBC: good jobs first". https://violationtracker.goodjobsfirst.org/parent/hsbc.

9. China File, "Document 9: a China file translation". 8 November 2013. www.chinafile.com/document-9-chinafile-translation.

10. Z. Zhang, "What is ESG reporting and why is it gaining traction in China?". China Briefing, 13 January 2022. www.china-briefing.com/news/what-is-esg-reporting-and-why-is-it-gaining-traction-in-china.

11. BBC News, "Nike, H&M face China fury over Xinjiang cotton 'concerns'". 25 March 2021. www.bbc.co.uk/news/world-asia-china-56519411.

12. J. Law, "One year on: how are fashion's boycotted brands faring in China?". Jing Daily, 6 February 2022. https://jingdaily.com/hm-burberry-nike-cotton-controversy-one-year.

13. PEN America, *Made in Hollywood, Censored by Beijing: The US Film Industry and Chinese Government Influence* (New York: PEN America, 2020). https://pen.org/wp-content/uploads/2020/09/Made_in_Hollywood_Censored_by_Beijing_Report_FINAL.pdf.

14. C. Marc, "'Spider-man: no way home': Sony reportedly refused China's censors request to remove statue of liberty". The Playlist, 2 May 2022. https://theplaylist.net/china-release-spider-man-no-way-home-sony-marvel-20220502.

15. Simmons and Simmons, "What you need to know about the Chinese Anti-Foreign Sanctions Law". 11 August 2021. www.simmons-simmons.com/en/publications/cks76w4g713a30a164jbve2zg/what-you-need-to-know-about-the-chinese-anti-foreign-sanctions-law.

16. S. Kaplan, "How to navigate the ethical risks of doing business in China". Harvard Business Review Online, 26 January 2022. https://hbr-org.cdn.amp project.org/c/s/hbr.org/amp/2022/01/how-to-navigate-the-ethical-risks-of-doing-business-in-china.

17. G. Møller, "China falls off H&M's top ten sales markets in the third quarter". Scand Asia, 6 October 2021. https://scandasia.com/china-falls-off-hms-top-ten-sales-markets-in-the-third-quarter.

18. BBC News, "VW boss 'not aware' of China's detention camps". 16 April 2019. www.bbc.co.uk/news/av/business-47944767.

19. M. Shroff, "China: sunset of localized version of LinkedIn and launch of new InJobs app later this year". LinkedIn, 14 October 2021. https://blog.linkedin.com/2021/october/14/china-sunset-of-localized-version-of-linkedin-and-launch-of-new-injobs-app.

20. A. Osborne, "Unilever boss Alan Jope must wash his hands of Russia". *The Times*, 29 April 2022. www.thetimes.co.uk/article/unilever-boss-alan-jope-must-wash-his-hands-of-russia-052wfh0z7.

21. S. Harvey, "Unilever stops Russia export". Just Food, 9 March 2022. www.just-food.com/special-focus/ukraine-crisis/unilever-stops-russia-exports-but-maintains-essential-food-supply.

CHAPTER 11

1. M. Green & S. Kennedy, "US business leaders not ready for the next US–China crisis". Center for Strategic & International Studies, 16 May 2022. www.csis.org/analysis/us-business-leaders-not-ready-next-us-china-crisis.

2. S. Roberts, "Embracing the uncertainties". *New York Times*, 7 April 2020. www-nytimes-com.tilburguniversity.idm.oclc.org/2020/04/07/science/coronavirus-uncertainty-scientific-trust.html.

3. B. Nelan, "How the world will look in 50 years". *Time*, 15 October 1992. http://content.time.com/time/subscriber/article/0,33009,976739-3,00.html.

4. R. Abrami, W. Kirby & W. McFarlan, "Why China can't innovate". *Harvard Business Review* 92 (3) (2014), 107–11. https://hbr.org/2014/03/why-china-cant-innovate; Allison *et al.*, "The great tech rivalry".

5. Abrami, Kirby & McFarlan, "Why China can't innovate", p. 107.

6. C. Rotblut, "Never bet against America: Buffett's screening strategy". *Forbes*, 11 March 2021. www.forbes.com/sites/investor/2021/03/11/never-bet-against-america-buffetts-screening-strategy/?sh=538675a07a42.

7. A. Peaple, "Joerg Wuttke on China's self-destruction". The Wire China, 14 August 2022. www.thewirechina.com/2022/08/14/jorg-wuttke-on-chinas-self-destruction.

8. Z. Dychtwald, "China's new innovation advantage". *Harvard Business Review* 99 (3) (2021), 55–60. https://hbr.org/2021/05/chinas-new-innovation-advantage.

9. E. Perry & S. Heilmann, "Embracing uncertainty: guerrilla policy style and adaptive governance in China", in E. Perry & S. Heilmann (eds), *Mao's Invisible Hand: The Political Foundations of Adaptive Governance in China*, 1–29 (Cambridge, MA: Harvard University Press, 2011).

10. Y. Wang, "For whom the bell tolls: the political legacy of China's Cultural Revolution", working paper (Cambridge, MA: Harvard University, 2017). https://scholar.harvard.edu/files/yuhuawang/files/cultural_revolution_0.pdf.

11. R. McGregor, "Xi Jinping's radical secrecy". *The Atlantic*, 21 August 2022. www.theatlantic.com/international/archive/2022/08/china-xi-jinping-biography-opacity/671195.

12. C. Parton, "Does the 'Beidaihe meeting' actually take place, and why does it matter?". Mercator Institute for China Studies, 23 August 2022. www.merics.org/en/opinion/does-beidaihe-meeting-actually-take-place-and-why-does-matter?

13. C. Xia, "The party that failed. An insider breaks with Beijing". *Foreign Affairs*, 4 December 2020. www.foreignaffairs.com/articles/china/2020-12-04/chinese-communist-party-failed.

14. C. Xia, "The weakness of Xi Jinping: how hubris and paranoia threaten China's future". *Foreign Affairs*, 8 September 2022. www.foreignaffairs.com/china/xi-jinping-china-weakness-hubris-paranoia-threaten-future.

15. B. Lee, "In China, a tale of two plenums: 'core leader' vs. 'collective leadership'". Carnegie Endowment for International Peace, 15 November 2016. https://carnegieendowment.org/2016/11/15/in-china-tale-of-two-plenums-core-leader-vs.-collective-leadership-pub-66129.

16. K. Huang, "Xi Jinping's reforms encounter 'unimaginably fierce resistance', Chinese state media says in 'furious' commentary". *South China Morning Post*, 21 August 2015. www.scmp.com/news/china/policies-politics/article/1851314/xi-jinpings-reforms-encountering-fierce-resistance.

17. X. Wang, "Hainan's Covid chaos exposes the bad, ugly – and scary – of China's virus control measures". *South China Morning Post*, 27 August 2022. www.scmp.com/week-asia/opinion/article/3190293/hainans-covid-chaos-exposes-bad-ugly-and-scary-chinas-virus.

18. P. Li, "Toward the geocentric framework of intuition: the yin–yang balancing between the Eastern and Western perspectives on intuition", in M. Sinclair (ed.), *Handbook of Research Methods on Intuition*, 28–41 (Cheltenham: Edward Elgar, 2014); T. Fang, "Yin yang: a new perspective on culture". *Management and Organization Review* 8 (1) (2012), 25–50.

19. R. Nisbett, *The Geography of Thought: How Asians and Westerners Think Differently, and Why* (New York: Free Press, 2003); K. Peng & R. Nisbett, "Culture, dialectics and reasoning about contradiction". *American Psychologist* 54 (9), 741–54.

20. N. Lynton & K. Kogh Thogersen, "How China transforms an executive's mind". *Organizational Dynamics* 35 (2) (2006), 170–81.

21. S. Upton-McLaughlin, "Why 'dual-culture management' is important in China". China Culture Corner, 15 July 2020. https://chinaculturecorner.com/2020/07/15/why-you-need-to-adopt-dual-culture-management-when-working-in-china/#:~:text=While%20this%20may%20sound%20similar,multiple%20cultures%20values%20and%20beliefs.

22. A. Adachi, A. Brown, & M. Zenglein, "Fasten your seatbelts: how to manage China's economic coercion". Mercator Institute for China Studies, 25 August 2022. https://merics.org/sites/default/files/2022-08/Merics_ChinaMonitor_EconomicCoercion_EN-4.pdf.

23. T. Van, "Lotte prepares to shut its China headquarters". Inside Retail, 23 May 2022. https://insideretail.asia/2022/05/23/lotte-prepares-to-shut-its-china-headquarters.

24. Green & Kennedy, "US business leaders not ready".

25. Y. Doz, "The need for strategic agility". *Globe and Mail*, 30 December 2008. www.theglobeandmail.com/report-on-business/yves-doz-the-need-for-strategic-agility/article20391771; Prange & Heracleous, *Agility.X*.

26. K. Beck *et al.*, "Manifesto for agile software development". 2001. http://agilemanifesto.org.

27. Mercator Institute for China Studies, "Is China facing a period of uncertainty?". 2 June 2022. https://merics.org/en/merics-briefs/china-facing-period-uncertainty.

28. V. Ni, "Beijing orders 'stress test' as fears of Russia-style sanctions mount". *Guardian*, 4 May 2022. www.theguardian.com/world/2022/may/04/beijing-orders-stress-test-as-fears-of-russia-style-sanctions-mount.

29. Shell, "What are Shell scenarios?". www.shell.com/energy-and-innovation/the-energy-future/scenarios/what-are-scenarios.html.

30. P. Cornelius, A. Can de Putte & M. Romani, "Three decades of scenario planning in Shell". *California Management Review* 48 (1) (2005), 92–109. http://strategy.sjsu.edu/www.stable/B290/reading/Cornelius,%20P.,%20A.%20Van%20de%20Putte,%20et%20al.,%202005,%20California%20Management%20Review%2048(1)%2092-109.pdf.

31. J. Treat, G. Thibault & A. Asin, "Dynamic competitive simulation: wargaming as a strategic tool". Leadership, 1 April 1996. www.strategy-business.com/article/15052.

32. Board of Governors of the Federal Reserve System, "Living wills (or resolution plans)". 19 July 2021. www.federalreserve.gov/supervisionreg/resolution-plans.htm.

CONCLUSION

1. Marxists Internet Archive, "Selected works of Mao Tse-tung: *On Contradiction*, August 1937". www.marxists.org/reference/archive/mao/selected-works/volume-1/mswv1_17.htm.

2. PRC State Council, "Xi: principal contradiction facing Chinese society has evolved in new era". 18 October 2017. http://english.www.gov.cn/news/top_news/2017/10/18/content_281475912458156.htm.

3. B. Milanovic, "Francis Fukuyama against mainstream economics". VOXEU, 2 April 2019. https://voxeu.org/content/francis-fukuyama-against-mainstream-economics.

4. A. Amari & A. Tanaka, "The urgent need to establish 'strategic autonomy' and 'strategic indispensability': economic security strategy for a digital transformation society", Japan Foreign Policy Forum 67 (Tokyo: Ministry of Foreign Affairs, 2021). www.japanpolicyforum.jp/diplomacy/pt20211013 08092511642.html#:~:text=Strategic%20autonomy%20means%20secur ing%20citizens,international%20society%20as%20a%20whole.

5. M. Pei, "China will be deglobalization's big loser". Project Syndicate, 14 April 2022. www.project-syndicate.org/commentary/ukraine-war-accelerates-deglobalization-and-china-will-suffer-the-most-by-minxin-pei-2022-04.

6. Morgan Stanley, "Five reasons for the trend towards multipolarity". 17 July 2020. www.morganstanley.com.au/ideas/five-reasons-for-the-trend-towards-multipolarity.

7. B. Kausikan, "China's strategic dilemmas". Asia Sentinel, 22 March 2022. www.asiasentinel.com/p/china-strategic-dilemmas?s=r.

8. C. Parton, "UK relations with China". China Research Group, 2 November 2020. https://chinaresearchgroup.org/values-war.

9. A. Peaple, "Craig Allen on US business confidence in China". The Wire China, 27 March 2022. www.thewirechina.com/2022/03/27/craig-allen-on-u-s-business-confidence-in-china.

Index